GW00854692

HOW WE DID IT

**100 entrepreneurs tell us the story of their struggles
and life experiences**

By

**Anand Srinivasan
www.EntrepreneurshipDaily.com**

Contents

Introduction

I'm a digital media consultant. More importantly, I am a struggling entrepreneur – I have had several false starts over the past seven years. As someone who is pretty risk-averse, I went through a pretty uncertain phase trying to come up with a strategy to make sure that I did not put my family's future at stake while committing myself to my business ideas.

This is not a story that is unique to me. Talk to any entrepreneur and the one common thread that runs through all their stories is the struggle that they went through during those initial few months. However, while we hear the story from the ultra-successful start-ups like Facebook or Google, we simply do not hear a lot about businesses that are relatively smaller, or ones that closed down. Stories about VC funding are given much more importance than stories about how the entrepreneurs built their businesses to reach that level in the first place.

In a way then, this book is meant to scratch my own itch. I have always been interested in the stories about entrepreneurs and have wanted to know how they executed their ideas. For this book, I talked to more than 100 entrepreneurs to know how they went about their business; be it validating their idea, or setting up their finances, solving business challenges or even talking to their families about the potential risks. I did not want myself to restrict this discussion to tech start-ups or those centered around the Silicon valley (which is exactly what most start-up related blogs and websites do). I have tried to consolidate information from start-ups that are extremely diverse and those that face vastly different challenges.

We have stories to share from Chris Grant, the owner of a family owned farm in Essex, Massachusetts as much as we have stories from Eren Bali who launched the popular Silicon Valley start-up Udemy.com. There are stories from Robin Turner and Andy Hart who did not have a successful run at their start-ups as much as we have stories from successful entrepreneurs like Matt Barrie who launched Freelancer.com at the Australian stock exchange recently. People like Cricket Allen (of The Perfect Snaque) and Aditi Kapur (DeliveryChef.in) tell us about their challenges as female entrepreneurs while Courtney Ilarrazza (Baby Bodyguards) and Dianne Crowley (Wild Wing Cafe) tell us their experiences as entrepreneur couples. The last few pages of this book contain a list of all entrepreneurs I have talked to and a short snippet about what they do.

The idea for this book is simple – there are challenges entrepreneurs face all the time. Aspiring entrepreneurs may also be worried about their job prospects in case their companies fold. And mainstream media that focus on the glitzy VC funded start-ups of Silicon Valley do not tell the complete story. I wanted a book that tells us the story from the horses' mouth. I couldn't find one and hence wrote one myself.

This book may not be the typical best-seller that gets reviewed on the New York Times. As an amateur writer, I am not even sure if I have proof-read this enough to fix all the issues with grammar and typos. But I believe this book will still be of terrific value to anybody who is either running or is interested in running their own business.

Good luck starting up – this is how 100 others did it!

Chapter 1 : Validating Your Business Idea

We have all had those moments – you are going about your life like any other regular day. You encounter a small pain point and suddenly a million dollar business idea hits you. This idea is so exciting; you can't stop thinking about it. You spend sleepless nights wondering how popular this business could become if executed. But what's the next step? Are you sure the idea is really something that could change people's lives? How could you really be sure before investing time and money into the idea?

I talked to Mike Matousek, the owner of FlashNotes.com, an online marketplace for students who want to buy and sell class notes, study guides and video tutorials. Mike was a junior at Kent State University when he launched this website. During one statistics class, Mike realized that most of the materials covered were something that he was already familiar with. However, for students following the subject for the first time, there was a vast disconnect between what was being taught and what they wanted. Mike decided to create detailed study guides for Statistics which he started selling at $10 apiece. The response was overwhelming. "*Not only did they sell, I was literally hunted down on campus by more and more of my classmates – easily making over $1,000. After this initial interest, I knew I was onto something, and had my friends test out the idea of selling study material in their own classes*", he says.

In Mike's case, the validation happened through an unscalable manual process that demonstrated demand. Once this was established, Mike would simply go ahead and build a marketplace where any student could buy or sell guides to other students.

With Mary Apple, the founder of Pretty Pushers (www.prettypushers.com), the process of validation happened through the birth of her two children. Mary is a fashion conscious lady who did not really like wearing those used unisex hospital gowns for what was "*the biggest event*" of her life. She decided to make her own yellow cotton dress to wear during her labor. Unfortunately, this dress did not accommodate the needs of the hospital staff. "*The anesthesiologist ended up cutting my little yellow dress off because it was blocking several access points for IVs. I felt disappointed and defeated. I felt like an ill patient instead of a strong woman giving birth*".

Mary spent two years working on the design of her hospital gown. She used all the feedback provided by the staff to create a new design that could be better suited for a woman in labor. "*That development stage lasted for about 2 years, and by the time I went back to the same hospital to give birth to my 2nd child, the Pretty Pushers brand was alive and well – and you'd better believe I wore one of our labor gowns. In the same delivery room, even with some of the same nurses, I wore the new and improved gown, proudly, the entire time! The staff applauded it and that was true validation of the brand!"*

Seeing your business idea get validated is a moment of great relief. I talked to several other entrepreneurs on their story of idea generation and validation. Here is a snapshot of how they all did it. *(Brief description of each business is available at the end of this book)*

Jordan Eisenberg | www.urgentrx.com

All of my businesses started around a problem – and a desire to solve it. All of the products I've developed were solutions to problems I had in my own life. I came up with UrgentRx (our fast-acting portable line of over-the-counter pharmaceuticals) since I was carrying medicine with me and my pills would get crushed and as a result were very unsanitary. They would taste awful when I had them when I had no liquid present. I solved this issue by creating UrgentRx - flavored single dose over the counter medications that taste good, don't need liquid, and could fit in my pocket or wallet.

To validate, I started by asking myself: would I buy this? While self-validation of an idea or concept should never be the only step in validating your idea, it is an extremely important one. Separating the fact it is your idea, objectively think about if you would pay your own hard-earned cash for the item. And would you be willing to pay what the actual price would be (you need to understand what the final price to consumers would be after factoring in the manufacturers' cost, shipping costs, wholesale margin, retail margin, etc.). A great idea that you would pay $10 for, but that you can only get to market at a cost to consumers of $50 is no longer a great idea. Once you've passed these steps, then take it to family and friends and ask them about it and get their feedback. After they've told you their (generally positive) thoughts – they're your friends after all - push them on what they DON'T like – then you will start getting to the truth (and come up with ways to make your concept even better – very important!).

After this, online surveys and leveraging social media is a great way to start moving from the qualitative feedback and into quantitative (which can help you drill down on things like ideal price-point, product name, etc.). Finally, bring your product – even if a prototype – to potential customers (trade-shows are a very efficient way to pitch many potential customers at once) and start trying to SELL it. There is no better validation than people committing to buy your product (and if they dor buy, ask why not – this feedback is the best way to make your idea better). Also, there are now online platforms like Kickstarter that allow you to do many of these in a one-stop shop (though I do not suggest skipping all the other steps). I brought UrgentRx to local pharmacies and got their feedback.

Rob Walling | www.getdrip.com

I've founded multiple start-ups, and the ones that have worked best were when I validated the idea before building anything. My most recent start-up, Drip, came out of a pain point I had just gone through in an existing business. We had spent several days writing custom software to capture email addresses from our website and realized there had to be a better way.

But I didn't go out and start building software the next day. Instead, I wanted to find 10 people who would be willing to pay a specific amount for the product once it was complete. This forced me to not think about features, but to distill the idea down into its core value - the single reason someone would be willing to pay me for the product. I took that, and emailed 17 people I know, or had at least heard of, who may have shared the same pain.

Of those 17, 11 said they would pay for it at the price I had mentioned ($99/mo). Later I lowered the price to $49/mo, but with the purchase commitment from those initial 11 people, I not only had my initial customers who could provide me feedback on the details of how Drip should work, I also had the start of an early base of revenue I could use to start growing the product.

Rob Infantino | www.openbay.com

It was the perfect storm. The combination of searching for the next big idea, my passion for cars, and what turned out to be a terrible personal experience when I brought my car in for service that ultimately led to starting another company. I've always loved cars, but had spent a career working in and starting companies in enterprise software. My last company, Astrum Software was acquired by EMC.

The outer edges of my tires were showing signs of wear, so it was time for a wheel alignment. I'd gone in to my local dealer for the service and wound up leaving after they gave me an estimate for $4,000 worth of repairs they had found. I declined all services and went home to do some research online. I was surprised to find there was no single resource where I could receive service proposals and estimates from shops near me, look at ratings and reviews, and schedule and pay for service. I knew there had to be a better way, and so the idea for Openbay was born.

I owe much of the validation process to Steve Blank. After formulating the idea for this online marketplace, I got out of the building and spoke to potential users of the service. The idea needed validation by real users. Since I was planning to build a two-sided marketplace, I had to speak to vehicle owners and automotive service providers, both of whom consistently offered valuable feedback about their challenges, their needs and what they'd want to see. I built a working prototype and shared it with the same groups with updates along the way. This took months of work. Before I knew it, I had validated my idea and development on a real product was to commence.

Jeb Blount | www.salesgravy.com

I started Sales Gravy in 2006. My primary intent was to promote my first book, Power Principles. The idea was to create a community for sales professionals and use that community to drive book sales and sell online training. The initial name of the site was "salesprofessionalsonline.com". However, after running the idea by some of my friends in the digital advertising community I was advised that this was a poor brand name. Honestly my feelings were hurt by their blunt feedback that the name was "*dumb.*" We had already started building the website and it was exciting. Starting over would be a setback.

At first I resisted the name change but thankfully I came to my senses and began a search for a more powerful brand. I stumbled on Sales Gravy as a name while having dinner with my family. It turned out to be a great choice. Short, sweet, and unforgettable.

We launched SalesGravy.com in December 2006 and over the next 90 days the business came together as much more than a place to sell books. I realized very early on that to monetize the site and create a self-sustaining business we had to have a more compelling offer. By March of 2007 I had a strategic plan for Sales Gravy. We would become a destination site and online community for sales professionals. We would then leverage that audience to sell employment advertising to employers that needed to hire good salespeople. We've stuck to that focus and today we are the market share leader in our niche.

Kyle James | www.rather-be-shopping.com

Way back in 2000, I was doing my Christmas shopping online and noticed the *'Coupon Code'* box when checking out at BestBuy.com. Since I had never heard of a coupon code I went and did some research. I quickly discovered that there were not many sites that listed coupons and organized them for quick retrieval and so the idea for **Rather-Be-Shopping.com** was born. My validation process was simply based on the fact that online shopping was growing by leaps and bounds in 2000 and there simply weren't many coupon sites to fill the demand. I knew I was getting in early on a niche that was growing quickly.

Jason Richelson | www.shopkeep.com

We validated it in my wine stores. I was solving an actual problem I had in my store, which was that my PC-based POS system continued to crash and get viruses and disrupt the businesses. I was spending way too much time and money on fixing it. I knew there had to be a better way for my store, which means there had to be a better way for many other stores too.

I also spoke with a lot of other retailers I knew. For most of them POS technology was too complicated or too expensive, so they would just use a cash register because that was easier. There was an obvious opportunity to create a less expensive and simpler alternative.

Jason Cohen | www.wpengine.com

Often the best ideas arise from your own life. You see a need, you see others struggling with something you can fix, so you invent a fix. However, many ideas cannot also sustain businesses. A business isn't just a good idea, it's also an idea that you can charge much more money for than it takes to produce, find customers, convincing them to buy and to support them after their purchase. Most ideas can't do that, much to the chagrin of millions of inventors with genuinely good ideas.

The way you validate the idea is to think about it as validating the business. You already know the idea is decent; that's not the question. Before starting WP Engine, I spoke to 40 potential customers before I had anything – no company name, no product, no slides, no presentation, no website, nothing. But I could ask whether they worry whether their website is slow, or whether it will stay up if they suddenly get a lot of traffic, or whether they worry about security, or whether they value being able to call any time and get friendly, knowledgeable help.

But *everyone* would say "*yes I want that.*" The question is, would they pay extra for that? Would they pay ten times more than they're paying today? That's a very different question, but since the answer was in the affirmative that showed that there's an actual *business* behind the idea.

Philip Masiello | www.800razors.com

For 800razors.com, we did a few things. First, we spent about 6 months researching the overall industry - the consumer profile, the competitive landscape and the present distribution model. We understood that whenever you have a competitor with over 70% market share, that channel is ripe for disruption. After our research, we set up a beta site about 6 months prior to launch and provided product to about 1,000 customers. We tested price points, product quality, site navigation and overall user experience. The response was so overwhelmingly positive that we knew we were on the right track for a successful start-up.

Jason Schultz | www.jason.me

Ideas for problems to solve can come from anywhere. Sometimes I discover a problem by hearing other people complain about it, while other times it's something I directly have experience with. Ideas by themselves are also quite worthless. The value comes from the execution, turning the thought into a working business.

Typically I try to validate an idea far before it becomes a business. I seek out potential customers (i.e. people who experience the problem first hand) and then ask them questions that clue me in to the demand for the service.

Here's another quick way to validate an idea and build a customer list. Setup a simple one page website that describes the product or service and ask that visitors simply leave you with their email address. Setup pay per click advertising to quickly generate targeted traffic to your page, then test test test. Try different pricing models and levels, different ways of describing the product or service, and so on.

Bryan Knowlton | www.appraisersclub.com

Before I got started building my business, I started by publishing articles in industry related magazines and on industry related websites, I then created a number of free give away products along with a blog to build my audience. I then moved on to producing a few industry related directories and epic resources that I could sell. After sales started to come in, I decided to create the company that later became a private membership site focusing on teaching internet marketing skills to my audience of real estate appraisers.

Matt Shoup | www.mandepainting.com

I worked for a college painting company while I was attending Colorado State University and that introduced me to the painting industry. Shortly after graduating, I found myself with a new wife (my college sweetheart

Emily), a new house and a job as a mortgage banker. I quickly realized that the corporate world and I did not get along at all and, before I could make the decision, I was fired in early 2005. With a lifelong passion for entrepreneurship and the experience I got in college, I founded M&E Painting in 2005 with my last $100 and over $100,000 in debt. Validating the idea was the easy part for me: I have always been an entrepreneur and felt I could best serve my community by moving into an industry that had a woeful lack of quality and service in the Northern Colorado area.

Joshua Dorkin | www.biggerpockets.com

I believe that the idea was validated the day that I could quit my job and rely on the business to pay my bills. In the early years, I had more than my fair share of naysayers who told me to stop while I was ahead. This included major VCs, angels, friends, and others. While I respected their opinions, I know that the idea had legs and fought on. As our budding user base started to invite others to come on board, it was clear that the concept behind the idea was proven. The key was to get the site to the point that the growth happened organically. I believe that the idea was truly validated when I started getting phone calls from the press, when private equity firms and other VCs began to reach out, and when I saw the site and our revenues grow in a major way.

Andrew Gazdecki | www.biznessapps.com

From the time I was in high school I always aspired to be a serial entrepreneur. I was fascinated with starting businesses and always found myself creating and then moving onto new ventures. Then when I moved on to college I set the goal of starting a company every summer.

While wrapping up my senior year of college at CSU Chico in 2010 it became evident that the world was shifting to mobile and fast. That's when I first noticed how expensive mobile app development was. At that time if a small or medium sized business was looking into developing a native app, they were looking at months of development time and sometimes as much as $50k. Thus where I found my opportunity; provide a solution that made taking businesses mobile fast, easy and at a low cost.

We validated the idea by starting to go after clients as soon as we had our initial product up and running. We believed if we could sell it to the local businesses in the area we could sell to any small business. Landing our first few clients and getting them to pay for the product was extremely validating and really gave us the idea that we might be onto something big.

I've been thinking about private space for a very long time. But it was the creation of an electronic lock that really made it all possible for me and my company to build something amazing. We did early experiments with students, seeing if they would reserve an apartment for a few hours to get studying done. That allowed us to figure out that others might enjoy private space as well.

There were a few cleaning start-ups with, supposedly, good traction that had raised initial rounds, so we decided it was worth investigating further since barrier to entry was really low anyway. We actually validated it without having any cleaners to do the cleanings. We threw up a site, a booking form, a phone number, and ran some PPC ads through Google and Bing, and saw what the conversion rate would be had we actually had cleaners—we would let customers get all the way to giving their credit card info, and then say we couldn't actually do it. I suppose it is a kind of MVP, if you like start-up terminology (I hate it, personally!)

The best validation we've done so far has been actually performing our service hands-on for our team members and our friends. You learn so much when you just do the work manually. There is a reason that bands start playing in garages for their friends – they can see which songs people like, then lean into that. The more we help our friends on a small-scale, the more insight we get into our customer base. A couple other ideas that worked for us: We sent out surveys to our users and asked what products they wanted us to develop next. We went to the local Starbucks and asked people to try our product, answer questions about clothing, or even give us copy feedback. I always call one of our customers on the way home from work and just ask them what they hate about our website – or what we could do to make it a game changer for them.

After working at the ABC television network and then a digital music start-up back-to-back in the late nineties, I realized the Internet was going to disrupt traditional media in a big way. I just didn't realize how at that point. Next, I worked at Sony Pictures Digital for four years and a couple of things happened: My ideas about digital content and how to make money at started to become clearer and the market caught up with some of my assumptions. I always wanted to be in the business of storytelling, but it wasn't until 2006 that I felt confident the time was right to start a digital content company. Even then it was too early!

In the beginning advertiser validation was key. We would come up with an idea or produce an idea someone pitched us and then immediately go out and try and find a brand to sponsor it. If we found a brand and they paid us a reasonable sum of money we felt like we had some validation. Admittedly, it was really about audience validation. Then things changed in 2011 when we launched Kin Community (the channel and multichannel network) on YouTube. Everything became about how engaged our audience is: how many views, watch-time, shares, likes, comments, etc. Now that we have one of the most engaged content communities online, we are back to seeking validation from advertisers. It has come full-circle.

Aditi Kapur | www.deliverychef.in

I founded DeliveryChef.in – a website that lets you order food online from your local restaurants for delivery. The first step to validating my idea was to evaluate whether I would use a service like that. Thinking like a customer is key – that's how you find the value proposition of your business idea, look at the pain point, and really think about how to address it. Once you have done that, then you can talk to others – friends, family and people whom you identify to be in your target audience to see if they would use the service.

Once you are sure you have a market for your venture, you need to talk to the people that are actually going to pay you, and make sure the economics work out. For me, it was the restaurants – would the increase in delivery orders add value to them? If so, how much could they afford to pay for it consistently over a long period of time? This would be my revenue model. Would this be enough for me and my business to make a profit in the long run? When all this fell into place, I decided to start up!

Adam Simpson | www.easyofficephone.com

The businesses I've started have always been "*early adoption*" scenarios. For example, with Internet advertising in the late 1990s, and now with cloud-based phone service starting ten years ago, we got into the game near the beginning. This meant that the basic idea validation was in place, and there were some existing companies in the space with proven models, but at the same time the market was open to new and innovative start-ups. I've found this to be a good starting point. You know the model can work, and you also have a certain amount of time to refine your offering and differentiate it before new competition shows up in force.

The idea for elevate DIGITAL really had its genesis in 2008 when I first became interested in finding a way to connect people – to objects, information, other people – differently than we'd seen in the past. This idea was primarily rooted in government - how can we provide access for people to engage with their local leaders and connect with city-centric information in a new way?

As I watched social and mobile take off so quickly, I identified an even greater void in the marketplace. Not everyone had access to those platforms and even today, many still don't. These channels are one-to-many and I wanted to look at creating an outlet that could provide equal access to information and connect with the groups of people that were forming in public places, on the ground-level. As a result, the idea grew to be much broader than its original government focus and in 2011, I founded elevate DIGITAL with the goal of connecting people to information and brands through engagement and interactivity at the street level.

Micha Kaufman | www.fiverr.com

The best way to validate an idea is to try a mini version of the product's larger vision. This is often referred to as 'MVP, 'short for 'Minimum Viable Product. An MVP should contain the unique, core value proposition your idea is trying to address. The MVP should appeal to the user of the product, taking into account that the first to try it have the special attributes of *'early adopters'* - those who are willing to test new products even if they are not fully backed.

If you want your product to get traction, have virality components built into the product so that the early adopters can spread their experience by tweeting, liking, etc. Put customer support as the center of the product. This ensures customers have an easy way to communicate their experience, both good and bad, directly to you.

As an entrepreneur, make sure to do as much of the initial support as possible, so that you don't miss precious feedback, which your first users will share with you. How did this apply to Fiverr? When we started Fiverr the larger vision was to create the next eBay for services. Like eBay, the initial product could not possibly hold all the features of a mature product, simply because it would overwhelm the first customers and confuse them as to what the core value proposition was.

eBay, started with hobbyists and collectors doing small price transactions and then evolved into a full-fledged marketplace that can also serve business and merchants. Fiverr was quite similar: we started with low-end transactions for $5 and then expanded to more professional and higher priced services. The MVP was a simple, intuitive and delightful two-sided marketplace, with a clear call to action, inviting people to offer their skills and for others to order those services without the need to negotiate with the sellers.

We made sure the experience was sticky and viral, so that customers spent a lot of time on the site, and wanted to share their experience with their friends. After validating this basic model and learning how to scale it up we were ready to move to the next phase of introducing more advanced features.

Zalmi Duchman | www.thefreshdiet.com

The idea for my start-up came during a call with a friend who is a chef. He was telling me about a diet delivery service in Los Angeles that he heard about. I did some research on the Internet & could not find a similar service in Miami, FL where I lived & decided to start a similar business. I validated my idea by actually jumping into my business head-on. Instead of spending time on market research I decided to start my business & see first-hand if this is a service that people want. After seeing that I was able to sign up 3 customers to begin the service for a month, I felt that I had enough to begin delivering my product.

Stacey Lindenberg | www.growyourtalent.com

I interviewed over 20 people that had successfully started their business in my industry and who had a proven track record of staying afloat. I asked questions about how long it took them to become profitable, what things they would do differently, and what advice they would give me. I also did market research to determine if there was a need for my services and how realistic it would be to start out on my own

Kathy Crifasi | www.hipzbag.com

My Product-based start-up was born purely out of necessity. I had a problem and there was no solution, so I created one. I felt strongly that there was a "*shift*" in the world revolving around our increasingly deep attachment to our cell phones. As we've seen time and time before, when there is a shift in the world, new products and practices are developed to accommodate them. Wah lah, the Hipzbag. I did not get a lot of validation on the product for quite a while. When I showed it to friends, they would just say it was not for them. My Mom, of course, loved it! So it was me and my Mom wearing the Hipzbag for the first 6 months.

After getting myself and the Hipzbag out into the world (anyone that would take us), I stumbled upon reps that '*got*' the concept instantly and wanted to present it to QVC. The Hipzbag was accepted immediately from the QVC buyer in 2010. They sold out on the first show! It was instant VALIDATION and our product has been a best seller and a customer favorite ever since. Now everyone that said that my invention "*just wasn't for them*" and I mean everyone wants one.

Mike Glanz | www.hireahelper.com

A couple of my college roommates used to make money loading and unloading moving trucks on the weekends in college. They got the jobs using a couple of small moving websites where they listed their services. But they were constantly complaining about the experience. We used to talk a lot about starting a competing service and doing it better. That's when the idea for HireAHelper was born.

I had multiple ideas for start-ups prior to HireAHelper.com, each one better than the last. Señor Stacks was going to be the listing service for home poker games; YouGotComments.com was going to be a MySpace desktop notifier so you didn't have to open up a browser to check MySpace. There were probably a dozen others too. For each one I had launched a website, generating content on my own and spending a little money on advertising. They all failed hard and fast. The biggest difference between HireAHelper.com and the previous sites was the model generated cash. I knew if we made $10 per order that we only needed 300 orders per month to support myself. 10 orders per day. When I compared 10 orders per day to 100,000 users required supporting myself via the other sites, it seemed like it couldn't be that hard.

A lot of my validation came very democratically. When I told that story to my soon-to-be co-founder, he immediately got excited. When I went and asked for money from friends and family they too seemed to buy into the model as well. Having people that believe in you can be a dangerous thing. It was all the motivation I needed to plunge in head first.

Mike Townsend | www.homehero.org / www.flowtab.com

Kyle and I were typical early 20 somethings, so the bars were a scene we were very familiar with. With knowledge about mobile technology potential, it was a long conversation at Copa D' Oro in Santa Monica with the manager one night that gave us our spark.

Debra Cohen | www.homeownersreferral.com

I was extremely uncertain that my idea would work and I met with a lot of naysayers. My business was very unique and a lot of people didn't "*get it*". Ultimately, I spoke with as many contractors, homeowners and realtors as I could and the majority of them were able to relate to the type of service I was providing.

I remember speaking with one decorative painter in particular when I was first thinking about launching my contractor referral business. She was so talented and did exceptional work but she told me that business was slow. I couldn't believe it. It made me realize that—while many contractors may be talented in their fields—they aren't always that good at promoting themselves and that's my area of expertise.

Rob Biederman | www.hourlynerd.com

We actually went door to door pitching our idea to every small business owner in Boston and Cambridge that we could find. A lot of them rejected us straight away, but our pitch really resonated with many of the business owners who had no ability to access high quality labor with the prices they could afford. We found about 8 customers and posted their projects to a GoDaddy starter page we bought for $10. This was enough to get MBAs coming to our site and placing bids to work for the businesses, primarily (I think) because they thought it would be a cool experience. There was no substitute for getting this initial traffic (on both sides of the market) to the original site; after we had proved to both sides we could cater to their needs, it became a lot easier to acquire new projects as well as MBAs to bid on them.

Raghu Kulkarni | www.idrive.com

It was late 1990s, and internet was the new Wild West. Lots of new things were happening on the web. We thought why not do backup on the web? The internet access speeds were very slow, so even moving small files was a big task. But it was doable and at least you could use the web to store small critical files. Emails were already very popular, so files and data were next.

Audrius Jankauskas | www.impresspages.org

The funny and, one might say, stupid thing is, we didn't do any idea validation. When creating ImpressPages, we did everything from inner passion and idealism. All of us had experience in the web industry and all of us felt the lack of a comfortable tool to work with. So when this idea of building a totally new CMS was born, we didn't look for much proof but dived straight to it.

We had that feeling of certainty and we held on to it when developing each stage of our product. Together came the positive feedback from users who liked it and it was the best idea validation an entrepreneur could want. To put it shortly, just do business and see what comes out of it. Do a market research, find your strengths and values, create a product and test it on actual users. That's our recipe of success.

Ryan Wallace | www.iphoneantidote.com

I had been looking for different types of businesses I could start for a long time, but I never found the courage to jump in on any of the ideas. I actually broke my iPhone one day, and looked up how much it would cost to fix. I was floored at the idea of spending $200, and when I looked up the price of the parts on eBay, I saw the parts were priced at only $40. I decided to give it a shot at repairing it myself, and after I fixed it, I sold my iPhone on eBay. Shortly after, I started buying broken iPhones on eBay and selling them on eBay. It didn't take long for me to realize that I was giving eBay too much money in fees, so I decided to create a business where people could sell their broken iPhones.

As I mentioned before, I really validated the idea because I needed the service. There were some other companies like ours, which purchase broken iPhones, but none of them paid what I believe to be a fair amount for the devices. Then I looked up their reviews, they were not great by a long shot. I realized that if we were to start an iPhone buyback service, that paid fair, and acted as promised, we would rise to the top.

Jake Sigal | www.livioconnect.com

I really liked music and technology throughout my life and career. I was working at Delphi within the XM Satellite radio group and learned about Pandora. I knew they were going to be great so I pitched the execs at Pandora to allow me to build a desktop radio for them. It worked!

Myke Nahorniak | www.localist.com

Our idea was validated when we found our first paying customer. The original idea for Localist was a destination site; a place to find all the upcoming events in a region. The response to the idea was almost universally positive. "*I've always wanted a way to find all the events that are happening where I live!*" In reality, translating that idea into a business was much more difficult, and met with far more resistance.

Fast forward a couple years and we ended up with a very sound business model that still immediately clicks with people who end up being fantastic customers, but not necessarily everyone. And that's okay, we're not building Localist for everyone; we're building Localist for people who "*get it.*" Any meaningful validation of an idea comes from having someone who is willing to pay for what you're offering. In that sense, validation of the idea is more a validation of the execution. Ideas per se are fairly easy. What's much harder is finding the people who not only agree that it's a good idea, they're willing to put their money where their mouth is.

Arnon Rose | www.localmaven.com

Typically ideas I have had for start-ups have come to me as a result of seeing a gap in a particular market or a need for a product or service that did not yet exist. My first company out of school introduced a product for skiing called Ski Valet. It was basically a wheel for the back of ones skis that allowed you to roll the skis to the slopes versus carrying them. In those days, skis were much longer and much heavier and I thought that there would be a market for something that made carrying skis easy. I learned from that experience never to launch a product that I wouldn't use myself. In the case of the wheel for skis you wouldn't have caught me dead with one of those on the back of my skis and as it turned out, most other people felt the same way. So now my rule is that a business must serve a need and deliver a product that I myself would use.

Jill Foucré | www.marcelsculinaryexperience.com

Initially my idea came from my personal experiences in stores/cooking schools of a similar nature and I liked them and liked the model. Once I decided to start developing a business plan, I did more formal research including studying market and industry trends, conducting focus groups, doing on site surveys of comparable stores, and interviewing other business owners.

Kevin Lavelle | www.mizzenandmain.com

The idea for Mizzen+Main came when I saw a Congressional staffer run into a building soaked in sweat from the sweltering DC summer heat. This was around eight years ago when the use of performance fabrics was on the rise, and I thought, why not make a dress shirt out of these performance fabrics? It seemed like a logical idea. In reality, it was a tremendous challenge for Web and I to create a product that looks like a natural, organic dress shirt but performs alongside the best technical garments worn by athletes on the field.

We spent a long time under the radar working on the nuances of the product itself before launching. Discussing it with friends and family you trust was a great way to get initial feedback, but ultimately, you have to create something to determine if it a) really works b) is something people will actually pay for or sign up for (should you plan to monetize in other ways) and c) is something that you really want to do because it will be anything but easy. The moment I knew my idea for a *"performance fabric dress shirt"* would work is when I showed the first prototype to my wife by wearing it home. She knew I had been working on it for an extended period of time, and knew that I would be wearing it home. When I asked her what she thought, she looked at me and said *"about what?"* I knew in that moment if she couldn't tell I wasn't wearing my standard dress shirt, and instead was wearing the world's first performance fabric dress shirt, that we could really builds a company around this idea!

Edward DeSalle | www.netirrigate.com

The original product concepts for Net Irrigate were validated by selling the product before it was actually built. I simply asked prospects, *"Would you pay for something like this if it works and how much would you be willing to pay?"* It turned out that in the agricultural community, there were plenty of people willing to test and experiment with new technology, provided they didn't have to pay for it until it actually met their expectations. I learned that it's critical to understand their perspective and the value they're deriving from the product; not your own. In essence, it didn't matter what I thought was cool.

Alicia Weaver | www.prestigeestateservices.com

My husband and I were always looking for an idea we could take and make our own. For every idea we came up with we'd do our homework and try to poke holes in it. Who was the competition? Was it profitable? What were the barriers of entry? How much money and time would it take to just get it started? Once we found an idea that seemed solid we jumped. We both agreed it was important to give it a go on our own so we waited until the right idea came along, there weren't obvious obstacles so we gave it a go.

Chandler Crouch | www.chandlercrouch.com

I dropped out of college. After a not so successful attempt at running a lawn mowing company, I took some time to reflect on the direction I was going. I saved $2000 and planned to take a 2 week break from work to figure out the career I was going to start. During that 2 week period I stopped by the leasing office of my $365 all-bills-paid apartment to pay the rent. The landlord, who owned 13 apartment complexes in town, happened to be in the lobby. He asked me if I had any interest in helping him start a real estate company. At the time I had hair down to my bellybutton and definitely didn't *"dress for success."* Considering the way I looked and the serendipitous timing of the whole thing, I thought surely this is some sort of divine sign. I thought about it for a couple hours and the rest is history.

Robert Livingstone | www.royaltext.com

We certainly weren't the pioneers for text message marketing. However, we saw a gap in the market as the existing providers in the marketplace seemed to offer a transactional and impersonal relationship. We wondered why there weren't any companies that catered to small businesses, helped them to build their customer lists, send out the campaigns and track the results. When we found the gap in the marketplace and discovered that there wasn't too much saturation in our local market, we decided to take the plunge and open the business.

Michael Kawula | www.selfemployedking.com

Validating a business helps you both validate and invalidate assumptions. My first 2 businesses I owned were franchises and as part of the process of buying a franchise you're required to speak to other current and previous franchise owners. This process of speaking with other owners helped me learn a lot and also saved me from purchasing other franchises because I was able to invalidate my assumptions. I'm a big believer that imperfect action beats perfect inaction, though I'm happy I took the time to speak with other owners prior to purchasing and learned more about the day to day life of the owner.

Have a set of questions prepared and try to speak to several different owners, those who are doing great and those that aren't also. This will help you in your decision process and make you better prepared for when you move forward. You'll also build great relationships of other people who you can use as mentors when you get started.

Rick Martinez | www.senorsangria.com

My idea found me. I was making sangria at home for get-togethers. Over time I started refining the recipe to make it taste better. Eventually friends started asking me to make them a jug

Eventually it became them giving me $20 for the hassle of making it. Then one day coming home from a party where I had made some sangria, my then girlfriend (now wife) stopped me as we were walking back to my apartment in Hoboken, NJ and said I've got the perfect business for you (I've always worked for start-ups but wanted something of my own. I had plenty of ideas but none ever really excited me). Maria said why you don't sell your sangria. Plus she had the name that night - call it "*Senor Sangria*".

I thought she was nuts but went to the liquor store shortly thereafter and realized that the bottled sangria on the market just didn't taste like what I thought sangria should. To validate, I made some of my homemade sangria and I took it to a few retailers and asked them if they would buy sangria in a bottle that tasted like this. All of them looked at me like I was nuts but agreed that the existing bottled sangria sucked. Each of them said if I could bottle my homemade stuff they'd buy it. They all seemed to really enjoy my sangria but didn't think I'd be able to do it on a commercial scale.

I visited a bunch of folks like this and made a list of who said they would buy it. What I didn't realize then was I was in essence "*pre-selling*" my product. Later on I would come back with my finished product and would remind them of the commitment they made to me. The 2nd level of validation was running the numbers. I created a fairly complex spreadsheet which I still use today. This spreadsheet allowed me to understand how much money I would need to commit to this business and how much product I'd have to sell.

It forced me to ask a TON of questions to people about the alcohol industry. Keep in mind that I didn't know anything about the alcohol industry. My background was internet software. This step to me was critical because it made me realize the HUGE task I was taking on. This made it REAL. These 2 steps were all the validation I needed to have me move onto the next step. The next step took me almost 3 years. I had to formulate my product, find a packer, design the packaging, sell my home to fund the company, quit my job to focus on this business 100%.

Julie Busha | www.slawsa.com

A non-natural version of the original Slawsa recipe was one based off of a very old family recipe that wasn't being sold in any stores when I came aboard to lend my efforts in 2011. If you'd told me three years ago that I'd be the owner of a condiment company that is in more than 6,000 stores nationwide and expanding abroad, I'd say you were crazy. You never know what hurdles life will throw at you. I was 34 when my former partner asked that I buy him out. I was shocked, but given the extreme efforts that I personally put into launching the brand, how could I not find a way to make that happen? You'll find that risks are worth taking when you believe in your product and your abilities to grow it. I will tell you that professionally speaking, there is nothing more fulfilling than waking up each day knowing that the success of growing a great brand in the hearts of consumers is because of your efforts. Pardon the pun, but I relish that feeling.

Validation for me truly came from grocery buyers who were willing to take a risk on carrying Slawsa. A seasoned grocery buyer has "*seen it all*" and is especially wary of start-ups because they generally lack knowledge of the industry. Remember, the first thing a buyer wants to see is your marketing program. In other words, do you have a clear vision and plan of how to sell your product off the shelf? Getting a retailer to carry your product is the easier aspect of selling at retail. Price, uniqueness, flavor/attributes are all important, but the buyer's job is to generate sales and you need to prove to them that you're taking steps in marketing to achieve your shared goal of selling. I went straight to major retailers as I have always envisioned Slawsa as a national brand due to its uniqueness and affordability. You need to prove to yourself and to prospective buyers that there is a market for your product. Friends and family will tell you what you want to hear so the best feedback you can get is from total strangers. They're not only going to provide honesty about improvements, packaging or things you haven't thought of, but they'll either buy your product or they won't. Sales, whether it be at a retailer, online or at a festival or farmers market, is the ultimate validation that you have a viable product.

Heidi Lamar | www.spalamar.com

In 2004 I purchased a commercial building which had 3 tenants. One of them was a struggling spa which had belonged to the building owner's daughter, who had recently passed away. The spa was sort of a "*gift with purchase*" I did some research and found that Scottsdale had more spas per capita than any city in the world so I knew it would be a very competitive business. I visited quite a few of the resort spas and found that many of them were offering "*the desert experience*" to visitors. I decided to offer an escape from the desert to locals by rebranding the spa as a "*cactus free zone*" Combining an island ambiance with prices that were 40% below resort-spas, I was able to attract the locals and the savvy travelers followed.

Zeb Couch | www.offmarketformula.com / www.speedhatch.com

The idea for Speedhatch came from being in the industry. I got my real estate salespersons license when I was a sophomore in college and started my own residential real estate leasing company right after I graduated. By the time the opportunity to launch Speedhatch came around, I was about two years out of college and had about four to five years of real estate experience under my belt.

Speedhatch is all about fast, easily scalable and useful websites for real estate agents. From being in the business, I knew how important having a web presence is but many of the options for real estate agents were expensive, antiquated and took weeks, if not months, to build. I had some pains that needed to be solved and Speedhatch was a personal solution. But, just because Speedhatch was going to solve my problems, didn't mean it was going to solve other people's. So, to further validate, I "*got out of the building*" (as Steve Blank always says) and talked to colleagues in the industry about their own pains around launching a web presence. I emailed agents, called agents, I also surfed around the web and found forums where real estate agents hang out and talk about their business. Forums are the best because they're unadulterated (I learned this from Amy Hoy). You're listening to customers when they don't know they're being listened to, which means they're really being honest about their pains and the problems they need solved. The forums were a goldmine, tons of questions like "*how do I get a cheap website?*" and "*any ideas on how to quickly build a website?*" Perfect validation for Speedhatch.

Google keyword tool is another great resource to help validate ideas. Put together a list of keywords and phrases associated with your idea that your potential customers might search for. Type these keywords and phrases into Google keyword tool and see what kind of volume there is. It's no science, but a good amount of search volume means there's a common problem that needs solving. This method will also clue you into any competitors.

Justyn Howard | www.sproutsocial.com

While working for an enterprise software company, I began to see a lot of potential customers using social media to connect with customers. However, every third-party social media tool in the marketplace was consumer focused and didn't have the power that commercial use demanded. Therefore, I wanted to build a platform that made social engagement, publishing and measurement more efficient and effective for business use. The result of that is Sprout Social.

Blaine Vess | www.studymode.com

I live by the adage: necessity is the mother of invention. Too many aspiring entrepreneurs over-think and over-complicate things by searching for the perfect idea when, really, they can probably find their best idea much closer to home. That was certainly the case when I started StudyMode and today we are financially self-sufficient, we employ 25 people and we help more than 90 million visitors each month.

In 1999, my friend Chris Nelson and I were struggling college freshman. We were facing the same challenges that students still face today – expensive tuition, intense competition for grades, and difficulty obtaining books and study materials. We decided to launch a site for our friends to share research materials and course notes. We realized very quickly that we had a marketable and scalable product.

Quite simply, our idea was validated by the instant demand we saw for our product. In fact, I had to learn to code in order to enhance our site to keep up with the growing demand. We also knew our product was solid because we found it helpful ourselves. And after all, we were representative of our target market.

Michelle MacDonald | www.sweetnotebakery.com

The validation of my idea was probably one of the most important steps taken at the beginning of the startup process. I had several ideas for what kind of business I would launch and what product to choose. It's crucial to be solving a problem with whatever your idea is. For me, knowing that my start up would be with food (as that is my passion and that an important ingredient in any business) I had a few product ideas. I started with cookies and started researching the market, finding what outlets I would be able to sell to. From my research I found that the market had a lot of competition and wasn't necessarily on the rise at the time. I was looking for something that I could offer that would differentiate my product from the competition. After much more research I found that gluten-free products were on the rise, and it hit close to home when I found out my grandfather was diagnosed with celiac disease (requiring a gluten-free diet). I found market research from online sources about the growing demand for products of this nature.

I then went straight to the outlets I would be selling to, for me it was cafes, restaurants and grocery stores. They all expressed a growing demand and interest. I looked at what gluten-free product was missing from the market and/or lacked a good tasting version and I found that a gluten-free bagel was something that needed to be improved on. All the options I found lacked a real bagel taste. I went back to these potential customers and asked if they would buy a bagel if I created one; the answer was yes. I then researched if there was a foundation and/or group for my industry and came across the National Foundation for Celiac Awareness; I asked them if they have heard a demand for a better gluten-free bagel alternative, their answer was yes. I then got in touch with a local blogger who blogs for the gluten-free community in my area and asked what he had heard, he responded the same way; there was a demand for a better option. All of this validated my idea that this product would indeed be solving a problem.

Danny Maloney | www.tailwindapp.com

We got the idea by failing. Alex (my co-founder) and I had been working on a different product that wasn't panning out. From that failure, we stumbled on a better opportunity. When enough customer pitches resulted in "*[your core business] is a nice idea but tell me more about this other thing*," you have to listen to the market. If we hadn't, Tailwind wouldn't exist today.

We "*validated*" our first (failed) product by having friends and family tell us how wonderful it was. Felt great, but they didn't use it. When we started Tailwind, we took a different approach- asking complete strangers who didn't care about us at all to sign-up and pay before our product was even built. We stood up a sign-up page, bought some AdWords traffic and people actually started offering to pay us! We didn't actually charge them, but we learned we were onto something.

Cricket Allen | www.theperfectsnaque.com

The Perfect SNAQUE product line is based on foods/snacks I was making for myself at home. I wanted whole foods with little to no processing, a great taste and a product where every bite counts.

Before The Perfect SNAQUE, I owned a beverage company that grew very quickly, and nationally, before all of the "*tweaking*" through the validation process had been done. I learned making changes on a big stage is expensive and exceedingly difficult with a start-up's resources (people and capital). Knowing this, we invested in a plan for The Perfect SNAQUE that gave us the time and measurement tools to validate the idea. What we now know is a product's first blush may not be what you ultimately deliver to the market, making validation somewhat of an evolution that requires being nimble and listening to feedback.

Overall, the number one measurement tool we use to validate our product is repeat orders from stores, distributors or consumers (direct). Repeat orders are the ultimate sign your product is working. If you aren't getting repeat orders, don't fret. Just get comfortable with the idea that validating can be a process of changes in areas such as: pricing; packaging; communication. I can say the original product we went to market with changed in all three of these areas. We didn't give up. We made adjustments that ended up being right.

The validation process continues to evolve for us because we continue to sell to various types of customers in different parts of the country (e.g., natural, independent, conventional grocery, gourmet, cafes, online, gyms, etc). Thus far, it is becoming measurably stronger every month and the validation has continued.

Nick Paradise | www.threadbuds.com

We prototyped our product and began showing it to friends and family and even strangers. We asked for honest, candid feedback because without that, we'd never be completely sure if we were on to something. The feedback we got was overwhelmingly exceptional and we decided to move on improving our prototype based on feedback we received.

In one of my previous start-ups, my partner and I made too many assumptions and didn't ask enough questions. We had a great idea that we lost sight of due to a feature we thought was very important. Had we done a more hands on and in depth market analysis or simply asked questions, we would have realized early that this feature was not as important as we made it to be. My advice here: Ask questions - lots. Learn about the industry you're getting involved with. Call some professionals or reach out to your networks to find someone who might have some really great knowledge or expertise in what you're doing. Friends and strangers alike who are great and knowledgeable in something, are usually more than happy to show or tell you how great they are in that industry.

Eren Bali | www.udemy.com

The key validation factor for us was to see if people would be willing to pay for online courses. There were two stages to validating our idea. First, we needed to build our course library and get paid courses onto the platform. Second, we had to find students that were interested in paying for these courses.

Our early courses were designed primarily for entrepreneurs and people working in the tech industry. We knew courses such as social marketing, raising capital for start-ups and python programming would be helpful educational content for this demographic. We then contacted partners who had a growing email list of people who fit this demographic. We reached out to organizations such as "*Start-up Digest*" and "*Start-up Weekend*" who we knew had a larger start-up following. Our success with this strategy was largely because we focused on creating value for the partner and also their customers. We created a revenue-sharing agreement with the partner and gave customers a discount on the courses. This was hugely successful for us and gave us around $40,000 in revenue.

Partnering with organizations with content and an audience was a game-changing moment for us and gave us the validation to continue our efforts.

Josh Rosenwald | www.unroll.me

We know that everyone has too many subscription emails in their inbox. It's a global problem so we didn't need to validate the need for a solution as much as we needed to validate the type of solution needed. We decided the safest route would be to build and push out the Minimal

Viable Product - the most basic product that could properly work - as quickly and as cheaply as possible. Admittedly, it wasn't our best work but it was the cheapest and most efficient way to test the market.

This inevitably backfired as our user base began to grow so large so quickly. It was also really challenging to build our later version on top of our shaky foundation. But at the end of the day, it was totally worth it because we were able to prove in a very cost effective manner that we had the right initial approach to a very large and under-served marketplace.

Christy Ferrer | www.vidicom.com

It was extension of two great loves - Fashion and immortalizing it by videotaping runway shows. No one had ever done that before and used it as news features back in 1979. Secondly, a love for New York City where I had just moved. I had so many people coming to visit me that I made a video tape of what to do and where to go in the city. I talked a friendly hotel owner into allowing me to play this on a channel in his hotel and now CityBuzz is in 140 hotels in NYC and 75 in Chicago. I created what is now called branded content meaning establishments paid to be covered in the show.

It is often hard for many to remember that ideas are cheap and good ideas are cheap. It's all in the ability to execute on those ideas then monetize them. So you have to continually tweak the business plan and see what catches.

Bas Beerens | www.wetransfer.com

The WeTransfer concept was borne out of a simple need to provide a solution for people to easily send large files online. At the time I was running an agency called OY that dealt primarily in high-resolution imagery and video – as many creative agencies do. We were spending a huge amount of time and money on couriers physically delivering files, and so we knew immediately that a service like this had a reason to exist from a business perspective.

For a few years, this tool, which we called OY Transfer, was used by OY's clients and suppliers in Amsterdam. Even big corporations like Tommy Hilfiger and Nike Europe were using it. Although they all had their own systems, they were increasingly using OY Transfer for its quick and easy functionality – it was free to use and deliberately didn't have any complicated registration processes, passwords or FTP environment.

For about three years we were working on improving the service, removing bugs and listening to user comments and feedback. With OY

Transfer the problems of courier costs and slow delivery times evaporated and I realized that a simple service like this would appeal to a much wider audience - but I hadn't yet found a business model to make a more substantial service a reality. Keeping the service free was central to the success of OY transfer, and banner ads or asking our users for money simply didn't sit well with me, so taking the service to the next level had to wait.

Around this time I met Nalden, a Dutch blogger with millions of international followers. Nalden was earning his money from full-screen wallpaper advertising on his blog – ads that weren't obtrusive, but instead were a simple, beautiful and integral part of the blog's user experience. Nike, Universal and others were paying a lot of money for (mostly un-branded) backgrounds.

Nalden and I shared the same passion for finding the Internet's potential by harnessing simplicity and design. We were looking to work together for a few years, then after one lunch I had the 'Eureka' moment and realised we could integrate Nalden's advertising model into the transferring tool. We knew this would work – so for a whole year all the developers at OY worked on this new tool, which eventually became WeTransfer.

Nalden mentioned WeTransfer on his blog the day we launched in September 2009 and the reaction was amazing. By the second day, we already had 70,000 visits. We had only expected 5,000 users in the first month, but this eventually turned out to be over 250,000! When user numbers increase that rapidly, the idea in its purest form validates itself.

We now have 50 million monthly users and we still pride ourselves on the simplicity of the service. There's no doubt that the simplicity and the ease of use of our platform are behind its success.

Iftach Orr | www.pix.do

Ideas come to me when I least expect them – while driving my car or taking the dog for a walk – but that doesn't mean they come out of thin air. I like to think of the things we experience and learn in life as ingredients in a stew. When you first put everything into the pot it's a bit of a mess and one ingredient is completely unrelated to the other, but once they've cooked for a while they begin to form this amazing new dish. I try to stay on top of the latest activity in the industries I'm interested in and talk about what I'm following with friends and family. Eventually the ideas will just start to come.

My validation cycles are rapid. I treat an idea as clay in my hand and in those first few days everything is flexible. I run ideas through a few friends and rather than focusing on specific features I spend my time improving the story around the product. Then I build a simple landing page (less than a day's work) and post it to a few blogs to see how people in the outside world react to it.

J'Amy Owens | www.billthebutcher.com

You are likely in love with your new idea, but be prepared to be heartbroken if your idea cannot pass an analytical validation, to really prove it should be launched. There are disciplined and rigorous ways to validate your idea, including: thoroughly researching the category, describing your strategy in a business plan with detailed financial information, identifying and interviewing the proposed user groups/customers and the proposed vendors, lenders, distributors, sales channels and especially the competitors. You would do well to conduct informational interviews and take copious notes. Be prepared to walk away from your idea if it lacks validation from people other than your friends and family.

Akbar Chisti | www.seamusgolf.com

I had a background in golf and finance, while my wife Megan, was an apparel designer by trade. She went to start making custom wool golf head covers for me and before she knew it, she had sewn over 100 for my friends and their friends. While this was validation that some folks might like our little craft hobby, it wasn't until the buyer of Bandon Dunes took an interest in our product that it seemed like it might have some potential as a business. Early support from the fashion editor of the most prominent magazine in golf was also very validating.

Monica Wreede | accessoryconnectz.com

I have been a children's clothing and accessory designer for over 9 years. Inspiration fell into my lap in 2004 when my beautiful daughter was born. My creative streak was in full swing. I knew I wanted all of the cute accessories for my daughter. So I took matters into my own hands.

Before I knew it, my little hobby had turned into a great little business which I named little*bow*peep, then years later, The Boutique Kids. Along the way, I saw a huge demand for embellished items such as flip flops, headbands, etc. My "ah ha" moment came to me and I knew I had to develop a product to interchange accessories to many items without being permanent! That is when my new product and company was born, Accessory Connectz®.

With LiveIntent, we built the basic version of LiveIntent tech, which allowed us to use machine optimization to serve an ad. It allowed a publisher to use a template again and again and not have to recode it. We then found a few publishers that were struggling to monetize their email newsletters and allowed them to test the product for free, as long as they agreed to provide us feedback. The feedback was overwhelmingly positive so we were able to raise another round of financing to keep the lights on.

Chapter 2 : Setting Your Finances Straight

Money, as they say, is the most powerful drug. Once you have gotten used to the luxuries that money can buy, it can be pretty daunting to let go off them in order to pursue your dreams. There is no one way to setting your finances straight when you start your entrepreneurial journey. Take the example of Debra Cohen. As the founder of Home Remedies (www.homeownersreferral.com), a home owners' referral network, she was hard pressed for cash flow during the initial few months. Debra's family had just purchased their first home recently. In addition to this, she had also taken a $5000 loan from her husband's retirement savings plan for the business. All these debts had to be handled with just one income from her husband.

To work this out, Debra took up a part time job at a local furniture store. Her family also learned to live with one car, stopped eating out, cleaned their own house, mowed their lawns and rarely ever hired a babysitter. By setting up a home office in the basement, she was able to save a few hundred dollars more on renting office space. "*I purchased a refurbished computer and fax machine and I even used my home phone line as my business line for a while. I did all of my own printing and bartered legal services with a stay-at-home mom in the neighborhood*", she adds.

Establishing a strategy to pay the monthly bills can be quite daunting at first. While it is hard, it really is not something unachievable. I talked to other entrepreneurs about how they went about paying their monthly bills during the initial days, if they had to go for months without getting paid, etc. Here are some experiences that they shared.

Andrew Gazdecki | www.biznessapps.com

Initially we were really bootstrapped and acted accordingly. The first office space we ever rented was a single room, $400/month, and ended up fitting 10 people by the end. It was an experience similar to living in a crammed dorm room, for better and for worse. The working conditions were far from ideal but I can't think of a better way to bond with your co-founders, stay focused, and motivate yourselves to work your way to a nicer working environment. Wal-Mart and Craigslist were our primary sources of furniture and equipment.

But the best way to handle those initial bills is to get your product into the hands of your target customers ASAP. Listen to their feedback and tailor your product around it. Find ways to provide real value to your users and don't be afraid to charge in return.

The single biggest factor to not starting a business is fear of no income. When we started The Quell Group there was not an income stream – just talent. A small reserve of funds provided a bit of a cushion to cover expenses for a couple of months, but there was real pressure from the beginning to get business. Although new customers were soon acquired payment for services was often delayed by 45 to 60 days per client requirements.

Again, the Quell Group business was started cold. We left our jobs on Friday and started launching our company on Monday. Bear in mind we are a married couple that left their jobs at the same time. The challenge was significant. We were incentivized by the need for income and we could devote full time and full attention to getting clients. Again, heavily working our network resulted in clients from the onset. As we produced work we were able to share what we had done with new prospects as proof of our capabilities.

There was a brief period of about two or three months where purchasing something as lowly as a mailbox was an expense that had to be carefully considered. Following this period we were getting enough momentum that we could rent our own office space. I don't believe we could have focused on the business and launched it as quickly had we dabbled at it on the side. The urgency of success is less evident when you are starting a company as a side job.

Sam Tarantino | www.grooveshark.com

About two years into our entrepreneurial journey, we had to go through several months without pay. Up until that point I was perpetually out raising money (since no one wanted to invest any more than what amounted to one month of expenses). When the 2008 housing crisis hit, investment money dried up. People at the time were scared to invest in anything. The company ran out of money for the Christmas payroll in 2008. In fact we paid zero (or partial) payrolls for 5 pay periods until April 1st of 2009. Raising money during this global financial crisis was virtually impossible, but we had a few large funds that would invest if we raised a full $1M.

Here we were in the middle of the worst economic climate since the Great Depression and we had to raise $1M; otherwise we would get nothing. We missed payroll time and again yet nobody left because our traffic was skyrocketing. People believed in the cause and in the fact that we were growing. By March, I was $150k short of the $1M goal and now in danger of not being able to make server payments that kept the site running and growing. We went to our landlord, who we owed 3 months' rent, to invest the last piece of the raise; and on April 1 we finished the raise and paid people 5 periods of back pay. I felt no greater relief on that day than I did in my entire 8-year career. That is why to this day I always emphasize that the heart of entrepreneurship is persistence in the face of the impossible.

Michael Lindell | www.mypillow.com

It really depends on the entrepreneur's situation. In my case, I went all in when starting MyPillow. My wife and I had $200,000 to our name and were raising four kids, and I ran it down to zero before even selling a pillow. One thing to be mindful of if you're the type of person who goes all in, be careful in getting too caught up in investors, because then you risk selling out your idea and product or selling too much of your stock if you own a company. I got caught up in this. I had to sell some of MyPillow to keep up with capital demands in the beginning. Overall, you need to see if it's feasible to go all in or work part time. It's really a personal decision rooted in an individual's circumstances. I will say this: If you are going all in and don't have cash flow, find the right investor who believes in your idea or product just as much as you do.

Patrick DeAmorim | www.decate.no

When I started, I was lucky enough to live with my girlfriend's parents (and my girlfriend, and child), so while I paid a bit of money just so I don't feel like a "*freeloader*", if I had no money, I still had a roof, food, and the general comforts. The first business I started was being a freelancer web side developer (I suppose it can be argued whether freelancing is "*really*" a business or not. I of course also had my parents as well whom we could have moved in with, but she preferred being near her family.

I had to go quite some time without an income, because when I was starting, I knew no one (connections can definitively help you get somewhere), I had no money to invest, no experience, no knowledge, nothing - so the start was more of trying 100 times, getting lucky a few of those times, and learning from when something did not work.

I doubt anyone who is just starting in business will start making enough to pay the bills in the first few months, unless you get lucky, or have very relevant experience, or have the right contacts. It's definitively a good idea to start your business on the side of a job, because until your business is stable, and you have savings in the bank, it will completely mess with your head when you're not sure if you'll have enough to pay the bills next month. Desperation and stress is a horrible mindset to run a business in, because not only does it not help you at all, it can harm you in so many ways.

If I had to do it again, and I had a job, and had my own bills to pay, I would have saved enough to live for at least 6 months without an income, before quitting my job. I'd also have made sure to have some kind of safety net, just in case. It can also be argued though, that if you have no choice but to succeed, you'll push even harder to make sure you do, but if you seriously want to be successful in business, having a safety net just means that you can sleep well at night, while fighting 100% day after day after day.

Raj Sheth | www.recruiterbox.com

We went through the first six months of the start-up without pay. In fact, we went through two years before that without pay, as well (failed start-ups). For Recruiterbox, we had an investment of $20,000 that got us through the first six months of 2011. This was an investment by family and friends against equity in the company.

Some people can pull off side jobs while working on the business, but it all depends on what you want to get done in your venture. For a lot of technology start-ups, you need to work 24 hours on your software product and getting customers. Working a side-job will take some time and quality away from the business; however, I understand that everyone's situation is different. I can't do it.

We got through the cash crunch challenge by selling fast! At six months, we were doing about $5,000-6,000 per month in revenue which started paying our bills.

Aaron Skonnard | www.pluralsight.com

My partners and I made a conscious decision at the beginning of starting our business to bootstrap it and not take funding. We started off by investing $5,000 each and we all came in with savings so we were prepared to go months without pay. This highlights an extremely important point: All founders of a start-up must have the same expectations when it comes to earnings in those first months.

Each of us did continue some side projects as well, including speaking at conferences, writing books and doing consulting. This brought up the question of, "*Where does this side income go? To the individual or to the business?*" You have to get along with your co-founders well enough that you can resolve tough questions like this among your core group. Another challenge of taking on side projects is that it distracts you from the company's purpose and goals. We had to agree as a team when it was finally time to let go of the side jobs and fully commit to only deriving income from the company. That's a hard thing to do, and we had several lean years during that time, but we rallied around our common vision for building a company we were passionate about and believing in what we were doing.

Micha Kaufman | www.fiverr.com

Not only did we go without pay, but we actually funded the initial project ourselves in the beginning (bootstrapping). At the same time we realized that we needed to validate the viability of the business concept. To ensure that this would happen, we came up with a business model that was built into the marketplace before we launched and which would kick in from the first transaction (we took transaction fees). As the marketplace scaled, the revenues the company generated scaled along with it.

Blake Smith | www.cladwell.com

We were pretty "*all-in*." We ended up quitting our jobs and going without pay for 9 months building out an initial product and raising some money from friends and family. During that period, my wife and I did some consulting (10-15hrs/wk) to reduce our burn rate. Towards the end we were paying our 3rd co-founder out of our personal savings as well – right when he and his wife were having their 1st child and moving to Cincinnati! Watching our money go down that quickly was really scary. It pushed us a lot in our faith and friendships. The benefit of jumping "*all-in*" was that it helped us attract investors and a great team.

Quitting your job and going without pay demonstrates belief and conviction – which is really exciting and attractive to partners and teammates. It also allowed us to focus our efforts. The disadvantage of jumping "*all-in*" is that we focused more on fund-raising early rather than building out a cool product. We probably spun our wheels fund-raising instead of focusing on our customers early on – just out of necessity. Is it a good idea to start a business on the side? I don't know if there is a one-size-fits-all answer to that question. The most important thing is to focus on helping and serving your customer whether part-time or full-time. Income is a peripheral benefit – chase it directly and it disappears – chase your customers and it grows.

Danny Maloney | www.tailwindapp.com

We thought it'd only be a few months until we were drawing full salaries. Way off. I didn't pay myself a cent until our 19th month, when we closed out first outside investment round. Today, I'm making 1/3 of what I did at my last corporate job. The keys to getting through the leanest of times were (a) save money in advance to cover expenses, (b) cut personal expenses dramatically and (c) only take what you need to cover the essentials. This let us grow faster by hiring great team members to work alongside us.

George Burciaga | www.elevatedigital.com

Every time I've started a company, there has been a time when I was not taking pay. Anyone falling into or discovering entrepreneurship should be prepared for that reality. You need to understand that you'll not only potentially forgo pay, but you should be prepared to give up almost everything to make your venture, project or start-up successful. It won't stop at pay. It won't stop at sleep or stress or finding ways to leverage different assets or taking loans to move things forward. You have to be committed to your company. Even successful entrepreneurs can find themselves not taking pay for several different reasons. You could even consider it an effort to show the board or investors that you're personally committed to expanding the company further and faster.

When I started my first company, I went nine or ten months, right out of college, without taking a paycheck. At the time, I was pitching my software to a handful of different clients and not taking pay became a huge motivator for me. I was able to sell the idea. I believed in my product so much and understood it so well, that every time I talked about it, people believed it too. I was so confident in its success - the metrics and the deployment. I don't think I would have been as effective at convincing other people to believe in my product too, if I hadn't developed that hunger by not taking pay for those ten months.

Jay Barnett | www.prioritypickup.com.au

I had a number of different businesses I could have pursued at this time. I settled on my current venture because it is an internet based business. I didn't need to set up a shop front, hire staff or purchase stock. My office, shop front and stock are all on the internet.

Because my business is online, I am able to hold down a job as well. I financed the early set up, pay my bills and save a little through my job. In time I am planning for the business to pay me back, and pay me a wage. It is important to give a business time. I have a 2 year plan initially. And I will be able to make it because I have kept my job.

Matt Shoup | www.mandepainting.com

I started turning paint jobs around very quickly so I was able to barely make ends meet for the first few months until the profits started rolling in. I wish I could say that we did it perfectly, but we did take out a line of credit to make sure we had cushion to fall back on in case things slowed down for a time.

Kevin Lavelle | www.mizzenandmain.com

Web and I both went for an extended period of time without taking a salary. We lived off savings, found other ways to earn money, and buckled down. It's not an easy journey, but it ensures you are in it for the right reasons and the long haul if you are willing to make those sacrifices.

Joel Simkhai | www.grindr.com

I had my own Internet marketing business when I started working on Grindr with $5k of my own money. I worked on both businesses during the time we were in development. Several months after we launched Grindr, I stopped working on my other business. I had always intended to remain an entrepreneur and in the early days stayed focused on keeping costs low and worked out of my home.

I rarely spent money on anything that didn't go towards the business. At the time, I didn't know what I was getting myself into. I did not have a business plan nor did I realize how much of an undertaking the technology aspect of Grindr would become. But surrounding me with the right people who shared the same passion and vision has helped turn Grindr into a reality.

One of our biggest challenges is coping with the pace of growth and finding tech talent in the Los Angeles market. We started working out of my living room in 2009. By 2011, we were moving into our Hollywood office. Since then, we've moved into a new space and continued to grow.

Edward DeSalle | www.netirrigate.com

I lived off my wife's salary during the first year of product development to cover daily living expenses. On the business side, I maxed out two credit cards for initial working capital. Eventually, I even had to take a day job to pay down the business credit card debt and I ended up doing product development in the evenings. After about two years, there was enough new customer revenue to pay myself a small salary out of the business. Eventually, the small customer base that was established led to an Angel Investment from local business people that heard about what Net Irrigate was doing.

Robert Livingstone | www.royaltext.com

We opened RoyalText.com as a sister company to an already established business, IdealCost.com. I started IdealCost.com with less than $2000 and bootstrapped it myself. We kept our overhead very low. I had a phone, fax, website and gas in my car. Our service was 100% labor based so it didn't require any staff or other hard costs. Our profits from IdealCost.com went into funding and expenses for RoyalText.com. We went without pay for about 5 months. If we didn't already have cash flow coming in from our other company, we'd have opened RoyalText.com on a much smaller scale.

As soon as we opened RoyalText.com we showcased it immediately to the public. It is a good idea to keep a full-time job while building a small business on the side. Having a steady paycheck takes the pain out of running a start-up at a loss for the first few months or years. The challenges of having both a full-time job and a side-business include time management of the job and the business, work-life balance and building the business quickly at a part-time pace.

Chandler Crouch | www.chandlercrouch.com

My saving grace was the preparation I did before I began. I didn't start on a whim. I intentionally reduced my living expenses as much as possible by making a lot of hard decisions and sacrificing pleasantries. It also helps that I didn't have a wife or kids. Starting out I worked at a restaurant as a waiter. This helped because I could take home a lot of free food. At some point I had the realization that every success story I've ever heard was also coupled with really spectacular stories of hard times. I realized that the only way my story would be considered a failure is if I quit during the hard times. I decided that no matter what, no matter how bad it got, I just wasn't going to quit.

During my time in Waco (when I paid off a 6 mo lease to "*collect my thoughts*") I also came to believe in God, before that I was agnostic. I didn't lead a perfect life, and still don't, but I pray for guidance. There is no way that I would be living the life I do today and there is no way I wouldn't have gone through what I went through if it weren't for my faith in Jesus Christ. It's been a messy path, and I've made plenty of wrong decisions, but in hindsight I can see a lot of purpose for the path I've taken.

Cricket Allen | www.theperfectsnaque.com

There is art and science involved here! We are cash flow freaks and extremely mindful of our expenses. Inevitably, you will find yourself in a cash crunch especially if customers do not pay on time. First, we put our own skin in the game – this will make you very frugal on your overall monthly expenses. And early on, we were not shy about turning to credit cards to handle some of the expenses where we could not find credit terms or outright pay for something. This did help in those early days and eased some monthly cash crunch. But be careful here. You don't want to have crazy debt especially when you seek out investors. I have mentioned a couple times about customers not paying on time. Never accept this by the way. Rattle the cage for payment!

Aditi Kapur | www.deliverychef.in

I went through many months without pay, but it's not easy. If you don't have any other form of financial support, I would recommend to think long and hard before starting up – the initial months can be rough – either save up some money to live off if you quit your job, or start a business that is profitable from day one (providing services such as styling, graphic designing, programming, etc). You could do a side job, but it is really really tough. Starting a business takes up more time than you can imagine. You need to work 24/7. In that situation, managing a side job is not easy.

Courtney Ilarrazza | www.babybodyguards.com

In the beginning I kept my job as an attorney, while my husband handled the new office and clients the first few years. I of course helped after-hours and on weekends. In 2010, we had grown too big for him to manage alone and I was ready to come on board full time and leave my legal career. It took years and a lot of sleepless nights of us to grow to the point where I felt comfortable leaving my security net.

We got to a point where my day job was a hindrance on our growth rather than a safety net. My advice for the starting out entrepreneur would be to test the water, see what works and build on it. Start slow and lean and be ready to adapt, be ready to grow. There may be months where you can't take pay and there will be months where you can take a big bonus. This is the road we choose, it's not always stable but it is always an adventure. Ultimately we have control, at least more control in our future than we would as someone's employee.

As scary as it was those first few months, there is no motivator like not having a fall back. We believed in our company and I think that made the sacrifices easier. We knew that reinvesting any and all profits back into the company was the best long term plan.

Kyle James | www.rather-be-shopping.com

Working on Rather-Be-Shopping as a side-job was the smartest thing I did in the early days as it took 10 months to earn significant revenue from Rather-Be-Shopping. My wife would not have been OK with it any other way. The biggest challenge was finding the time to work on the side and still have time for family life. Fortunately I did not have kids yet so I had more free time to put toward the business. I found time by working smart and not wasting any free time. It takes a lot of discipline to be a successful entrepreneur and excellent time management skills.

Julien Smith | www.breather.com

I'm lucky enough that I had successes before this. So my co-founders and I ran off my personal cash for a while. If you have that opportunity, it makes things much easier.

Dan DeLuca | www.grownsmall.com / www.classchatter.com

I built my site specifically to have low overhead. If I could not pay the bills out my pocket I would shut down a long time ago. I also took donations. This did not bring in a lot of money, but was a huge motivator. If people were willing to donate a few dollars then I must have been on to something. This lack of revenue was a blessing and a curse. It certainly kept me from exploring certain opportunities, but it made me focus on my niche. In the long run this is what saved me when people with much deeper pockets then I entered the field.

Jill Foucré | www.marcelsculinaryexperience.com

I did not pay myself until the store had been open for three months and at that point it was (and still is somewhat nominal). I spent a lot of time on the financial portion of my business plan so I was realistic about what we were going to have to spend, what the absence of income was going to mean, and how I was going to compensate for that in our household, since I am the only income earner. We have managed by reducing personal expenses, leveraging our existing assets, and ensuring that the rental properties upstairs from the store (we purchased our building) continue to generate income.

Morris Miller | www.xenex.com & www.rackspace.com

I was very fortunate with Rackspace because I had recently sold another company that I had founded. After graduating from law school, I was an attorney at a law firm and I came up with the idea to digitize Texas case law and publish it on CD-ROM. That's how Curtis Hill Publishing got started. Starting Curtis Hill Publishing was quite challenging. I presented my business plan to 168 potential investors and I was almost ready to give up when the first investor said "*yes.*" In that case, my persistence paid off.

After selling Curtis Hill Publishing, I was meeting with companies and considering different opportunities when I was approached by 3 young guys who had an idea for a company. I talked it over with one of my business partners, and we decided to invest in them – which was Rackspace. We didn't pay ourselves at Rackspace for quite some time, but we were able to do that because of our previous business success, which isn't necessarily the case with other entrepreneurs.

Adam Simpson | www.easyofficephone.com

Our early revenues went entirely to sustaining the company and reinvesting in it. My co-founder and I were able to go without salaries in the early stages, so we didn't have to cannibalize cash flow.

Mike Matousek | www.flashnotes.com

I have always looked at this in a slightly different way. I am very cash cautious, but at certain times as an entrepreneur you need to take risks. Whether it's people, a marketing activity, or a feature -- you need to push your budgets when you see an opportunity. If you always play it safe, you will slowly fade away.

Zalmi Duchman | www.freshdiet.com

I did not take a salary for the first year. For the first 5 months I actually held a full time job & was working on my business. After that time I had to quit my job & focus fully on my new business. I think in the beginning it was a good idea to keep my job in case the business did not work out. I had many challenges in the early stages as I was doing almost everything myself & was under a lot of pressure. I did whatever it took in the early stages to keep the business afloat, whether that was paying for things out of my own pocket or going to family for help. I also gave special prices to customers who were willing to buy more months of food in advance so I had extra cash to pay the early bills. I remember very early on while I was doing deliveries (I used to do deliveries all night) I called my wife and told her I just could not do this anymore & was very close to giving up. Thankfully she was very supportive & talked me into continuing the fight. Without her support I don't think I would have been able to keep it up.

Kathy Crifasi | www.hipzbag.com

I didn't quit my day job when I started my company. I used my day job paid for my Hipzbag habit as it was Hipzbag that I was passionate about. I came up with an amount of money I was willing to risk on this project and that was my investment. I decided early on that once that money was out – that was it – Hipzbag needed to make a profit on its own by that point. Luckily, my initial investment was returned to me in a big way and my passion was transformed into a profitable business.

Michael Wayne | www.deca.tv

My situation was a bit atypical. I had saved enough money to give myself one year to get the company off the ground. I had other motivations to not spend the whole year's savings however: my son had just been born. I knew when I was 6 months into the start-up and we hadn't closed funding, I needed to hustle. Thankfully we closed our A round funding almost exactly one-year after I started writing the business plan for the business. When we started the company my salary was less than half of what I was making previously.

Mike Townsend | www.homehero.org / www.flowtab.com

Flowtab was a night and weekend project initially. We officially jumped in the pool and quit our jobs after 15 of 20 bars said they would use it if we built it. It's super important to sell before you invest to build, make keynote, photoshops and powerpoint your best friend on day one. On day two, go out and sell *"vapor ware"*, and pay particular attention to the expression on customers' faces when you first present the idea. If they immediately understand the problem and your solution, keep going.

We had enough personal savings to last about 4-6 months. It's extremely important to understand cash-flow, make sure you have enough capital saved up to start a company. It's a shame when a promising business fails because you don't have enough to pay rent.

Audrius Jankauskas | www.impresspages.org

ImpressPages was started as a side project. At the time all three of us were employed at a web agency on a full-time basis. But as they say, the day has 24 hours so we used them all by spending our time after work to create what was interesting for us. We did it like that for two years.

With respect to finances, it's always a safer option to start as a side-job because on some level you will always be cash positive. It takes out a lot of stress in the beginning as you don't have to worry how to cover your bills. But what goes around comes around, and juggling two things at once is really challenging on a totally other level.

It sucks your time and energy. You do twice as much work which has to maintain same level of quality. You have to keep up with your social life. You have to get your family/friends on board as they will be the ones dealing with your shit if you fail. Forget time for myself – it has to be reduced to minimum.

The key is to notice when to drop out. Either from your full-time job, or your side project. Take your time to test every option possible, set clear goals and only if all of them fail, quit. On the other hand, if you feel like it's escalating really quickly and no time can be wasted, drop everything else and concentrate on what might be your billion dollar idea.

To optimize our everyday spending, right from the job-related stuff to buying pens and pencils, we asked for favors, discounts, free trials on everything. Some gurus advise to spare money for a few months and then dedicate 100 % to the business you want to do – sounds like a good motivational lesson but doesn't work in practice. So it's really better to start off easy, with a side project and then scale it till you become confident and start earning money.

Ryan Wallace | www.iphoneantidote.com

Luckily, I had some savings built up. But honestly, it would have been fine either way. I designed the business to operate at a profit, so there were no big problems with cash flows. As long as we bought more iPhones, we always had good ways to sell them. As long as we weren't holding too much inventory, there were not going to be any cash flows issues. iPhone Antidote was designed to be low overhead, so other than our variable expenses, we didn't have too many monthly bills other than our web hosting.

Adi Bittan | www.ownerlistens.com

It's stressful for sure. I ensured the finances were taken off through several ways:

a) I have some savings so it's not that I was staring at a financial abyss.

b) My husband has a steady job so of course that helps although it does not feel great not to contribute to the family's income, especially for entrepreneurs who tend to want to be self-sufficient.

c) I worked in a consulting capacity and was able to bring in about 50% of my previous income through that.

There are of course advantages and disadvantages to each approach (working side-job or taking it full time from the start). If you keep your job, income is of course the main advantage. It buys you time to keep exploring and prototyping until you feel confident in your approach. On the other hand, it's distracting and costs you time. Everything will take you much longer and it will be hard to do any research that involves talking to potential customers who might not be available on weekends. It's doable but you will have to get very creative with your time and very efficient at work. My advice, stay employed while you're in the exploratory phases and once you've settled on a path you've researched thoroughly, burn the boats.

To be clear, "*research*" does not mean reading a bunch of reports on the internet. It means talking to customers, validating needs and iterating through the product and business approach.

John Brady | www.protempartners.com

We had savings and my spouse's income. We also had to curtail our standard of living significantly. We examined every dollar that went out in any given month. It's amazing what you can cut out when you need to. It was especially difficult to live within different means later in life; feeling like we were just starting out all over again. And once we made the first cut, we went through and cut again.

Akbar Chisti | www.seamusgolf.com

Everything was a side job for me; however my wife decided to quit her job early on to focus on production and fulfillment of product orders. In fact, she quit her job without telling me, and when I found out that caused a huge drive on my part to sell since it takes a lot of head covers to supplement the income of a designer. The luck of being in Golf Digest early let us open an e-commerce sales channel which basically underwrote the wholesale model that is more demanding for working capital.

Having Megan sew for the first year or so allowed us to retain all the resources in the company and pay for more wool, sewing time, and other stuff that could get the business going. It wasn't until about a year and a half into it that I could finally quit my job as CFO for a real estate developer and really focus on managing/growing the business.

Michael Kawula | www.selfemployedking.com

For the first franchise I started, I did part-time until my business was up and running profitably. I worked 7 days a week and 18 hour days to be able to break away from the paycheck that I was so addicted to. I had my first child on the way and didn't want to make the leap without a little cushion.

When I bought my next franchise, I created a C-Corporation and took part of my 401K to buy stock in my newly formed corporation. This gave me a cushion while I built up the business and ultimately helped me outperform what my 401k could have done alone by investing in myself.

Rick Martinez | www.senorsangria.com

I ended up selling my home and taking that money and funneling it into the business to get things started. From there we tried to be as savvy as possible by wearing multiple hats and juggling a TON and putting in lots of hours. On top of that we took it slow. Our first production was small. Also instead of producing 2 SKU's which we knew we need we only rolled out 1 SKU. Also, before we had our first production run we ran a trial run to make sure the process was going to work.

The product for this trial run would not be able to be sold. But we used it as samples to pre-sell. We hit as many locations with these samples so that we could go to production with a bunch of orders already queued up. In addition we produced a small amount of product instead of a large amount. It cost us more but at least we didn't have a large bill to pay. Once we got more successful we negotiated longer payment terms with our vendors who we were spending the bulk of our money with (60 days versus 30 days). We also worked with our biggest customer who was a HUGE fan of our brand and negotiated a line of credit with them

Michelle MacDonald | www.sweetnotebakery.com

My plan when I started my business was to use the $15,000 I had saved up for the business and personal expenses and put the rest on my credits cards. I continued working my regular job for a while until it became necessary to devote all my time to the business. I also carefully managed my profits and used those to put back in to the business. I shared a facility and equipment until I had the funds to purchase equipment of my own and just recently got a place of my own. With our current growth investors and banks are our next source to be able to handle the growth and pay the bills at the same time.

Jordan Eisenberg | www.urgentrx.com

Simple answer: expense reduction. I stopped eating out, cut back on all unnecessary expenses, and went into "*financial kernel mode*" where I could live largely off of savings and minimize my personal burn rate. Not fun, and it doesn't last forever, but if it were easy to start a business and didn't require considerable sacrifices, everyone would do it.

Tracey Noonan | www.wickedgoodcupcakes.com

We were fortunate in that my husband had a good job and was able to support us personally while Danielle (daughter & co-founder) & I worked to grow the business. All the money we earned went back into the company. We did not have a big budget to start the company and we were adamant about not incurring debt so we pinched every nickel and penny we could. Danielle moved back home. Neither of us took a pay check for the first year. Poor Danielle had zero money for any social activities with friends but that didn't stop her. We didn't take any vacations, spent nothing on ourselves and kept our focus on the bigger prize. Every purchase for the business had to be justified. We simply didn't have the financial safety net to be careless.

In retrospect this was a good thing because it taught us how to be profitable and how to do more with less. We definitely had some lean times but it was necessary to help us have the cash to innovate, expand and grow.

Chapter 3 : How To Fund Your Start-up

So you have this great idea that you are extremely passionate about. How do you go about funding this idea? A lot of entrepreneurs convince their family and friends to lend them money for the business. But it's not always the most feasible idea.

Take the example of Myra Roldan, an entrepreneur who owns a popular vegan cosmetic shop on Etsy. When her first business was growing, Myra started attending a number of networking events in New York trying to find an investor who will be interested in her business. But the funding never happened - "*I didn't have the "books" (Profit and Loss, 3 year projects, etc) to look attractive enough to any of the investors. I was too small for them with an insufficient amount of annual sales to be taken seriously. I always felt like I literally was entering shark tank, being chewed up time and time again to only be spit out in shambles. I would leave every event feeling defeated and would cry in my car all the way back home.*"

Myra didn't get any support from the banks either. Finally, she decided to borrow money from her 401K and from her weekly paychecks to fund her start-up. She thinks for businesses that are not big enough for investors, self-funding is the only way to succeed. "*Today, I still self-fund and I reinvest almost all of my profits back into my business. I also learned how to invest in the stock market in order to get the necessary capital to keep my current venture solvent.*"

Jordan Eisenberg | www.urgentrx.com

In the beginning, it's largely a numbers – and effort – game. You need to "*kiss a lot of frogs*" and not get discouraged when people don't rush to whip out their checkbooks. Without exaggeration, once I decided to go for it and start UrgentRx, I made a point to meet a handful of new people (over breakfast, coffee, lunch, beers, etc.), at least 6 days a week – with the singular goal of looking for investors and those who knew them. I met with literally hundreds of people – many of them unqualified – but in every meeting I made sure to get the name of someone else I should speak to. Some of my largest investors were found as a result of creating this networking "*spider web.*" It required a tremendous amount of effort and time, but it paid off in the end.

Also, in addition to meeting as many potential investors as possible, following the initial meeting it's important to not be afraid to ask for the close. A "*yes*" is great, a "*no*" is second best – but avoid "*maybe*" like the plague. People telling you "*maybe*" are 99 times out of 100 going to end up as a "*no*" but will waste massive amounts of your time. If you don't have continued, thoughtful dialogue with potential investors, it's not going in the right direction. Cut bait and move on.

Another great piece of advice is that if you want money, ask for advice – and if you want advice, ask for money. It is a subtle tactic but it can lower the inherent resistance the potential investor feels of "*being sold too hard.*" In the end, remember that money is a commodity – there is a lot of it out there – you just have to go find it.

-

Monique Tatum | www.beautifulplanning.com

When I first started my company I will never forget cashing out my 401K. I was terrified. Yet, it had to be done. I knew that I just needed something to stay afloat and manage the costs of computers immediately. Within my industry, it is not common for clients to pay their retainers upfront, however being a start-up, many were not so easily convinced. We would do 50% upfront and 50% 15 days in. This grew client trust and I really hit the ground hard scouring for new clientele. Then I would be on sites like Craigslist daily looking for small jobs or a person that needed a PR or marketing campaign.

However, cashing out my 401K was key as it really jump-started us. The rest came from filling in clientele quickly. It was a lot of hard work, face glued to the computer screen and ear glued to the telephone chatting and making new client friends. Also, when I left the software company I was lucky enough where they loved me and did not want to see me go. They stayed with me as I left and they were my first annual retainer client.

Monica Wreede | accessoryconnectz.com

When starting both of my businesses, I had no other funding than my husband and I. It is extremely hard to grow without funding. My husband and I have put all available income into my new product just to get it retail ready. I am currently selling, manufacturing, marketing, running my website, graphic design and all of the above myself! It is almost impossible to grow without outsourced manufacturing & funding so please keep this in mind when starting a business! When I started my accessory company in 2004, I started out selling my hair accessories for .99 cents on Ebay! Within a year, I was selling one hair bow for $20-$25 bucks!! My first hair bow instructions E-Book sold for $200 on Ebay! If you put your mind to something, you really can accomplish it!

Mary Apple | www.prettypushers.com

I will be honest that there was a lot of personal $$ outlay just to develop and manufacture our first product to hit shelves. For 2 years I shelled out money without having anything to sell. I had no investors and no bank loan. I used my cash in savings and maxed out credit cards to bring my dream alive. A finance person once told me that a '*wide portfolio'* looked the best to any party or institution.

He said "*If you can get a variety of things and stay in good standing with all of them; a small loan, a family or friend investment, a VC investment, a merchant processor loan, etc. makes you look more credible to any future investors*", and I still live by this advice. We have acquired capital from all of these mentioned sources, and each time it becomes a smoother transaction.

Lawson Nickol | www.allamericanclothing.com
Funding to start the All American Clothing Co. came from personal income I earned during my 30 years working for other companies. I used a lot of my savings and credit cards to get this started.

Bryan Knowlton | www.appraiseallrealestate.com
I started very small and on a shoestring budget. By keeping expenses down to an inexpensive self-hosted blogging platform using Wordpress and forming an affiliate partnership with industry magazines and websites where they would get 50% of the sales of my products, I didn't have to have a huge marketing budget.

Matthew Griffin | www.bakersedge.com
I wish I knew how to convince strangers to give me money for something that "*could be*". Our start-up funds primarily came from personal savings and a business line of credit from a local bank (with our house and cars as collateral on the note). What we experienced is that outside investment takes notice only after you have considerable traction. Ironically, we only had offers after we didn't need the start-up money.

Andrew Gazdecki | www.biznessapps.com
For Bizness Apps I initially invested a little less than $20k of my own savings to get the prototype up and running. Which at the time was a biggest amount I ever wagered and in college that is a boatload of money. I believed in the business and worked closely with small restaurants. My first clients were in the local area. The CSU Chico school gym was our first client and was our first iPhone app. Everything just grew from there.

George Burciaga | www.elevatedigital.com
In a capital-intense business like ours, where equipment is involved, balancing investors and clients becomes a tricky game. Investors want to see interested clients, but you need money to be able to show and deploy products for clients.

When I needed capital, I took a clean concept of the company and some projections to secure a line of credit that I had to personally guarantee. That gave me the leverage to move forward and bring in other resources, but it was not easy. You really have to believe in your company, if you're to personally guarantee that financing.

The best thing to do in that catch-22 situation is to look for an investor that is familiar with the type of company you're developing. If your concept is catchy enough, they will deploy capital to get you off the ground. Oftentimes, if an investor is familiar with your industry and the space and can believe your vision, they'll devote the dollars to allow you to move forward.

Chris Grant | www.grantfamilyfarm.com

To get my capital to begin making my product, I scrimped and saved. I had to seek out the buyers of our products ahead of time and make sure that our relationship could support us growing products for them a year in advance. The materials and supplies I needed were bought as needed, in order to make sure I didn't have stagnant products on hand. Now in a retail setting, our products are sold at farmers markets, and are perishable. There is a narrow window to produce vegetables in New England, so when the markets open, we need to be ready to sell. We had to prove ourselves with our products and build the reputation with our customers n a very crowded market.

Debra Cohen | www.homeownersreferral.com

I took a $5000 loan against my husband's retirement savings plan. It was terrifying but making that investment in myself proved to me that I was committed to making my business work. And, I was able to repay the loan in 6 months.

Rob Biederman | www.hourlynerd.com

We were lucky to begin as a class project at HBS and received $5,000 in seed funding. Funnily enough, though, we spent almost none of the money before we had traction, all using a $10 website and a ton of word-of-mouth marketing through friends. It's incredible the traction you can create with a simple starter page if customers are aware of you.

Kevin Lavelle | www.mizzenandmain.com

Personal savings, borrowing money, extending credit cards, or family investments are the only ways to get an idea off the ground. That being said, if you can prove how popular your idea/service/product is on a limited budget, conversations change with investors quickly. Though many investors want a track record and a sizable customer base, some savvy investors recognize that if a concept proves its value quickly, (every time you produce a limited run it sells out, for example), they may be able to make you hit scale much faster than if you were to get to that "*ideal*" fund-raising stage. Bear in mind, this path means you will likely have to part with much more of your company to raise the money.

Michael Lindell | www.mypillow.com

I can't say it enough: MyPillow's success started with local craft and county shows. This is not only a great way to get your product and company's name out publicly, but also a great opportunity to get feedback from people who stop by to try the product. They let you know what they like and don't like about it. These same people also become your clientele. That's how you start your cash flow. This is also a great way to find investors, especially since it's hard to get a loan from the bank to start your start-up.

Iftach Orr | www.pix.do

I've heard from many investors that they don't invest in an idea, they invest in a team, and so being able to build a strong team can really help in the case of lack of customers. One way to prove demand for your product, even before it's ready, is to allow potential customers to pre-order. In this instance, even though you do not yet have a paying customer you are able to prove your potential. Another common misconception is that attracting capital is all about the big bucks or bust, but in reality, raising a small amount of capital can be more realistic. With a small and efficient team you'll buy yourself the time needed to build your customer base and then attract more capital at a later stage.

Jeff Kuo | www.ragic.com

Before doing Ragic full time, I actually planned our start-up for quite a while when I had my day job, but a lot of times it doesn't work out too well because it's really hard to meet clients face to face or even get on a conference call in the working hours. Meeting customers and getting feedback is especially important in the early stages of product development. I think it doesn't hurt to try it first, but if the progress is slow, then he should probably consider doing it full time. Start-up is a lot of work. We bootstrapped, and still have not gone for any outside funding. The service projects provided us a nice early cash flow for us to survive. We are also very careful about spending and expansions, so we've always have enough capital to keep our small, lean start-up running.

Heidi Lamar | www.spalamar.com

In my case, I continued working as a realtor for the first year. Unfortunately, my spa was in Scottsdale Arizona and my real estate business was in Portland, Oregon. Luckily, I had a good reputation in real estate so I was able to work remotely by phone and travel to Portland on the weekends. I would work at the spa Mon-Fri, while negotiating listings on the phone. I would fly up on Friday night to list the properties I had been discussing, sell them over the weekend, open escrow on Monday and fly back to AZ.

Nick Paradise | www.threadbuds.com

This is always difficult for any start-up but we are completely bootstrapping this start-up. I have always known I wanted to build businesses so I've been saving for these types of situations. I think there is a great degree of pride I find in building a business with money I earned somewhere and saved. You question purchases and define needs and wants more clearly with a bootstrap mentality.

That's not to say that getting investors isn't important, especially if you can't bootstrap. My advice is to find the nearest business incubator and get them involved with helping you shape your idea, product or business. A lot of times, getting input from companies or foundations that cater to this very thing, helps you not only make better decisions in the beginning, but help form new relationships that can help you network to possible investment opportunities.

Morris Miller | www.xenex.com & www.rackspace.com

Rackspace was a different kind of company. When Rackspace launched, we didn't make a big splash. The founders put something online about their data center and ability to manage servers, and immediately began attracting customers. They allowed customers to pay month-to-month instead of requiring long-term contracts, which was unique, and had a customer service commitment, which was unheard of in our industry. Customers flocked to Rackspace, which was part of the reason I decided to invest in and get involved in running the company. We needed little capital to start and prove the model, and the customers were seeking what Rackspace was offering (managed hosting). As Rackspace grew, we invested much more heavily in marketing and were able to expand our data center.

Hill Ferguson | www.zong.com (Chief Product Officer, Paypal)

This is the "cold start" problem. You can't attract capital because you have no track record, but you can't build a track record with no capital. In the past, I have blown through personal savings, borrowed money from family, and run up credit card debts to overcome this.

I don't think this is uncommon for first time entrepreneurs. One piece of advice when trying to attract a lender or investor is to have a clear vision of what success in your product and/or service look like in the future. Breakdown that future into discreet milestones or checkpoints. This will not only give investors more confidence in you (because you have a vision and an execution path), but it will also be helpful for you to hold yourself accountable.

If you're a first time entrepreneur and you don't have product-market fit yet and you don't even have a product, you have to focus on creating and offering a sustainable product that doesn't need venture backing.

For example, in my first business, Pulsepoint, my three partners and I put in $100k each to get started. We were fortunate that the business was very profitable and we didn't have to raise the first round of financing until the company was very far along. Our Series A was $60 million dollars. Since then, my positive track record has made it easier to raise financing.

Today, a young, smart team can put something into the cloud quite inexpensively. One of the things I see in my office is that many of my youngest, smartest guys have side projects, dreams of being entrepreneurs. I certainly can't blame them. And as an entrepreneur, I support them.

Marketing is key. I sometimes meet young engineers or CEOs who are forming start-ups that say, "*I'm just not good at sales or marketing.*" And I look at them and I think "*you're going to fail.*" Because if you can't sell your ideas, you're dead.

Chapter 4 : Finding The Right Manufacturer

For people venturing into a business selling physical products, finding the right manufacturer is extremely critical. Not only is the quality of the output crucial, but you must also ensure that the manufacturer is trustworthy, can deliver during peak demand and can scale their supply seamlessly to meet your growing demand.

Finding a manufacturer who is on the same page as you is the hardest part of starting up, according to Nick Paradise, who owns the company ThreadBuds (www.threadbuds.com) that make colorful earbuds that do not tangle. With discussions happening mostly over emails and phone calls, Nick says he found it more comfortable dealing with manufacturers who could speak in English. Finding the right manufacturer however was a trial and error process considering that manufacturers who make earbuds are almost everywhere and it is difficult to zero in on the right partner. "*After acquiring samples from various manufacturers, assessing pricing, lead times and ease of communication, we decided on our partner. I bought a flight and went overseas to see the machinery we'd invest in and to meet the factory owners and workers. This was the most fun part so far about starting our company. It also allowed me to feel very comfortable about who I was partnering with on this venture.*"

Like Nick, other entrepreneurs had pretty interesting stories to share. Here are a few of them

George Burciaga | www.elevatedigital.com

Working with manufacturers as a start-up company is not easy. You're just not given as much attention as a multi-billion dollar company would. So when you're determining who you want to work with and what products you're going to use, you're guessing at a lot of it up front.

When it came time to work with a manufacturer, we went about it through a process of trial and error. We found ourselves in a prototype environment, testing out different products and integrating our own software. Once we felt comfortable with the equipment and design, we called in manufacturers to show them what the product would ultimately look like and then worked with a master assembler to put all the parts together. With our assembler in particular, we were able to create a unique, mutually beneficial partnership. Though they were a fairly large assembler, they weren't building products in our specific category at the time. By working with them, we were able to help them grow a new category of business, while moving forward with our own development. Getting the assembler interested in our product and building a partnership that benefited both of us both was crucial.

Eight years ago when I was first gathering supplies and having our garments and packaging manufactured, I was determined to sort through all the bad and find the '*perfect vendor*' for each component of the business. However, I soon learned that there is no such thing. Your once grateful vendor might ignore you when he's got a bigger customer, or your timely guy might have a factory fire and go out of business for a few months. I mean these scenarios are endless. The key is having a handful of good or OK vendors that you can bounce between. That keeps their pricing competitive, too.

Many of ours came through referrals, so the initial vetting process was already done. Then there were some that we used blindly and they messed up, but it's rare that they wouldn't fix it or refund us. Also – and this is a major point – we manufacture in America, and in most cases, within driving distance of our office in New York. Most vendors won't try to burn you if they know you can walk right in and look over their shoulder. If you have to get a translator just to talk to a factory overseas, well, that's a whole problem in itself, and likely there will be more problems to come from that kind of situation.

Rick Martinez | www.senorsangria.com

I asked a TON of questions to anyone that would listen. I was amazed with how much information people would provide to me for free. I also used a professional lab to formulate my product and they had many contacts in the manufacturing space. That led me to who I thought would be our first co-packer. Unfortunately about 2-3 months before we were going to have a trial run with them they backed out on us because of one of the requirements I had. I didn't want my product to be filtered at all. This one packer needed some level of filtration for us to work with them and that was something I would not budge on. So I ended up going back to the drawing board and started asking anyone. I found other brand owners on line and would call them out of the blue and introduce myself and ask them for suggestions.

Finally I realized that maybe I should contact bottle suppliers. Those bottles end up going to the folks I needed to use. One bottle supplier in particular directed me to our current packer. A lot of ground check was just in person. We met with them, toured the facility. We knew they were old school in how they did things (slightly more than a hand shake). We were nervous but we really didn't have any other option due to some of the requirements of our product. So how we compensated for this was to be involved in everything they did so we can help but more importantly guide the process.

Lawson Nickol | www.allamericanclothing.com

Network with people in your industry; building relationships is important and these people can help point you in the right directions. Research the people you want to do business with and don't settle for the first one you find, make sure you have options. Visit the plants you want to do business with. An advantage we have in being USA Made is that we can visit any of the plants we want to do business with and see how they operate.

Kevin Lavelle | www.mizzenandmain.com

Finding manufacturers is an incredibly difficult process because, unlike programmers, for example, they tend not to have a virtual presence and regularly seek out business online where it is easy to find them. Depending on the industry, it may be virtually impossible to find the manufacturer you are looking for without insider knowledge or a straightforward introduction. It's important to check out their references. Who have they done work for? Who else is in their supply chain? Take small steps when first working together – you won't regret it!

Philip Masiello | www.800razors.com

I had plenty of experience working with manufacturers so I knew what types of factors to look into. A manufacturer should be large enough to purchase correctly and efficiently. They should also have a great industry reputation. With 800razors.com, the manufacturing landscape for quality products was limited to 2 players, so it was a matter of getting one of them to be our supply partner. We always work out a relationship where the manufacturer benefits from our success. This provides and incentive to provide us with what we need.

Michael Lindell | www.mypillow.com

MyPillow does all of its own manufacturing because I am so particular. I stay away from overseas manufacturing because a product can be copied. In the USA, you sign non-compete and disclosure forms to protect your product and business. For raw materials, make sure all your ducks are in a row so that you aren't being taken advantage of.

Peter Mann | www.oransi.com

This was an e-commerce business and I was interested in carrying the higher end brands. It took a lot of hustle in the beginning to convince these companies to allow us to source product from them. I had to sell myself and this business to them. Since we were selling online and shipping product directly from the manufacturers there was no inventory risk.

Chapter 4a : Setting Up Your Own Manufacturing

If finding a manufacturer is daunting enough, imagine making the product yourself. Lawson Nickol, the founder of All American Clothing (www.allamericanclothing.com) – a manufacturer of apparels and accessories that are all made in the United States, has some wonderful piece of advice when it comes to setting up your own manufacturing plant. According to him, location and people are the two most critical things to look out for. Unfortunately, Nickol stumbled upon a challenge which is ubiquitous to entrepreneurs who want to make products in the US.

In the apparel industry, close to 85% of the jobs have been shipped out to foreign locations. "*This made it impossible for us to setup a manufacturing plant in our hometown because not enough people know how setup a production line or operate the equipment*", says Lawson. To resolve this, Lawson set upon finding a location that would not only solve the human resource problem, but also optimize their logistics, "*we try to keep the manufacturing plant close to other resources that we will need. For example, the cut & sew plant is located only hours away from the cotton mill and only a couple miles from the washing facility. This means we can get raw materials faster and save on freight.*"

Myra Roldan | herbanluxe.etsy.com

Before you even go into the expense of starting your own manufacturing with your own equipment and employees you need to visit your local government website and/or make some phone calls to see if you are required to have any type of special license or certification. Once you get that out of the way and have the green light to move forward, you need to explore costs and have some planned alternatives. Equipment is super expensive in many cases so you need to have a healthy budget. Depending on the equipment you need you should explore renting or purchasing used equipment to start.

Hiring employees can be tricky, especially if you are running a home-based business or small business. Again, it comes down to dollars and cents. Take the time to set a budget, understand what type of profit margins you need in order to justify the hiring of employees. With employees, you gain extra expenses and responsibilities – are you ready and do you have the financial resources to pay for worker's compensation insurance, pay employee taxes, and pay your employees (just to name a few of the expenses)?

When I started my first business, I operated on a shoestring budget. I purchased used equipment and came up with creative ways to do the things that more expensive equipment I couldn't afford did. For example, I desperately needed a paste filling machine. I couldn't rent the machine and even a used machine costs over $1,000 which I couldn't afford. I did a ton of research and one day a light bulb went off in my head – I could use a jerky gun with a long nozzle to get the job done at a fraction of the cost.

I also kept my operation small and implemented an independent sales representative program that allowed women from different parts of the world to start their own website offering my products. Since they weren't employees of my company I did not have to incur the expenses of having employees. This model worked for a while.

Cricket Allen | www.theperfectsnaque.com

Our mantra in manufacturing (and overall) is crawl, walk, run. Below are areas where I'd recommend this approach:

a) If you are making a food, first see if you are able to find a commercial kitchen where you'll have the equipment and/or square footage to reasonably produce quantities for a test small market. Aim for a month-to-month lease if you can. Local caterers are a good place to start. If they aren't a good fit, ask them for recommendations.

b) Do not invest in any fancy equipment until you are in dire need to meet the demand. Be as manual as you can be at first by using people power and/or low investment tools. When you are ready for the commercial grade equipment – do your research. Look at the equipment demos on YouTube; talk to various equipment manufacturers; send them your product so they can give you feedback on whether their equipment can handle your product. And most definitely go visit the equipment manufacturers with a sample of your product before you pull the trigger. Also, I recommend leasing the equipment if you can (lease to buy). You'll have less capital output this way.

On the above two points, you will earn serious sweat equity! Know that if your product works, you'll grow out of this completely crazy stage, but it is a valuable part of the growth process allowing you to become more intimate with your product needs.

c) Hiring – if you are able to find quality temporary help this is a great way to go. At first, you won't be manufacturing every day so it would be a waste of money to pay for full-time employees when you might manufacture only a few days a week, or less, at first. Also, manufacturing demands a great respect for detail, rules and regulations. You want a staff you can trust on this level. So even if you think you are ready to hire, I would not pull the trigger until you see them at work for three months. If you are able to have a "temp" opportunity with chance for full time work after three months, you'll become familiar with the work ethic of this person before that big hiring commitment. From my experience, employees' true colors (whether temp, consultants, full-time) come through between the three to six month mark.

d) Do not make any big commitments to packaging right away. If you can, start with "*stock*" packaging, not proprietary. Since you will make changes to your creative and likely your packaging, you don't want to throwaway proprietary packaging that cost you a lot of money. Also, when you do proprietary packaging, go for digital at first to avoid a big expense on printing plates.

e) Food Stuff – you'll need to work with a professional who can do your nutrition facts and guide you through the FDA guidelines and requirements on how you list ingredients, packaging claims, allergen info, etc. Don't try and do this by yourself.

f) Ingredients – get samples galore before you go and order a ton of inventory on any ingredient. You need to be aware of textures, weights, shelf life, quality, etc from all of the vendors with whom you will deal.

g) Credit & Terms – as a new company, you might not be able to get credit right away from your vendors. But, over time, you will get credit/payment terms that will help immensely with cash flow. Try to buy small quantities of all your raw materials at first so you don't dole out a lot of capital. Then work to build up your credit resources one-by-one and pay on time. These will be your future credit references. You'll find credit/payment terms will be of immense value as you grow your business.

h) Do invest in doing it right. You want a quality professional product so make sure when you do invest in everything from your ingredients, bags, labels, etc., that your product has a professional look with a high quality product.

Owning the manufacturing of your product will allow you immense control of your product and minimize spending unproductive money. If someone is manufacturing for you (co-packing), they are going to have minimum production quantities. If you don't have places to sell your entire product at first you will be sitting on inventory, and that will tie up cash. Also, food products have date codes so it's tick-tock on the expiration. Lastly, you will likely tweak your product in the early stages of your start-up. When you are the manufacturer, this tweaking is a lot easier to do at a micro, inexpensive level. All of the above scenarios were why we decided to own the manufacturing for The Perfect SNAQUE. And while a hair net may not be glam, it's truly productive and satisfying. YOU are making something tangible and putting it out there and that feels good at the end of a long day

Jordan Eisenberg | www.urgentrx.com

The most important step is to find people who are experts in your particular field or industry and leverage them. Experts are generally very proud of their expertise and want to show it off – let them. I initially went out and, through persistent and directed networking, found my way to people who had very specific domain expertise that was relevant to what I wanted to create.

For UrgentRx, I needed expertise on pharmaceuticals, over-the-counter medications, contract manufacturing and FDA compliance. I asked them about a million questions and was a sponge for information. Concurrently, I did my absolute best to learn as much as possible about my industry as I could. I scoured the internet for information and subscribed to all of the industry journals and publications (these contain massive amounts of information). I also attended trade shows for the industry simply to get the lay of the land. Beyond this, I leveraged the internet to find contract manufacturers and convinced them to work with me on developing prototypes (there are great resources like ThomasNet for domestic manufacturers and Alibaba for international). The best news is that you can generally do all of these things outside of your 9-to-5 job – it's just up to you to have the persistence to make it happen.

Akbar Chisti | www.seamusgolf.com

I suppose our competitive advantage is that Megan did a lot of the sewing from the beginning. When it got to be too much for her, she offloaded to her aunt, then a couple of accomplished contract seamstresses that were her friends. She had the contacts to make sure we could grow and have the appropriate sewing team in place.

Chapter 5 : Finding A Development Team

If you are shipping software or have your business operating primarily through an online channel, then finding a development team that can execute your ideas is extremely crucial. Unlike manufacturing where you can ask for samples to gauge the quality of the product before ordering in bulk, development teams are mostly hired based on past reputation and references.

Myke Nahorniak is a 30 year old entrepreneur who founded his web calendar software start-up, Localist.com five years ago. Myke feels that freelancing sites are a great bet when you have small specific tasks to be accomplished. However, if you are looking at a more sophisticated application, remote teams only add to the frustration since you usually end up spending more time and energy getting the same work done. When he got started, Myke started visiting a lot of tech meet-ups to discover the kind of developers his start-up will need who he would eventually contact. He says that sites like Dribbble.com can be great when you are looking for design work.

Here are stories from other entrepreneurs who have experience finding development teams.

Michael Kawula | www.selfemployedking.com

Originally when my company outgrew our own technical abilities we tried different services from freelance sites and researching companies online. I had some great experiences and some terrible ones. I outsourced a piece of software we needed to help automate our orders on our website that we had priced at $18,000 by a USA company. The company we found in India was able to perform the same service for $1800 and created a much better product.

Shortly after that we hired another company for SEO work and after 3 months we found out it was a scam. They were providing us with reports of work they were doing on our site each month and billing us. After being uncertain of what they were doing on my site I changed their pass-code and the following month they sent another bill. When I asked them how they got onto my site to do the work, they never responded back.

Since then I've found most of my help through networking on LinkedIn and even on Twitter. I've worked recently with individuals in Pakistan, El Salvador and the Philippines. We use TimeDoctor to record the hours they spend working for those paid per hour and for others we pay per task. This seems to work the best.

Finding a development team has been one of our biggest challenges, mainly because I'm not a programmer — just a hack. It is difficult to evaluate the work of a programmer if you have no understanding of their code. My first experiences with developers didn't go well. I hired an outsourced development team to build the first version of our social network and it was a disaster. I put faith in them because they had someone in the US "managing" the project, but unfortunately, his job was really just to sell me. In the end, the team did terrible work and communication was a nightmare. I ended up losing the 5-figures I had spent on the project and all the code was tossed in the trash. We had to start over.

I found a site called ODesk that allows you to hire remotely and manage their work through a tool that takes screenshots at random once every 10 minutes. This tool lets you see that your developer is working on what they say they are working on, and keeps them accountable. Through that site, I found my first few good developers, and as we've grown, we've begun hiring these folks directly, without the aid of outsourcing sites.

I definitely recommend using outsourcing sites, but I strongly encourage readers to make sure the person you hire has worked with others through those sites and has positive reviews. I always recommend doing a very small test task to make sure you can communicate with your developer and that they can handle the job at hand.

At first we didn't need a developer. It was only until we started doing a significant amount of cleanings a day that our initial process (it was just Google calendars and Gmail) wasn't cutting it. I actually used reddit's forhire to find an initial developer with extra time that was looking for a new project to work with. He agreed to equity and a small paycheck, and later we added a couple contractors off freelance sites.

While I do love a lot of the freelance sites, it's mostly because I feel like I'm strong at gauging how good other people are at what they do with just a little time getting to know them. That's one of the reasons I prefer reddit—you can see someones post history and get a pretty damned accurate reading on how ambitious they are, how they view their work, etc. Of course with a lot of the freelance websites you can search names (or usernames) and find their social accounts if they have them.

Over the last few years, I have been through several stages of development. The first web developer that I hired was at college, and he built the initial version of Flashnotes.com. It barely worked, but at that point in time, it served its purpose. I remember staying up all night just to push the shipping confirmation button in order to send out the first set of class notes for students. This stage answered the first of three questions – Can you build it?

The second development team I used was outsourced in Seattle. These guys were fantastic, but when you deal with an outsourced U.S. firm, the price is steeper and timing is an issue. My piece of advice is that you should always assume that projects will cost twice as much and take twice as long. The quicker you can own that, the better off you will be.

Eventually when I closed my first round of funding, I was able to bring on a CTO who changed everything. We still used an outsourced firm for a period of time, but he was able to talk their language and ensure all deadlines were hit. The key lesson I've learned throughout the process is that while you will always want a newer, faster, cleaner version of your product, it is important to know that you can only sell what's on the truck. Do not chase shiny objects.

Jojo Hedaya | www.unroll.me

You won't find great developers for a start-up by sitting back and putting up postings on job posting websites. We went to networking and tech events almost every night and used every connection we could think of to find leads. I also found the book "*Who*" by Geoff Smart & Randy Street really helpful for our hiring process.

We've tried freelance websites and they weren't right for us. The most important aspect about a hire at a start-up is passion. People don't come work for start-ups because they pay well - especially not one in its early stage; they come because they love what we're trying to do and they want to put all their effort into bettering our company and helping it succeed. That's the best thing about a start-up, everyone that surrounds you, lives and breathes what we're doing in such an amazing way.

Rob Biederman | www.hourlynerd.com

We actually made our original website using Odesk. The product really wasn't great but it cost $890 and it met our needs for a long time! We even raised $750,000 of financing based on that site. We also used a more hands-on outsourced development firm in Boston to build our next site. They did good work but there are certain things you just need to do in-house. Technology is one of them.

Matt Keiser | www.liveintent.com

I started working with my current partner at my last business. He's the first technologist I ever worked with who actually was able to deliver all that he promised. Now part of what made the possible is that he wouldn't promise me what I wanted. He's mature and had built enough technology to know that it's not easy. So part of it was creating a relationship between the two of us where he could say, "*That's unrealistic or too expensive. Let's start with a much smaller build.*"

You need someone technical who can call bullshit. You need to be realistic – so whatever you're told, double in cost and time. And you have to trust your insider. No matter how many times you build something. Whenever a new team comes in, they'll tell you what you built already is crap.

A large part of the value of what you build isn't what works; it's what didn't work. You'll hear about companies like Yahoo that buys a company like Bright Media and aren't actually able to execute and deliver on the next generation of the product like you'd expect because they don't know what didn't work in the prior generation.

Adi Bittan | www.ownerlistens.com

We started with freelancers. The advantage: low commitment so if it doesn't work out, you're not stuck with them. The disadvantage: they can disappear on you at a moment's notice when a better gig comes along.
Quality wise, we tried to avoid at all costs someone that didn't have solid references from people we knew. We made that mistake once and never again. The guy we hired had everything right on paper. We even spoke to a former boss of his but after working with him we realized that boss was just a friend and the guy could not produce anything near the level that was needed. It was a huge mistake.

If you already have a team, that's great. However, if you don't, it takes a very long time to find a great team to work full time on a project so I would work with freelancers to get basic prototypes out for testing but continue to search for full time collaborator. Of course, there are some projects where that's not possible. The product might be super complex and require years of development. In those cases, the team needs to be solidified from the beginning.

Robert Livingstone | www.royaltext.com

We spent a year of research learning the mobile marketing industry inside and out. We spoke to multiple development teams in the industry and found our team by an industry referral. We were very pleased by their work. We have used freelance sites in the past, but not for major development work. We've found them successful for smaller projects, but required ongoing support from our development team. Therefore, we needed a stable company that couldn't just disappear on us. We self-funded the development process with profits from IdealCost.com.

Jeb Blount | www.salesgravy.com

My cousin owned a web development company and I turned to him for the first iteration of SalesGravy.com. About three years in though we began to outgrow his capabilities. Clearly, finding the right development team is critical to success, especially when you are pouring your own money into developing the site. Unfortunately, we hit a wall with my cousin's company and we were forced to find better people.

We turned to Odesk – a freelance website – and found a developer to augment the work my cousin's company was doing. That was in 2010. Over the next two years our relationship with that developer grew and we turned over more and more of the site development to him and his associates. In 2012 we shifted 100% of our business to his company and today we are very happy with the outcome. I encourage entrepreneurs who ask me to use freelance sites because we have had great results.

Jason Richelson | www.shopkeep.com

I went into the Ruby on Rails groups and found a guy who was answering everyone's questions. He was smart, experienced and I could see he had a great attitude. I contacted him and he became my Chief Technology Officer in October of 2008. He recruited developers from his network and I found others in the co-working space we were renting in New York City.

Danny Maloney | www.tailwindapp.com

Alex and I both have engineering degrees, but neither of us had coded much of use. We couldn't afford to hire a developer in NYC and never found a CTO co-founder to join us. Instead, we (almost entirely Alex) rolled up our (his) sleeves and figured it out. Along the way, we brought on advisors to accelerate our learning. It took 15 months to hire our first full-time developer, but today we have a great team to work with- and they all know way more than us. Don't wait for that perfect hire, though. If you build the initial prototype, it'll raise the odds of finding that person.

We've used some freelance help along the way, but only in limited, highly targeted ways. I do not recommend outsourcing any of your core product development if you are a technology-driven company. Freelancers' incentives don't align with yours, leading to more challenges than benefits. Plus, outsourcing development entirely will make fund-raising much harder.

Joel Simkhai | www.grindr.com

After coming up with the idea for Grindr, I scrambled to find a developer. With a bit of luck I found Morten Bek Ditlevsen. He lives in Denmark and worked remotely. I tried using the freelance websites but didn't find anyone. It's been five years – so they may be better now. We have used freelancer websites for non-technical skills with a lot of success. I've been fortunate in finding a great team of people who are truly dedicated and passionate about our business and serving our users, and that's helped us grow to where we are today.

Raj Sheth | www.recruiterbox.com

We developed the product ourselves for the first year. We never hired freelance engineers as the product was going to be experiencing ongoing development for years, and we felt more comfortable having people in the same room to think of solutions and what they wanted the product to stand for. After one year, we began hiring engineers full-time assisted by job listings on StackOverflow.

Eren Bali | www.udemy.com

We were lucky. Oktay and I went to college together, and we created some long-lasting friendships with engineers. We hired many of our college friends to join the Udemy team and we kept close relationships with our college to tap into the talent pool. We also asked our early engineers to recommend their friends to us and this allowed us to hire some very talented engineers.

Jason Cohen | www.wpengine.com

I'm lucky in that I myself am an engineer, so I haven't had to solve that problem. I find that freelancers are great for website work and other marketing material. But, if your start-up specifically depends on non-trivial technical work, you need a technical co-founder to get the requisite amount of devotion and thought, at a price you can afford, meaning someone else who also is working their butt off for free.

Chapter 6 : How To Get The Very First Customers

Once you have launched your business, the next step is to start spreading the word about your product or service. In my experience, even press mentions from the biggest websites and newspapers only take you to one level. Many times, the sales die down soon after the news gets old. Therefore, your business needs a solid marketing plan to ensure you build a slow and gradual customer base over time that is not solely dependent on PR.

You must have heard of the extremely popular music streaming service, Grooveshark.com. Sam Tarantino, the founder of the application tells us that the initial marketing strategy included a number of crazy stunts around the University of Florida campus where Sam studied. *"I had a friend dress up in a homemade shark suit costume and argue with some of the crazy folks in the "free speech zone" on the University of Florida campus. People thought it was hilarious and crowds gathered around filming YouTube videos, and word got out who we were"*, he says.

But viral videos were not the only way they got the word out. Sam tells us that he started sharing the application to bloggers around the world who did not have any sort of music product like his before. The simplicity of the app drove adoption and helped in word of mouth virality. For about three years, GrooveShark grew by as much as 200K-300K active users per month.

Here are the experiences from other entrepreneurs on how they got the word out for their start-ups in the early days.

Philip Masiello | www.800razors.com

This is the challenge for any start-up. We decided to look for opportunities that could get us in the press for something that is fun and complimentary to the business. We targeted a famous baseball player with a standout beard and offered him $1 million to shave with our razor. He did not take the offer (as we expected) but the outrageous stunt garnered over 200 press mentions, putting our company on the map.

Micha Kaufman | www.fiverr.com

In order to effectively scale, consumer web, and certainly two-sided marketplaces, should have a number of components built-in. Pre-launch, we understood that the future of the marketplace relied on an organic/viral effect. The marketplace needed to be sticky, addictive and capable of incentivizing people to share it with in their social circles.

It might sound counter-intuitive, but marketplaces almost always start with supply and not demand. If you have a market that has a surplus of supply and no demand, you simply don't have a marketplace. Assuming your product has value to a substantial audience, you should create inventory before you bring in customers. It's similar to starting an e-commerce store with or without very few products.

With that in mind, we focused our efforts on bringing sellers to the marketplace. We did that by stimulating and spreading word of mouth marketing to people we thought might be interested in offering their skills to others. We then worked to make the on-boarding experience as friendly, fast and friction-free as possible.

On the product side, Fiverr's design created incentives for sellers to get involved in the marketing of their own services. That kick-started a cycle of bringing customers and this created a snowball effect.

Rob Walling | www.getdrip.com

I start with my own audience. These are people who follow something you do in public: your blog, podcast, Twitter feed, Facebook, etc. Spread the word, offer a time-limited discount, and try to determine who is using your product and why.

The next outer circle is my friends' or colleagues' audiences. Now that I know who's using my product and willing to pay for it, I run through my network of friends and colleagues and try to determine who has an audience that might line up with that demographic, and figure out a way to contribute content to that person. Either by writing a guest post for their blog, appearing on their podcast, or creating a great piece of content they are likely to re-tweet.

Lastly, there's the outer circle, and that includes every other marketing approach you can think of: advertising, search engine optimization, content marketing, join ventures, etc. This is where you get your biggest reach, but it's far more expensive and time consuming to find new customers in this circle. Hopefully by the time you get here you have an exceptional idea of who should be using your product and where specifically you can find them. Circles 1 and 2 are mostly about learning. The third, outermost circle, is when you really start to grow a business.

Jake Sigal | www.livioconnect.com

I had experience in the consumer electronic industry, which really helps. I think nowadays if you want to start a business in a field without any experience, you really need to rely on crowd-sourcing or getting an advisor to help you break in. Of course, if you make an app or software to solve some specific problem, you can just launch it, call reporters and let them know why your product solves this problem, and away you go.

Matt Shoup | www.mandepainting.com

Hard work and long hours! I was out hitting the streets for 12 hours a day every day to make sure that everyone knew about the new painting company in town. Knowing a couple of paint crews that did fantastic work was the most important part of my early success because the proof was in the pudding, so to speak. Getting the first few jobs turned around and having them come out fantastically got the word-of-mouth started and, coupled with me putting the work in; people started calling me before too long.

Lawson Nickol | www.allamericanclothing.com

While developing a product and marketing strategy you need to define exactly who your customer is and how your product can UNIQUELY fill their needs. After defining this, it was easy for us to find industry trade shows, niche magazines and to implement a much focused Google Adwords campaign. We also reached out to contacts we had from previous business relationships. Once again, networking is very important.

Giancarlo Massaro | www.viralsweep.com

Getting the word out in the beginning is one of the toughest things any entrepreneur will face. You'll have all of your marketing materials and initiatives set up for launch day, and when you finally open the doors, no one comes.

For ViralSweep, we were talking with businesses before we even launched the product. This is a huge part of why you need to validate your idea before you even build something. By talking to businesses before and during the process of building, we were able to figure out pain points and problems people were having, which allowed us to build solutions for those people into our product. When we launched, we just reached back out to those businesses and they immediately became paying customers. Putting it into perspective though, it was only 2 or 3 people who immediately paid us, we went weeks and sometimes months until we found our next paying customer – it definitely wasn't easy.

In our first 8 months, we would see anywhere from 2 to 5 sign-ups per week. Per month, we would only see 1 or 2 paying customers. The one thing that really turned the tables in our favor was the content we started producing. Initially, we were writing blog posts – long form, 3-5,000 word posts that would get some traction with a decent amount of social sharing, and a couple sign-ups. These posts, however, were not 100% targeted to our niche, and we knew we could do better.

We spent 3 months producing a 12,000 word, interactive guide that has tremendously helped our business. The guide has been our biggest driver of sign-ups and paying customers. So, when something is working, you duplicate it, right? Following the guide, we launched The Growth Series in January where we are helping one of our customers hit certain goals to help grow their business. With their first two promotions using our service, they've already generated $34,000 in revenue. The Growth Series is performing extremely well for us, converting even more readers into customers than our Advanced Sweepstakes Guide.

So, while you can always use social media, paid advertising, forum posts, blog commenting, and a million different tactics out there to grow your business, you need to find something that works, and scale it up from there. Rather than taking the shotgun approach and doing everything, find one thing that works to grow your business and keep doing it.

Andrew Stanten | www.altitudemarketing.com

In the very early days of Altitude Marketing, my business partner, Stan Zukowski and I tapped into relationships we'd built over the 15 years we worked at Rodale and Lehigh University. It was a lot of personal relationship-building followed through with delivering exceptional quality, high value and unparalleled customer service.

The best way to get things moving is to deliver something of exceptional value, do great work and create evangelists who love what you provide. Within the first six months, we were getting referrals. And within the first year, we were on third-generation referrals. Beyond our personal network, Ben Franklin Technology Partners (BFTP), a state-funded economic development organization that funds and assists technology start-ups, was instrumental in helping Altitude Marketing get out of the gate.

I worked with them in my role at Lehigh University and they became one of our very first clients. Soon, BFTP began referring its own portfolio of start-up companies to Altitude. I also networked nonstop. I offered to lead a marketing 101 course at Lehigh University's Small Business Development Center; I provided feedback to start-ups and established manufacturers in "*Tiger Sessions*" through BFTP; and I guest-lectured for one of my professors from Lehigh each semester. All of these I continue to do to this day because maintaining those organizational relationships works to keep connecting you with new faces, new talent and fresh technology.

Finally, we took a dose of our own marketing medicine. We invested in all of the things we were telling our clients to invest in: a smart website; public relations efforts; a view book; thought leadership blogs; social media. We always make a concerted effort to ask happy clients for testimonials that we can share on our site and on our social media accounts.

Jason Schultz | www.jason.me

When I started my first tech company, there weren't nearly as many options for marketing as there are today. Back in the 90's we had banner ads, SEO, email marketing, and loose knit affiliate programs. Today there's an endless stream of PPC, SEO, mobile advertising, display advertising, video advertising, re-targeting, affiliate programs, and social marketing channels.

Start small with advertising networks such as Microsoft AdCenter. Grow the campaigns based on the ROI you're getting. If you're not getting the right ROI, go back and test new things. It's your start-up, you've got complete control over what and how you offer your products and services to people.

You have an advantage because you're a small start-up. The smaller you are the easier you can try new things and change parts of your business that larger companies can't easily change. Use your small size to your advantage; you're faster and more nimble than the bigger competition.

Bryan Knowlton | www.appraiseallrealestate.com

By blogging about industry related hot topics like problems in the industry, I was able to reach a large audience of appraisers looking for solutions to those problems. I answered questions on industry related websites and forums and hosted free webinars discussing the industry in general while giving valuable information on how to use the internet to get more business. The articles that were published in industry magazines also gave me credibility in my field. I used all these platforms to get my name out to my audience without hard selling them on any of the products or services I was creating.

Courtney Ilarrazza | www.babybodyguards.com

We reached out to "*mommy blogs*" and local news outlets. We sent stories about child safety to newspapers, magazines and television shows. We did free events and promotions at Baby Stores. We advertized places where our clients would be. A popular mommy blog hired us and then wrote a great review about her experience. We then got a trickle of business from there which we turned into a stream of word of mouth referrals.

We strove to turn that stream of referrals into a tsunami of thrilled clients that would spread the word about us everywhere they went. It then became our goal to make sure that every client, not only was satisfied, but that they loved us. We wanted to make sure they would tell their friends and family about the experience they had with us. This grew geographically until we became a major presence on parent's boards and blogs all over our geographic area. We are now aiming nationally because we are franchising.

Matthew Griffin | www.bakersedge.com

This is the least mysterious part of starting up. Look up people via the internet, call them, repeat as necessary. To get the word out we relied on local press (college paper, local papers), special interest web media. We reached out to bloggers and asked them if they would like to test our products. This was a slow but building process – always leveraging any exposure to pique the interest of the next media opportunity.

For sales we targeted smaller independent specialty stores and catalogs. We looked up their "*contact us*" info and made some cold calls. The success rate wasn't high, but it wasn't zero. The singular best thing we did was to sell direct via our website and list our products on Amazon.com as a third party. There is no better way to get the word out than good online reviews and actual sales. This also helped convince the retailers we were courting that we were a legit product and business.

Jay Barnett | www.prioritypickup.com.au

From previous experience, in other businesses, I already knew how to get business instantly. And that is through Internet Marketing. Firstly I set up a Google Adwords account. Of course you will need a website to attach your Adwords account to – so that will have to be set up first. Based on the quality of the words in the ad and my budget, I was able to attain a high position on the front page of Google, instantly, at key times of the day.

If you are new to Google I recommend taking some time out to study the online tutorials they provide. They are really informative, and there is plenty of support, so don't be shy in asking Google a question or phoning them. They have great customer service. Go to www.google.com/adwords and that is where I started.

Another thing I did at the same time was to engage the services of an internet marketing specialist to begin my SEO campaign. SEO stands for Search Engine Optimization. It works differently to the Adwords account. Unlike SEO, you don't pay per click or impression. SEO is based on traffic to your website and backlinks etc. It is an industry in itself, and not something I have time to get involved in, so I recommend getting someone in to manage that for you.

It is best to start SEO at the same time as your Adwords account. SEO takes time to get a high position on Google search pages. Allow approximately 3 months. You have to be careful who you choose as your SEO specialist. Some "*so called*" specialists can promise instant results, but will use back handed tactics to do it.

This is likely to cause damage to your website or can even get you blacklisted on Google. It has happened to me before, and it was devastating! I lost the domain name which was the same as my business name, along with my entire website. Basically, I had to start again from scratch.

Monique Tatum | www.beautifulplanning.com

In the beginning, I used to place my resume on Craigslist within the resume section with the subject line of what we do. I had written a very sassy (but extremely personable) little preamble. It got the phones ringing. I am a firm believer in guerrilla marketing and I will never forget printing out about 500 fliers and walking around NYC posting them to poles and trees that read "*Need Marketing*" or "*Have An Event?*"

To think back I was definitely barking up the wrong tree, but it was fun and an experience. I will never forget an older woman calling me and telling me that what I did was against the law and I littered her neighborhood and she was going to call the department of sanitation on me. I shook in my boots for a second and then went on to my next lead generation plan. I used to send nice little email blasts to friends and ex coworkers about referral programs and I truly maintained a good relationship with old contacts from old positions.

Betsy | www.betsyandiya.com

I knew my business needed a foundation of wholesale accounts for bread and butter, but also knew that any opportunity to get retail margins was one worth jumping on. Once I'd designed the first collection, I found my first wholesale buyers the good old-fashioned way: I pounded pavement. Anytime I visited family or friends back east, I'd take my sales kit with me. Finding the right fit with shops and building solid relationships with their owners and buyers has always been a huge component to our success. When I took my husband on as a partner in 2010, his main focus to start was continued growth in wholesale. To that end, we loaded the dog and a cooler up in our car and drove across the country 3 times, meeting with prospective wholesale accounts along the way.

As for retail in the beginning, I never said no. I did every craft fair I could find, every street festival, every trunk show, every church bazaar, and every pop-up shop. And of course, I got online as quickly as possible. For the first 3 years, I was on Etsy.com exclusively. Getting noticed online has never been easy. In 2008, social media wasn't the player it is today. Back then (and still today), I wrote a blog and worked to be featured on other blogs to be discovered online.

The through-line in all of this, though, is our focus is on providing an incredible customer experience in every way -- in the quality of our product and the other products we carry in our brick & mortar, our brand and story, design, customer service, in making sure you feel great while you're shopping with us. We've work incredibly hard at this and thankfully, word has spread.

J'Amy Owens | www.billthebutcher.com
First, make something so good, it commands attention and deserves loyalty. Do something iconoclastic and transcendent that offers a better alternative and is attached to a mega trend that your target consumers are already an integrated part of. Then, design a brand that is positioned properly so that you easily attract the desired audience. Of course, the secret sauce in making all of these mission critical tactics take hold is having unconditional love and respect for your customer.

Andrew Gazdecki | www.biznessapps.com
If you're lucky enough to target the small business market there's typically hundreds, if not thousands, of potential clients within a few miles. Our first few clients came from in person meeting with local business owners. Apart from that, my past experiences left me with a fairly adept understanding of search engine marketing and SEO. We also began an aggressive cross-country cold calling effort targeting several different verticals. Those combined with a very modest campaign on Google Adwords helped us start to add a couple clients every month.

Julien Smith | www.breather.com
Breather is such a crazy idea that it gets talked about a lot anyway. So we started with friends, who shared it with their friends, then we shared it to Twitter, and then it started going through strangers.

Google's AdWords and Bing's AdCenter. This was to validate that people would pay for our service. Once we knew they would, we had to find cheaper ways to acquire customers since the cost per acquisition in cleaning is too high on a one-time sale at our price point and most clients are looking for last-second cleanings, not recurring service. Keeping clients is also incredibly difficult. I've never struggled with repeat business as much as I have in cleaning. Your product is critiqued like no other, you don't have full control over the service being provided, you're always being undercut (and as a result clients are always considering trying the cheaper guys), etc.

Dan DeLuca | www.grownsmall.com / www.classchatter.com

In the beginning I got the word out using internet forums. People were actually quite willing to try things, especially since I was offering my service for free. I really supported those early users. I answered a lot of emails and built custom functions for my users. Back in 2004 the site was amateurish, but the concept was solid. People who stuck with it were in it for the ride, they were helping build the site and they knew it. I am sure plenty of people hit the homepage immediately turned away, but the users I did attract became my evangelist. They went out and showed people the site. Remember this was before Twitter and before Facebook, so when they showed people the site they actually showed it in person and demonstrated it. I was building a small army of experts.

My passion is building technology that blends the online world with real world activities. It may be old fashioned but the biggest thing that helped me attract users was having people on the ground demonstrating the product. It might not come as much of a surprise but teachers are great at this. It also helped that teachers are very active creating professional development lessons for other teachers. What started as a few teachers sharing my service with their co- workers eventually led to ClassChatter being part of the official professional development curriculum of several states. Its great having users doing this work for you, but especially in the beginning you are going to have to get out there and do it yourself. Have demonstrations and offers classes.

Nellie Akalp | www.corpnet.com

With my first company, we literally put up a one page website and the orders started rolling in in literally minutes! With our current company, put it this way, I do not know anyone who has more gray hairs than me at the age of 42. It was much harder the second time around since we were up against many competitors in the industry. However, I rolled up my sleeves and got to work being active on social media, sharing content across popular blogs and news outlets, making a presence for the brand as many places as possible to increase awareness. As a result, we celebrated our third expansion last year and I am so ecstatic about that!

Michael Wayne | www.deca.tv

When we launched the company in 2007, there was a wave of VC investments in digital content studios, Next New Networks, Revision3, etc. We got a lot of PR attention because we were one of the leaders of this wave. The lesson is: ride the wave. There is power in numbers. If there are lots of companies getting funded in the same space, make sure you are the perceived to be the best of the class. In terms of audience we opted early on (pre-2011) to partner with companies that already had audience - CNET, Yahoo!, BlogHer, etc. We didn't know how to build traffic organically on websites and YouTube was still not the best platform for premium content that advertisers would get behind. That changed after 2011.

Aditi Kapur | www.deliverychef.in

One of the first tools that we used to get the word out was social media – specifically Facebook. It was free, our concept was new, and generated a lot of buzz.

Adam Simpson | www.easyofficephone.com

Look for ways to multiply your sales team, without necessarily employing multiple salespeople. One of our early strategies was building a network of partners who had a symbiotic interest in offering our product in return for commission. When you get out there and learn your industry's ecosystem, you may be amazed at how many potential partners exist.

George Burciaga | www.elevatedigital.com

Since the very beginning, I've always been out and about and present in technology organizations, chambers of commerce and networking events. Being involved with groups like the Illinois Technology Association and the Chicagoland Chamber of Commerce have given me the opportunity to get in front of the right people and build a buzz without burning through marketing dollars.

Not every entrepreneur is a great salesman, but it helps. You have to be out there talking about who you are and what you're doing. You cannot just sit back and assume people will hear about you. Even sending an email isn't good enough. Being physically present, engaged and confident allows you to really sell your idea and your product and even more importantly build their belief in your capabilities.

In the beginning, it was all about networking, word of mouth. When we did get a customer, we treated them like gold. We were responsive, followed their business, their competitors and asked them about their business regularly. It was never about how we could sell them more of our stuff, but how we could help meet their goals.

Those early clients liked us a lot so they kept coming back for more and invited me to strategy and brainstorming sessions because they knew I wouldn't turn them into pitches for my company. We acted like an extension of their business and treated them like it was our own.

When it came time to give them our recommendations re expanding services, we were flexible on how we approached pricing and gave them everything from '*cheap and cheerful*' to '*wow me*' options.

Our strategy was to go after large companies, but that didn't mean we could compete head on with the global multinational suppliers they were used to dealing with. I called it the remora strategy. We would go after all the small projects that the bigger guys didn't care about. Over time, the customer gave us incrementally larger scale projects until we became a preferred global supplier ourselves.

Mike Matousek | www.flashnotes.com

I hustled -- customer service built Flashnotes.com. In the beginning, we had a lot of tech issues, but I was able to build relationships with my initial users through negative experiences that they had on the site. It may sound strange, but user complaints were always so exciting for me. This showed me that these individuals saw enough value in my idea that they were willing to reach out for a resolution.

This stage separates those entrepreneurs who are successful from those who are not. You need to decide if you're willing to get in the trenches and work through all the "*nos*," to get that first "*yes*." Find the early adopters to be successful. There are 7 billion people in the world, and if no one has your idea, it's probably a bad one. It all comes down to execution : can you get someone to pay for your product?

I remember walking around Minnesota's campus passing out $10 bills in the freezing cold to fraternity houses and students who would give me a minute of their time. It was 0 degrees, but I knew if I could get in front of them, I had the ability & passion sell them on my idea.

Zalmi Duchman | www.freshdiet.com

Since I started my business pre-social media it was not as easy as it is now to get the word out. I took local ads in the newspaper & I started a

Google Adwords account with specific keywords to my business like *"diet delivery"*. That is how I got my first few clients. Eventually I started to use direct mail as well as a good source of sales leads.

Joel Simkhai | www.grindr.com

In the early days we did not have a marketing or PR budget. We did do some guerrilla marketing by showing up at Pride events and we hosted Grindr parties at gay bars. We've also had a lot of great press mentions and mentions on TV shows and movies.

Our users understand that the more guys on Grindr, the better the service is. This gives our users a natural incentive to spread the word so more guys join the app. I recommend that every business look for ways to incentive their users to spread the word.

Stacey Lindenberg | www.growyourtalent.com

I believe starting within your own network is critical. People may overlook this step, but we all tend to do business with people we trust and like. We recommend people based on their character and our belief in their abilities. Starting with trusted contacts and asking for help is extremely valuable. Secondly, offering to write articles for trade publications, volunteering to speak at conferences and trade shows, and being visible in your community is also valuable.

Other tips include being visible. Continue to look out for the best interest of others, volunteer your time not just in your industry (writing, speaking, etc.) but also for your community. You still need face to face contact with people, and it is fulfilling to help others. It gives me immense joy to give back, and somehow it gives me courage.

As an entrepreneur, you are often playing the roles of everyone in your company, at least when you begin. You are your own accountant, cheerleader, marketing department, and more. Be prepared to put in the time to fill the roles. When you can afford it, pay for or barter the help you need in these roles if they aren't strength for you.

Myra Roldan | herbanluxe.etsy.com

When I was ready to start getting word out about my business I hit the pavement hard. I'm big on word of mouth advertising. I had business cards and small postcards printed. I posted them on library and local business bulletin boards; I even paid a few kids a couple of bucks to canvas a mall parking lot adding my postcard to every car windshield in the lot. Annoying, I know, but I wanted as many people as possible to know I was in business. I also joined the local chamber of commerce. I was on a mission to get in front of as many people as possible with the least amount of effort.

I also offered a "*business opportunity*" that was a mix of affiliate marketing and independent sales representatives. Women (and men) could sign-up and pay a nominal fee. In exchange they received a personalized landing page that contained text areas they could customize and a long with a link to my online store. Since it was a hybrid program. Whenever an independent rep made a sale, I would get notification and ship the order out. In exchange the independent reps earned anywhere between 15% - 40% depending on the size of their sales. This was one way to get in people talking about my product. There were some minor bumps along the way but we worked them out. A lot of people want to get it on the ground floor level of an opportunity and this was perfect.

Today I run a new web-based business, so I do a lot of web-based marketing including using Project Wonderful to get my button ad on as many sites as possible with the lowest investment. I sponsored giveaways, send product samples to several bloggers and Youtubers, wrote and submitted press release via PR Web, and sponsored several small woman-based events.

Project Wonderful has definitely lived up to its name. With a mere $20 a month, my ads are published across several blogs and viewed by thousands. I also use blogads, which is a bit more expensive but just as good. Bloggers also provide a great deal of web traffic, especially because I do not pay them to write the reviews – I ask for honest yet fair reviews.

Kathy Crifasi | www.hipzbag.com

Getting the word outside of your friends and family is always tough, especially if you have no experience trying to promote/sell a product- which was me. The first step is education. Today, like never before, you can find resources online to create a business online and actually make money from your home with little out of pocket money. Leaving your house has benefits as well. I went to every event, gift show, trade-show, expo I could find. Many times, I would go to an event with a goal in mind. Every time, I would come out with many more take-aways as it was the case of "*you don't know what you don't know*" – getting surrounded by the industry, asking questions and participating, helped me gain knowledge/contacts that I didn't even know I needed. I was at a gifting suite for the Emmy's when my QVC Rep found me. I was at a gift show when I learned about ways to get press. Each time I left an event, I created a new list of things to do.

Mike Glanz | www.hireahelper.com

We didn't really know anything about marketing or advertising, except limited experience playing around with Adwords and a passable knowledge of SEO. So we made the website "*SEO optimized*" and opened an Adwords account. We also started affiliate marketing accounts with Shareasale.com and eventually built our own affiliate marketing platform (where we give a commission to partners who refer us customers). Those are the cheapest way we've seen to generate sales, and to this day most of our orders come from one of those three channels.

In business school they will tell you to make long term marketing plans, but in reality you have no idea what your customers want, so you can't really do that effectively. I opened an Adwords account and started spending money on key words in order to get our first customers. Even if your customer acquisition cost doesn't make sense when you start off, you need to get those first customers in order to start getting feedback.

Mike Townsend | www.homehero.org

We arranged a few bar crawls to with our initial bars. We used Thrillist, Meetup, and Facebook events to promote our events. We would incentivize people with drink coupons (although in hindsight, I don't think we needed to).

Debra Cohen | www.homeownersreferral.com

My first promotion was a direct mail campaign to homeowners. I created it with the help of a friend who worked in marketing. I networked locally to find a new homeowner mailing list and, after each batch of mailers was sent, I called as many of the recipients as possible to introduce myself. I remember that I wouldn't let myself stop calling each day until I landed one new client.

Rob Biederman | www.hourlynerd.com

Aggressive door to door hustle, shaming family and friends into soliciting their connections. We also hired a PR firm who helped us place a few key stories about our early customer successes. That created a lot of inbound flow to our website.

Raghu Kulkarni | www.idrive.com

It was mostly through Google Adwords advertising, and we enjoyed good organic rank/position on Google and other search engines for the important keywords related to backup.

Audrius Jankauskas | www.impresspages.org

In 2011 we participated in start-up accelerator "*Different Engine*" in England. This helped us to clarify the idea and focus on the most important goals. We learned that sharing ideas is very useful – don't tuck them away in your closet, but rather speak to different sorts of people, find mentors, leaders who can advise you. This results in a wider contact list and a wider outlook in general.

Nevertheless, from the first days we concentrated more on making the actual product than telling people about it. Our media coverage was fair, but we worked really hard to create a close community of users and in the long-term this paid off really well – we got unsolicited reviews, articles, testimonials from people who were using and enjoying our product.

Still, in order to expand and monetize (!) we had to work more with publicity. Since ImpressPages is a really global product, we started scanning the Internet to hunt all forums, websites, blogs, etc. that cover related topics (such as content management, programming, coding, website development, web design, the list goes on and on...). We sent out numerous pitches, press-releases, tried making contact with reporters, bloggers, developers, everyone who's in the industry.

I was everywhere: filled out hundreds of participation forms, applied to various events, and appeared on different media channels. In my mind, potential users must see your message multiple times and from multiple sources to finally decide to try it.

Ryan Wallace | www.iphoneantidote.com

We naively thought that by providing the highest prices and the best service would just instantly get us out there. We were actually worried that we would get too many customers. It wasn't quite the case. We started actually getting customers mostly by word of mouth. After the concept had been proven a bit we started using Google Adwords. But a word to the wise - learn everything you can about Adwords before spending a dime on it. We literally wasted over $2,000 on Adwords before we realized what we were doing. Then we stopped our ads, and did a complete refinement after reading several books on the topic.

Ashok Subramanian | www.liazon.com

It may not be exciting, but it came down to the tried and true old school gumshoe tactics - knocking on doors, attending networking events and speaking to anyone who would listen. We even did a product demo in a Starbucks bathroom! There were certainly days where I didn't think we would ever get a client, but we kept moving forward and believed in our product.

Traditional sales and cold calling. We knew we had a good product, but weren't sure who made the buying decisions, or how much they were willing to pay. We just knew we were providing something of value. The only thing you can hope for in that situation is to have as many conversations as you can with prospects. We tried to keep it as conversational as possible, not chasing a sale, but chasing information. We asked prospects things like, *"what are your goals with your calendar?" "How much time would you say it takes you to create an online event listing?" "What percentage of your website traffic is to your calendar?"*

These genuine attempts to learn more about our customer gave us powerful metrics to develop our sales strategy on. We learned the terminology that resonated with them, the target decision maker, and the typical expected budget. Through these conversations, you land on folks who are interested, and some of them are even willing to buy what you're selling. We repeated this strategy for different markets, trying to maintain a constant sense of curiosity. Never presuming.

Arnon Rose | www.localmaven.com
I am still somewhat old fashioned when it comes to getting the word out. I believe that building solid prospect lists is where it all starts and that a lot of effort should be put into such data gathering up front. Sales drive an organization and it has always been a very early focus of mine in every business. Yes, product development is important, but to me a focus on building one's prospect list starts at the founding of a business.

Gathering information can be a manual project one does on their own or an automated process that is outsourced. Typically I will use overseas data entry companies to help me compile publicly available data and sort it in a way that I can use for outreach in terms of emails, print mailings, or creating prospect lists that I can enter into a CRM system for manual calling.

Good old fashioned selling and getting on the phone with potential customers is something every founder should be doing regularly. It keeps you in touch with your market and you can learn more about your business by talking to a customer on the front line than nearly any other activity. In today's world, it's so inexpensive to prepare detailed and customize email campaigns to different market segments that there is no excuse to avoid doing such mass outreach early on in the start-ups life.

Michael Folkes | www.mafolkes.com
I let my actions speak for itself along with the quality of my work. I also

leveraged the relationships between customers and my suppliers. I would often ask them (my current customers and supplier base) for business referrals. Xerox was my first customer. I found an opportunity within their organization that reduced their annual spend enormously year over year. It took well over a year after my proposal was accepted by Xerox, numerous meetings and negotiations followed and eventually a contract was awarded.

Jill Foucré | www.marcelsculinaryexperience.com

My first communication was via Facebook and my objective was to create "*buzz*" via my Facebook page. I didn't have my website up and running until shortly before the store opened so Facebook was my primary vehicle. I also had a very visible construction project going on in the space that we renovated and since we are on Main Street in our town, we had a lot of vehicle and foot traffic. We used our windows as an ongoing tease to generate chatter in the community and that was extremely effective. I also set up in front of the store at several community events (JazzFest, Sidewalk Sale, etc) and passed out information and got contact information to build the start of my email list.

Kevin Lavelle | www.mizzenandmain.com

In order to get the word out in the very beginning, you will have to do almost everything you can. From pinging friends and family, to spending a majority of your day refining your marketing, your selling efforts, and your customer service, do whatever it takes to grow, especially at the beginning. It is important to remember, however, not to alienate customers, existing or potential, by overselling or becoming something that you are not, just for the next sale.

Edward DeSalle | www.netirrigate.com

I got the word out in the very beginning by cold calling prospects. I did research on the Internet to identify organizations that might benefit from our technology. For every 50 I called, about 1 or 2 would show interest in beta testing Net Irrigate products. These test customers ultimately evolved into actual paying customers.

Rob Infantino | www.openbay.com

If you follow Steve Blank, he gets on his soapbox and yells, "*Get out of the building.*" This is exactly what I did. One of my initial goals was to acquire about 20 - 30 shops in the Boston area and then drive customers to those shops. Without appointments, I'd visit repair shop after repair shop asking them to spend a few minutes of time with me on a new idea that would help them generate more revenue and acquire new customers. Some spent more than a few minutes and some politely told me there was no interest and asked me to leave. I reached my goal in a short period of time. Next step was to get vehicle owners to try the service. I reached out to friends and family to try the new service and provide feedback along the way.

Iftach Orr | www.pix.do

One way to attract these devoted users is to understand your market audience and be active in the forums they themselves gather in in order to communicate with one another, be that a Facebook group, chat room or a professional conference. Use discussion websites to raise any interesting dilemmas you've encountered and link to your website when suitable. Disclose details about your project, this will make your users to be more devoted as they will feel they are a part of your venture.

Aaron Skonnard | www.pluralsight.com

The key was starting with building a solid product that we knew would get people talking and excited. This allowed us to use the least expensive channels to start marketing it through word of mouth, primarily on social media and at industry events. Our main objective was to get as many people as possible to experience the product, and then have them tell our story for us. This meant giving away our product for free for a while to thought-leaders who we knew could influence a lot of people. We didn't start spending substantial money on marketing until well after we'd already proven our model and had success from our word-of-mouth efforts.

Alicia Weaver | www.prestigeestateservices.com

We put up a website and Adwords immediately. There are a lot of good business directories; we added our business to any that even seemed relevant. We didn't fall into any business category easily so it was important the client could find us wherever they looked. We reached out to all our possible partners. We defined this as anyone who provides services in the same category. Chances are, every now and then people will contact them needing YOUR service and it's nice to have someone to refer. Do as much networking you can in person, it is much more effective and memorable when you remember a face for a company, not an email introduction.

Mary Apple | www.prettypushers.com

For me, when first creating the product, I would think about the types of outlets where I thought it could be sold. They went hand in hand – the product helped me curate the outreach list, but the store names also helped me curate the product. Right from the beginning, I thought of 2 family friends who owned small businesses. One was a Spa and one was a Hair Dresser. I went to them with my widget and they took it (probably just to be polite), but I absolutely built upon those 2 small stores. They proudly went up on the website and I would mention them in every sales call after that. After reaching a goal of 100 wholesale outlets, we started selling directly on prettypushers.com. That might not be everyone's order of attack but for me; it was a way to validate our brand before saying to the world "*Hey, come buy from our website*".

John Brady | www.protempartners.com

Old school shoe leather and outreach: friends, family, colleagues, professional contacts new and old. I also offered steeply discounted pricing in the first six months (so operated at a loss) to those initial customers with the understanding that if they were satisfied, they would provide testimonials, serve as references, be quoted in press releases, etc. Going this route though, it's imperative that the discount be visible in invoices, and that the return expectation is spelled out clearly, otherwise you risk devaluing your offering in the marketplace for the long-term. If they do not wish to be public with support after the experience, it should be an expectation that constructive, confidential feedback be offered so that you can improve and iterate quickly.

Mike Niederquell | www.quell.com

Being entrepreneurial also means being opportunistic. When starting our company we worked steadily to reach into the market as many ways as possible to make connections with potential customers. When The Quell Group was launched, it was done so by two people with skills in public relations and marketing that left 9-5 jobs – with no immediate income stream or prospective clients.

We immediately alerted our "*network*" of former colleagues, friends, friend-of-friends, family and more through letters and email that outlined the uniqueness and value of the services we provide. Our very first customers came about through people we knew who, in turn, recommended The Quell Group to others. (Yes, networking is key.)

Two clients immediately surfaced through referral from our networking effort. One, a small manufacturing company, and two, a division of a U.S. Car maker. At the onset, we quickly put into place the basic tools of marketing. Inexpensive business cards and letterhead were produced. Business cards were handed to everyone we knew. Letters of introduction explaining our unique value (how we bring something different to the table) were distributed to a long list of organizations we wanted as clients. Our first, very simple company website was launched as well (back in 1994).

Decisions to engage our type of branding and marketing services could take weeks, even months as our clients generally enter into long-term engagements. Advertising was not appropriate to our sales efforts – referrals were extremely important.

Jeff Kuo | www.ragic.com

We pitched the product to our clients in the service projects and got some of our early customers, and begin getting more and more by words of mouth.

Robert Livingstone | www.royaltext.com

We actually marketed our services on barter networks, which are large groups of various companies that trade goods and services within the network, but not necessarily in a one-to-one relationship. This is where our first clients came from. We also hired telemarketers and internet marketers. Most importantly, we hit the streets and hustled in finding clients and strategic relationships with a variety of advertising agencies.

Michael Kawula | www.selfemployedking.com

Having systems and strategies in place from day one on how you're going to attract customers is KEY in and business for success. For both my local franchise and my Online business I used targeted direct mail marketing which today is getting even easier with less businesses mailing. This helped my online business grow rapidly.

I also believe partnering with other businesses that are already working with your type of customer can help you grow rapidly. With my local cleaning business I partnered with local chiropractors who referred patients, realtors who referred new home-owners and several other businesses. I incentivized my referrers better than anyone and treated them like gold. This helped me expand faster than my competition.

You also need to provide amazing customer service so that you can ask for referrals and customers are happy to do it. Referrals were a HUGE part of my business and I always made it a habit to ask. Lastly win-back campaigns from previous customers or asking competitors to handle work they can't perform can get you going. Just make sure you have systems in place to not drop the ball and to maximize every customer/prospect touch point. Remember also to treat employees like gold because they are also an amazing referral source.

Rick Martinez | www.senorsangria.com

Start selling before you have your product - You might need to get creative but it is less expensive to do that then wait for the product to be complete. Next, Leverage your existing customers. Ask them if they know anyone that would be a good candidate for your product. Many times I've had retailers say my brother or cousin owns a store. Next thing you know I'm visiting that store and landing it as a customer. Though this does lead you to having customers all over the place and tons of driving but who cares you need to sell sell sell.

Also, find an employee at your customer location who will be your ambassador. Make sure that everyone in the organization knows your product and they've tasted it. Seek at least one ambassador in at the customer location who will sing the praises of your product. This will make sure that the location will not forget about you. This person will make sure all of their consumers will know of you

Make sure the customer knows your story. People love underdogs. Talk about your challenges and how you've overcome, talk about the hurdles you have in front of you, make them know that you are really committed to making a difference.

Finally, CARE. If your customers see that you care about not only your product but them they will support you beyond belief. Walk in telling the retailer or sales lead that you need their help and opinion; ask them for their thoughts about your brand. If you have a good product after they taste it and give you advice they will want to carry it. This is the no pressure sale; you are not going in there to sell them something. Instead, you are going in there to get their advice from years of experience.

Jason Richelson | www.shopkeep.com

We did a lot of SEO early on so that people would find us online. We had a great name and a great domain, which really helped. In the very early days we did some outbound calling, but we quickly learned that driving in-bound was the way to go for small business. So we continued to invest in our website and SEO and soon coffee shops started calling us.

Julie Busha | www.slawsa.com

Financial constraints force entrepreneurs to be very resourceful to get out word in the most cost effective way possible and much of that is built on sweat equity and creativity. Knowing I had a food item that people were unfamiliar with, I knew I needed to get our flavor out. While I would have loved to receive a national feature in a big magazine like O, starting my focus in the areas where we had distribution was more important. You can capitalize most on a national piece when you have national distribution, as it's likely you'll only get that national write-up once per publication or media outlet. Don't play that card until the timing will benefit you the most.

So, I reached out to every food writer, food blogger and local magazine in the areas where Slawsa was sold. I offered to send product samples, shared a little about my story and product and even gave a little pitch about why it would appeal to their readers. For the costs of samples and shipping, I was able to get some editorial content that spread across more consumers than who I could reach myself. I also tackled many festivals, expos and markets as well. Not only could I generate immediate sales to fund those grass-roots marketing efforts, but I also made sure those consumers knew where to purchase Slawsa once again - at their local retailer. The profits from our first major retail sale was spent on a creative month-long radio campaign of a syndicated program that reached that five-state area that the retailer covered. Social media is leveling the playing field for start-up companies to get out awareness amongst the deep pockets of much larger competitors, so the more creative uses of social media to market your product, the better.

In terms of acquiring our first retail partners, I have been relentless in knocking on buyer's doors, requesting meetings and presenting my brand. Having never sold a food product before, that first meeting was very intimidating. But, the more you do it, the easier it gets and the more confidence you will gain. Just like anything, as you start your business, you have to not be afraid to jump in the deep end and tackle every obstacle, whether or not you've done it before. Understand that you're not going to get a yes every time, or even most of the time. The more you can educate yourself about your industry by reading articles or interviewing more mature businesses is extremely important to putting yourself on the right path and avoiding mistakes early. Networking with other entrepreneurs or finding a mentor in your industry, perhaps a few years ahead of you, and who can guide you with knowledge, will provide a world of support and insight.

Heidi Lamar | www.spalamar.com
In the beginning, our marketing budget was quite limited so we did some creative bartering. The NBA Phoenix Suns Dancers got free spa services and in exchange, we got our logo on the scoreboard just like Bank of America and Coke. The result was that we looked bigger than we were and we suddenly had a spa full of guys!

Zeb Couch | www.offmarketformula.com / www.speedhatch.com
Good question. We looked into paid advertising online, but the keywords and phrases associated with our product were already heavily bid on and too expensive. We decided on a three-pronged approach. First, contact details for agents are really easy to find so we collected a list of emails and phone numbers for agents in our immediate area and began direct marketing to them with a free trial.

Simultaneously, we sent out a press release and also signed up for Help a Reporter Out (HARO) and actively made ourselves available for stories in associated industries and topics (great for free press and credibility boosting). We also put together a list of potential strategic partners to reach out to. At the time, lots of agents were signing up for listing management services like Rentjuice.com and YouGotListings.com. We figured if we could partner with one of them, we'd exponentially grow our user base while providing a value-add to our partner. We ended up partnering with YouGotListings, which is where the highest number of our new users came from.

Justyn Howard | www.sproutsocial.com

Fortunately, being in social media means that happy users naturally multiply. We've been lucky to have very loyal and vocal customers from the beginning, and using our own platform to nurture and engage with that community is a significant advantage.

Blaine Vess | www.studymode.com

At the beginning of StudyMode, we only told our friends and began emailing other students at our college. It was a very organic process. At first, we had a very small base of traffic – maybe 100 people a day. But the word got out and the site grew steadily. Today, we serve more than 90 million visitors each month.

Michelle MacDonald | www.sweetnotebakery.com

I got the word out by the following actions- starting a page on Facebook for my product/brand, account on Twitter, Linked In and other relevant social media outlets. I did a lot of cold calling to my potential customers to let them know my product was available; I also walked in to many places with samples. I found local shows and opportunities to demo my product and get it into the hands of potential customers.

By these actions I was able to get my first few buyers; they were a few cafes I walked in to with some samples. They saw the demand for my product and the passion I had in making and selling it and decided to give me a try. The first customer only ordered 3 a day and, my product being gluten-free bagels that was not a lot at all especially when being in the wholesale business volume translates to profit. It was a small starting point and one that I was determined to make grow, within a week the word got out that they carried my product through word of mouth and advertising materials such as signage and social media. Their order grew to 7 times more than the initial 3 a day. They are still ordering that same amount 1 1/2 years later.

After the successes of that account I research the next place I wanted to sell to and went in with a sample and that data and got in front of the owner. He ordered the same amount that my first account is now at, seeing that if they could sell that many his place good too. With each new account I noted the numbers and quickness of how the product sold so I could make order projections and take that to new accounts. The specific tactics I used was persistence, and learning about the market and sales process of my product and then continuing to expand that to my new buyers. I always asked for suggestions and especially when I got and still get a "*no*", I learn why so I can evaluate the reasons for hesitation. This way I can learn how to educate them and work through their hesitations to make a sale or in some cases I may see that it is not the best fit for my product.

Danny Maloney | www.tailwindapp.com

We acquired our first 20-30 customers purely through AdWords. It cost us ~$300. As we gained traction, we turned to content marketing. We were investing in a new market category, which meant education was essential. The more we educated people, the larger the market would become. That strategy paid off. Today, our typical blog post is shared hundreds of times, bringing relevant customers to our site and raising awareness of our offering and brand.

Cricket Allen | www.theperfectsnaque.com

I did a lot of events in markets where our product is sold and sampled the product myself. I still sample a lot in-store because it is extremely valuable to interact with your consumer. I want to hear their feedback, their food stories, health challenges, shopping habits, etc. And consumers really value meeting the founder and hearing your story. These hands-on type initiatives help get the word out and the product moving off the shelf. Also, your retail partners will appreciate you investing your time in their store with their customers.

Some of our first buyers came through our local market in were small independent stores. These are valuable relationships and should be respected because they took a risk on a new product. Other chain buyers came through dogged networking and/or trade shows. Also, don't be shy about finding products similar to your own and seeing who distributes then. Then call those distributors, get them samples and pricing and follow up!

Eren Bali | www.udemy.com

A creative tactic we employed in the early days of Udemy was producing our own courses. We realized that the production process (i.e. filming & editing video content) was a big friction point for our instructors. We produced a few of our own courses in the beginning and focused all our marketing capabilities on promoting them. This wasn't scalable, but it did allow us to build powerful social proof points, which were critical to our long-term success.

Our marketplace revenue-sharing model itself is a powerful tool, which allows instructors to monetize their knowledge. Instructors are able to keep 100% of the revenue when they pro-mote their courses themselves. Thus, our instructors are often out in the market, promoting their courses and bringing new students to Udemy, which benefits the whole marketplace.

Jojo Hedaya | www.unroll.me

Growth Hacking - This has been the number one reason for our rapid and exponential growth. Every start-up needs to figure out what it is about their company that will make users want to "*pay*." For us, it's the unsubscribe feature of Unroll.Me; this is the feature that gets our users most excited to try us out. The next step is to figure out how these users will pay and how much they're willing to pay. Sometimes a start-up decides that payment should come in the traditional form of money. We decided this wasn't right for Unroll.Me. Instead, we ask our users to share our service with their friends via an email, Facebook share, or Tweet after they've hit their 5th unsubscribe. It is by and large one of the best decisions we've made. Our users love Unroll.Me and since we let them "take a test drive" first, they're more than happy to pay the small fee of telling their friends.

Christy Ferer | www.vidicom.com

I kept my day job as a TV news reporter. Since all my friends were reporters like me, they helped spread the word. I also sent out generous copies of videotapes to a lot of people. At that time this was an unusual but expensive thing to do. An article about me being the creator of fashion videos in the New York Times helped too! Clients had to be targeted to those who would understand what I was doing. The younger companies that would get this kind of marketing.

Scott Perkins & Shawn Boday | www.vube.com

Vube gained traction and created awareness through advertising online. Our product is free to everyone that uses it, so creating usage just requires incentive. We have created that incentive with video contests where fans vote to decide which videos win money.

Bas Beerens | www.wetransfer.com

We have always worked closely with influencers, agencies, brands and key media outlets to get the word out and highlight the value of our service. This has included, amongst others, the likes of Nike Europe, tech-site The Next Web, and creative agency It's Nice That. Even before we launched WeTransfer in 2009, we had an established user base with OY Transfer that was generated this way - through the viral effect of agencies sharing our website with the brands they represented.

When we first started out with WeTransfer, user experience was at the heart of every decision that we made. This involved offering 50% of our ad-inventory to forward-thinking young creatives from across the globe, free of charge. By not relying entirely on marketers for content, we were able to tell great stories, improve the user experience, and ultimately show the huge opportunities available to commercial advertisers from our service. This began with Samsung and Canon and now includes a wide range of brands including FedEx, Getty Images and G-Star RAW. Until this day, the user experience remains at the heart of the business.

Tracey Noonan | www.wickedgoodcupcakes.com

In the very beginning, we were operating on a limited budget thus didn't have the luxury to spend money on advertising and promotions. Due to the visual appeal of Wicked Good Cupcakes, we quickly recognized that spreading our message using various social channels was a very cost effective means of getting the word out. We spent a lot of time growing our social networks. We focused on creating meaningful conversations with our followers and as a result those followers started turning into customers. It's important that you're not always "*selling*". As people began to request our product, Dani and I were more and more convinced that we had a viable business. Word of mouth kicked in and there began the journey of Wicked Good Cupcakes.

Dianne Crowley | www.wildwingcafe.com

Prior to opening Wild Wing Cafe in June of 1990, I worked in the advertising industry for nearly three decades. During this period, Cecil and I became firm believers in the power of advertising.

Here are my suggestions:

a) ALWAYS budget for advertising; Create the most impactful advertising campaign within the constraints of your budget

b) If you want consumers to think of you as a high quality restaurant, you need to run high quality ads.

c) We teased the grand opening two weeks prior. We ran three good-sized inserts in the newspaper. We advertised on the radio and paid for a radio remote the day of the restaurant launch.

d) Be careful with price point advertising. Don't set prices so low that you can't catch-up. Keep prices competitive so that you can eventually bring up the price structure and maintain profits.

e) Coupons only attract loyal discount shoppers. To attract loyal customers, you need to sell great products and services, not just low prices.

Final word of advice – "*Come out with your guns blazing!*" – Bring force and energy to your business. Express your passion is everything you do. Be the spark plug that ignites the whole community!!!

Beth Shaw | www.yogafit.com

I was a teacher for a pretty large yoga school, so I was able to get the word out through my network of students. I received initial funding from one of my students.

I was successful in selling so many copies of my DVD were because I listened to my customers. I always asked them what type of DVDs they would be interested in. In no time I had a long list of different ideas and potential DVDs. I would go through the list, make the DVDs, and market them to the customers. Because the DVDs were of high quality, word of mouth definitely helped.

Kyle James | www.rather-be-shopping.com

I would actually go down to our local mall and hand out flyers talking about Rather-Be-Shopping.com and some of the benefits it gave shoppers. Things like convenience, easy to comparison shop, and the use of online coupon codes to get a great deal. I literally hit the streets and pimped my online business. I would probably get laughed out of town today.

Akbar Chisti | www.seamusgolf.com

The outreach began as soon as our first customer came. I started cold calling all of the private golf clubs on the West coast, along with several on the east coast. When I realized this wasn't working very well, I decided to pack up my bag with a few of our best styles and head to the merchandise show in Orlando, Florida. A friend let me hang out at his booth, and I showed the product to everyone I saw, whether or not they wanted to hear my story. This led us to a number of invaluable connections, including the writers for many prominent press channels in golf.

Jason Cohen | www.wpengine.com

Guest blogging is a good way to get moving. Find places that your potential customers already frequent, and write excellent pieces. Another good way is cold-emailing people on LinkedIn, because you can target exactly the type of customer you know will be interested in your product.

Morris Miller | www.xenex.com & www.rackspace.com

Launching Xenex to the healthcare marketplace was very different than what I experienced with Rackspace. Xenex offers a UV room disinfection system for healthcare facilities. Our germ-zapping robots eliminate deadly pathogens like MRSA and *C.diff* that lurk on high touch surfaces in hospitals and cause healthcare associated infections, the 4th leading cause of death in the U.S. We were/are targeting hospitals and the infection control/prevention community with a technology solution they hasn't previously existed. In order to be successful, we had to prove to them that the technology worked and could help them reduce infection rates in their facilities. And the decision-making process in hospitals is very different than the server/hosting business.

Early on, we were fortunate to introduce our technology to a very well-known hospital with a progressive infectious disease doctor who was frustrated by healthcare associated infections caused by microorganisms like VRE and *C.diff*. He was interested in the science of how our device worked and listened to us as we explained what the robot could do – destroy those deadly pathogens in just a couple of minutes. He agreed to conduct a study on the efficacy of the device. He saw what the device could do in a lab setting and was willing to try it in the hospital. With the Xenex robot, it's a much more complex sale than managing hosting. We need to meet with different hospital leaders and educate them about how the technology works and what makes it different – a much longer sales cycle than in hosting.

Hill Ferguson | www.zong.com (Chief Product Officer, Paypal)
A critical first step is enlisting your friends and family. This will not only help you get the word out, but it will be even more useful when getting great feedback on your product and/or service. After this initial phase, you need to go where your customers go. If your customers are other start-ups who congregate and attend meet-ups, then go to every meet-up.

If it is within budget, maybe sponsor a meet-up, this will give you the opportunity to raise awareness to a whole group at once. If your customers are likely to be using other products and/or services, then try to reach them there, as well. SEO and SEM can be very cost-effective ways to experiment your way into finding the right cost per acquisition. I emphasize the experimentation here because there are a lot of ways to attract customers.

The real trick is to attract customers at a cost that is lower than the revenue you can generate from them using your product and/or service. Finally, expect to be surprised by what you find out when searching for good customer acquisition channels.

Michael Lindell | www.mypillow.com
The best way MyPillow got the word out and acquired new buyers was by doing local shows and fairs. You can't just put up a website and expect sales, because the potential customer can't find you—they don't know who you are. Start locally with people who know you, like your local newspaper reporters, then rely on word of mouth. Reserve a booth

at local shows and fairs. It's an easy way to get great feedback on your product and start developing a clientele. Get your story in your local paper or TV station in combination with the shows. After the shows, try a kiosk at a local mall.

Monica Wreede | accessoryconnectz.com

When selling in my earlier days on Ebay, I just listed and hoped for a sale! I listed and listed until the $$ started coming in! You really have to be persistent with what you do or else it will fail! I started out with a crappy camera & not so good accessories, but I kept at it! In one year, I was working with many top designers and selling my accessories as soon as I listed them! It was a guaranteed sale! A few years later I got contacted by The San Francisco 49ers! I was honored to design for many of the players' wives. Do not give up on your talent & dream! It is a hard road, but will pay off in the end.

With the new product & company of mine, Accessory Connectz®, is another story! With investing so much money in the beginning on the patent process, packaging, traveling, trademark, supplies, etc. it has been tough! I honestly didn't realize that bringing a product to market was so hard!

We have been blessed to be in Inventors Digest multiple times, was one of the top 3 finalists in the nation given by The Dallas Market Center, names one of the top 200 leading women in business award given by start-up Nation, features by many news & editorial features & more!

Matt Barrie | www.freelancer.com

We practice what we preach at Freelancer by using our own platform. We have run global marketing campaigns by drawing upon the crowd-sourcing aspect of our site. By galvanising the masses, you can run a highly effective campaign that reaches people across the globe.

Mark McClain | www.sailpoint.com

We didn't sell to friends and family (we developed software for very large companies – and I didn't know any corporate CIOs), so we had to find our way into early buying situations. We did try to leverage relationships, but we learned (through trial-and-error) how to identify an "*early adopter*" who would consider working with a new company (and an unproven product) in order to gain competitive advantage.

Jordan Eisenberg | www.urgentrx.com

The biggest thing I did early on to get customers was to remove any roadblocks and make it so they have no reason to say no. In the beginning, you need them more than they need you (so they think) and the way around that can be to quite simply prove it to them without risk on their end. This can mean providing deeply-discounted product(s) and/or a willingness to do limited-scope tests. Anything you can do to reduce the financial or headline risk of the customer makes it easy for them to say yes early on – and this is a worthwhile investment on your behalf. If you are looking to build long-term value, don't be penny-wise and pound foolish – get early customers on board, milk them for feedback (read: ideas on how to make your product even better) and leverage them to other customers (no one wants to be the first!). It's not uncommon for potential customers to be hesitant to invest heavily into a new, unproven, or unknown product / technology / service. Make it easy for them to say yes and then exceed their expectations.

Eric Schiffer | www.digitalmarketing.com

I was very aggressive and I began to target prospective buyers. I'd pick up the phone and write hand-written letters to buyers. I was rejected in the early stages a number of times. However, to me, no is nothing but yes in a matter of time. I knew I would find success with perseverance. Once you get your first yes, you build upon it and draw new buyers using it. It can be slow, but you'll see your base grow. It's like building muscle. You do reps and you find resistance. Eventually if you keep going and going, you'll grow!

Matt Keiser | www.liveintent.com

To attract beta customers, look for customers who have problems your product solves. Offer your services for free in exchange for being able to use their data and that they'll advocate for you if the product works for them. Also, you have to be remembered and warm introductions are key.

Chapter 7 : Getting Those First Big Customers

Unless you have already established your credibility in your industry, it is often quite difficult to convince the big customers to talk to you, let alone buy your product or service. It's a catch-22 situation in a way because unless you do manage to get a couple of these big customers, it becomes difficult to convince other major brands to talk to you. So how do you get the big brands to talk to you?

I asked this question to Hill Ferguson, one of the founders of Zong.com, a mobile payments service which was later acquired by Paypal. Hill currently serves as the Chief Product Officer at Paypal and according to him, the mantra to land a customer – big or small – is to simply solve a real problem for them. However, executing a big brand sale is plainly an *"exercise in persistence"*. He says, *"In the case of big brands, though, you need to do more than just solve a problem for them. You have to make sure the right person at that company knows what problem you can solve and that he or she values your company's solution. This can take months and months of cold-calling, online and offline networking events, and yes, even borderline executive stalking. Once you have your internal champion at the big brand selling your product internally, you're on your way to a contract."*

Eren Bali | www.udemy.com

Early on, we only had around 10,000 students on the platform. When you don't have a big community, it's hard to entice instructors to join your platform. It's also difficult to convince instructors to offer content on a platform when you don't have any social proof from other successful instructors.

So we reached out to experts that we had close relationships with. In our case, we approached our early investors who were successful tech entrepreneurs. Although we were operating a marketplace at that time, we did something very unscalable. We started filming and producing our own courses and hosted live events with our instructors. We were able to get a few thousand dollars from these initial courses; through these self-produced courses, we were able to convince two other instructors to teach a course on Udemy. This resulted in our first iOS and Python courses on Udemy. We made sure these instructors were really successful, and they made over $50,000 in early months of their course. We used their success as social proof for acquiring other instructors.

Bottom line, you have to use a few unscalable tactics in the early days to get the social proof you need and then the much-anticipated snowball effect takes over.

Getting the first big client was a key moment for sure. I didn't start selling to billion dollar corporations overnight. I needed to work my way up, but it didn't take too long. There were a few things I did in the early days that I would advise any start-up.

1. Make every client a fanatical supporter. That helped us on 2 levels. First, loyal customers became repeat customers and second they become reference for our new prospects.

2. Act bigger than you are. When we had 5 employees I acted like we had 10. At 10 I acted like we were 20, at 20 employees act like your team is 50 strong. This applies to your marketing materials, you internal vocabulary, how you present yourself and your company.

3. Make it easy for companies to do business with you. Believe it or not, large companies are taking a huge risk dealing with a small company. We packaged ourselves in a way to de-risk the investment in our solutions by signing agreements where if we went bankrupt, the code would be available via a 3rd party. We also worked through some large partners, and while getting an official partnership can be long, we always tried to bring our partners sales out of the gate. If you bring them revenue early, then the rules change and they will work with you.

George Burciaga | www.elevatedigital.com

It's all about relationships. When I'm out networking and at events, I'm always building friendships and relationships. You have to go beyond meetings and acquaintances. I've built a number of relationships through 15 years of networking and meeting people. My list of friends spans different industries and locations, but they are all interested in the idea we've developed.

When you think of some of the larger names we've worked with – Groupon or BMO Harris – it's easy to get intimidated. But you have to remember that there is someone behind those brands making a decision, you just have to figure out a way to get in front of that person. In my case, I either had those relationships directly or I knew people who could introduce me to the right person and set up a meeting. But again, I can't stress it enough; you have to know your product so well that you can make those people believe in it too. Once they believe in what you're doing, the rest takes flight on its own.

Monique Tatum | www.beautifulplanning.com

Here's the thing – we didn't. In the beginning, we were all over the place. We sold marketing plans, wrote business plans, did public relations. We focused on small companies because we were small and, in hindsight, I'm happy this was our focus because it allowed us to find our niche. No matter what anyone says, start-ups are always experimenting. If you are considering launching one you will be too. You can look at all the data and info but it will come down to what's right for you and how you want to run your business. So you will experiment and that will be okay.

It was not until a few years in when I sat down, was losing a bit of hair and decided we are going to focus on one or two expertise and that's it! So we looked at what focuses were the most profitable for us and also which were the most fun for us. When we spun that wheel we landed rather excitedly on PR. Once we decided our focus, we started doing a lot of work for other PR firms under their name. Then eventually we decided to stop hiding our name and by that time we were already working on big projects. I realized why should I hide my name if they could not do the work we were doing anyway? Our name slowly spread by referral and we grew to what we are today.

Nellie Akalp | www.corpnet.com

I just picked up the phone and called them. Literally! And that is how we were able to partner with companies like Staples, Kinkos and network solutions back then. Today I'm thrilled to be on Fox Business regularly and write for outlets like Mashable, Forbes and Entrepreneur.com. If you want it that bad, you have to go after it and get it! It is not going to come to you.

Lawson Nickol | www.allamericanclothing.com

We were lucky to have made some solid connections while we were at Rodale and Lehigh University. And the foot in the door at BFTP really helped to kick start our business. Eventually, our word-of-mouth referrals started bringing us bigger brands. One of the most validating moments for me was when we had Bob Teufel, former president or Rodale – a heavy-hitting publisher with titles like Men's Health and Runner's World – in our offices checking us out.

Betsy | www.betsyandiya.com

We did several cross country road trips where we courted other independent retailers like ourselves to carry betsy & iya as stockists. We never went after big retail shops – we've always traded on our values as small business people who craft a personal product that wearers can feel the humanness behind. So we looked for, and found, like-minded retailers as wholesalers. By that point, we were able to let others run the shop.

Eric Schiffer | www.digitalmarketing.com

There's a saying, *"Fortune favors the brave."* You have to be willing to knock on doors, make calls, and get people's attention in the best ways possible. It is paramount that you understand their needs as well or better than they do themselves. When you do that, pitching your product is easy! You understand how to best align your services to solve their pain. The best way to crack through is to solve their troubles by letting them sample your solution. Give it away for 2 weeks, 3 weeks, and a month. Or guarantee it. Make it easy for them to get into the game. Then at some point, start the billing process and keep them for life.

Matt Keiser | www.liveintent.com

It's hard. We hustled and made sure we had great decks and demos. One thing you have going for you usually in a start-up is that you're a domain expert. If you're a junior player and you're trying to start a business, that's a poor combination. So if you are an expert it is pretty easy to find someone who needs your expertise- you just may not get paid for it at first.

And that's why often you're eating Ramen and working really long nights. But those are the most rewarding times in a start-up that you remember with great affection. That's when you're failing and succeeding rapidly and you're honing in on what hopefully becomes your future business.

You need to find the customers that really need your solution. For example, one of our very early clients was MSNBC. We had a bunch of small pubs at the time with which we were testing the technology. I then met Celia Wu at a conference. Celia was in charge of email newsletters for MSNBC, she didn't have much of a budget and it was taking her time and energy. The relationship we formed was symbiotic because she needed solution that would allow her to focus on other aspects of her job.

Michael Folkes | www.mafolkes.com

I worked for Xerox as a contractor and I also worked for a supplier to Xerox. Management at Xerox knew about the quality, consistency and integrity of my work. I was fortunate enough to catch the attention of an upper-level manager during my performance at work. I was later able to provide Xerox Corporation with a significant cost savings proposal. This got their attention even though it disrupted their current business model. The innovated idea and cost savings were too appealing for Xerox to ignore. They remain a customer today and still enjoy enormous savings.

John Brady | www.protempartners.com

Starting at age 40, I had a strong network built up over a career of contacts and a reputation I could lean upon. When I didn't have direct connections to people who worked for the big brands, I was usually able to get someone one-degree removed who could make an introduction. Honestly, it wasn't easy. The hardest part wasn't big brands saying; "no" so much as it was them not saying anything. This made it tough to know which real opportunities were just moving slowly through a large organization, or deals that were going nowhere.

Jeff Kuo | www.ragic.com

We did this for about 2 to 3 years, and got quite a bit of connection to big companies. So when our own product is ready, these companies are willing to listen to our pitch because they know that we are good at what we do, and is worthy of their trust.

Mark McClain | www.sailpoint.com

Sometimes, it was lots of "*banging on the door*" (figuratively speaking). We did have some prior connections or relationships we could use, but a lot of times, it was pure salesmanship ("*Our product is such a better alternative to what you're doing today, isn't it worth a try?*"). We did some aggressive pricing, and as soon as we had a credible reference, we asked him to talk to almost every key prospect, till we built up a bigger base.

Akbar Chisti | www.seamusgolf.com

We designed our product specifically for sale at the big accounts we sought. Further, when we went to sell to them, none of the story involved selling elsewhere. We didn't know it would sell in other stores well but knew the product would do well in their high end shops. I think that too many startups decide early that their product belongs in more shops than in reality. What we've learned is that you have to prove the demand exists before the other shops will take an interest.

Rick Martinez | www.senorsangria.com

Many times I didn't go after the big accounts. In my experience they all wanted something from you. I found it easier just to deal with the mom and pops. And that's what I told the mom and pops when I started. I wasn't going to pull any favors for anyone or do anything under the table. Eventually once I had enough mom and pops and I made them successful then I went to the bigger stores.

At that point I showed them what the mom and pops were doing and they were impressed. They knew they could do better. They also didn't pressure us to treat them special because we already knew the potential. If a big account did push their weight or want something special. We would kindly just move on. We don't want to be dependent on one account or a group of big accounts. It's harder to manage many little accounts but long term it is healthier for the business because we don't lose a big chunk of business if we lose an account

Justyn Howard | www.sproutsocial.com

Our customers typically find us and try out our product before buying. In such a rapidly changing space, there tends to be a lot of experimentation. We've built something special that is compelling enough to turn many of those experiments into long-term relationships.

Danny Maloney | www.tailwindapp.com

Hustle, hustle, hustle. We worked our personal networks, called in favors, sent emails and InMails, attended networking events. We talked to anyone who would listen. Big brands were slow to adopt, but we gained traction with fast moving midsized brands. We over-invested in those relationships to learn what we were doing wrong and build brand loyalists. The resulting product improvements and positive word of mouth brought us to the point where big brands started coming to us.

Mike Niederquell | www.quell.com

Again, being entrepreneurial is being opportunistic and it's also being very confident in what you can deliver. To get big brands we offered them something they were not getting from their current supplier or vendor.

In one particular case, a company was experiencing unflattering coverage by the media. We simply wrote a note to the executive at the company and told them we could do better and how. We were afforded only a ten-minute interview that turned into a one-hour discussion. At the end, they fired their current agency, hired us, and the company became our largest client for many, many years. We continue to write notes and letters to CEOs who we would like as clients and give them insight as to how things could be done better – through our services.

Raj Sheth | www.recruiterbox.com

When we launched in March 2011, we thought we could just put our product on the Google apps marketplace, invest in some Google AdWords, and collect some money from family and friends for online marketing. We spent $30,000 for online marketing over the first year. This helped us discover that our customers found us through AdWords, app stores in HR software (getapp.com, etc.), and Google apps marketplace. I also did a lot of the SEO work – it two years to rank on the first page of Google for relevant keywords, and more than 50 percent of our website traffic comes from that. This remains invaluable because we cannot pay for that!

At first, our conversions turned slowly. We eventually realized that small companies, for whom we built Recruiterbox, need confidence if they move a process to your company; it becomes more about the time spent with the product and trusting the product. We began to cater to this knowledge, and at the end of the first 12 months, we started getting 20 new customers each month. Then, six months after, it became 30 per month, and after another year, we got 40 per month. It took some insight into our audience and some tweaking of our strategy to get there.

Big brands came to us entirely based on their impression of the first four screens of the product. They found us through Google search!

Morris Miller | www.xenex.com & www.rackspace.com

At Xenex, we were fortunate to partner early on with a very well-known hospital that was willing to utilize our device(s) to study their efficacy. But changing the mindset of the healthcare marketplace is hard – we have the only product that uses pulsed xenon (instead of mercury) and we have proven results (hospitals experiencing fewer infections when they use our robot to disinfect rooms).

But there is still a lot of confusion about UV room disinfection, so some hospitals have purchased less expensive competitive systems that don't have the same technology, and therefore don't have similar results. Sometimes the purchasing manager at a hospital doesn't understand the difference in the technologies and is only looking at the price – which is really frustrating and something we work on every day. Well-known hospitals like MD Anderson, Stanford and UCLA are using our robots, and what's really exciting is seeing these hospitals have results – patients suffering fewer infections AND patients recognising that the hospital is doing more to keep them safe.

Chapter 8 : Tackling The Chicken & Egg Problem

A number of businesses face the classic chicken-and-egg problem while starting out. For example, would you have joined Facebook if your friends weren't there to start with? Similarly, would you be posting ads on Craigslist if there were not enough buyers?

Some businesses fake activity till they gather critical mass. It is true for a number of online forums and message boards, including Reddit. Grindr, a dating social network for the gay community faced this exact problem when they started out. The problem was aggravated because not only did the application need a critical mass of active users, but because of the nature of the site, it required a critical mass of users locally.

Joel Simkhai, the man behind the app figured that his company had no budget for PR or marketing. Guerrilla marketing was the only way out. He achieved this by showing up at Pride events and organizing 'Grindr' parties at gay bars. This strategy not only helped Joel reach out to his targeted audience but because they reached out to them through parties and bars, were able to quite easily achieve critical mass within a neighborhood. From here, he only had to repeat the strategy across the various gay bars.

Joshua Dorkin | www.biggerpockets.com

When I started BiggerPockets.com, which is today the leading online community for real estate investors online with over 160,000 members and 550,000+ monthly unique visitors, there was definitely a chicken and egg problem. In order to get visitors to our new community to engage, we needed to have some content. All I could do was to seed the community with questions that I had and information and news that I was aware of. When people came and saw that there was something there to work with, they began to interact little by little.

By no means was this a fast process, though. It took a considerable amount of time to get enough activity to get people excited. It also took quite a bit of time before I could stop seeding discussions; one of the most important tipping points for us was when the community took over in that role.

That all said, getting those first users to come and visit was also a challenge. With no budget, I couldn't advertise to let people know who we were, so instead, I used my sweat equity. I went to quite a few online communities and got active. By doing so, I began to build my reputation as someone who was credible and little by little, people would come and visit my website thanks to a link to it at the bottom of my posts (in my post signature). I never participated on competing sites, because I felt that doing so with a goal of building my site was disrespectful to those communities, so I focused on ancillary niches.

Alex Brola | www.checkmaid.com

The fact is that in home cleaning specifically, there is way more demand than there is easily findable supply. For example, people need move out/move in/cleanings before guests arrived (emergency type cleanings) all the time. There is always a crazy amount of demand next-day or for weekends that to this day we can never fill, at least not without having a really substandard product (i.e. hiring untrained cleaners). It's something we're still working on.

As far as the maids go, not many of them depend on us for work full-time. They typically have a primary job (many of them work for hotels), and our system allows them to set their own days and hours so they can fit in extra work. So if there are lulls it's really not that big of an issue.

The chicken and the egg problem can always be solved by "*gaming*" one side or the other though, if your product requires it. Reddit, PayPal, and many other big companies employed a lot of tactics that the FCC would frown upon to get initial traction. At the end of the day if that's what it takes and it's really not hurting anyone, then it might be worth looking into.

Micha Kaufman | www.fiverr.com

It is true that a two- sided marketplace which depends on the submission of services by users (UGC) has a chicken and egg problem. That said, except for commodity marketplaces, other marketplaces usually start to build liquidity from supply. With that in mind, Fiverr also focused its early efforts on making the creation of supply as simple, fast and friction free as possible.

Given the high friction of the onboarding process in marketplaces that existed before Fiverr we had a real opportunity to disrupt this flow. Our target was to reduce the process of joining Fiverr and adding a listing to less than 5 minutes and make it free, so that for potential sellers it would become almost a non-issue to try the marketplace. At the same time, we made sure that buying would not take more than 30 seconds so that buyers would not have any frictions on their way to getting what they were after. No long registration process, no need to write specifications for your desired project and no price negotiation. We made buying a service as simple as buying a product on an e-commerce site like Amazon or eBay.

Patrick DeAmorim | www.decate.no

I actually started Decate about 6 months before it really took off. And then is when I really had a chicken/egg problem. This was before the dominant social network decided to close, so I was basically a new, inexperienced, worse site, competing against an already established site.

While I tried posting on that competitor's site, as well advertising with popular Norwegian bloggers, I noticed the issue where I got members, but spread over such a long period that there was never really anyone for them to communicate with, so then they left.

The way this was fixed was that when the dominant social network decided to close, from about 1 month before they were going to close down (at the time I made the announcement), I started getting a stable, large influx of many hundreds of users a day, which soon lead to critical mass. I have not advertised or even spent a dollar marketing Decate since that period, as the past 4 years I spent on the product itself, and also learning about this field, so all of the growth I have has been from word of mouth, people telling friends about the site, etc.

Matt Barrie | www.freelancer.com

When we acquired GetAFreelancer, it already had one side of the necessary two sided market – they had a critical mass of freelancers in select categories. We had to focus on building up awareness amongst the global business community that outsourcing projects online, was a cost effective and highly efficient way to build or grow a business. We tackled this challenge by being as proactive as possible. Presenting at conferences, working with journalists, meeting as many business owners as possible and giving them a great experience on Freelancer.com. Word of mouth from employers who have worked with exceptional freelancers helped us build up the number of employers who knew about the company.

Mike Glanz | www.hireahelper.com

We accidentally did it right by tackling both at once. We were able to acquire customers by using Google Adwords - and organically by doing some basic search engine optimization. The site was designed from the beginning to be easy for the major search engines to index. This helped HireAHelper show up in web search results for terms like *"moving labor"* and *"cheap movers."*

We also did everything we possibly could from a customer service standpoint - making sure every customer walked away happy and said positive things about HireAHelper. For example, my co-founder Pete and I once drove over 100 miles to unload a moving truck ourselves for a lady that had an issue with her order.

On the other side of the equation, we acquired our partner "*helpers*" by rolling up our sleeves and making calls. Lots of calls. Every day for months, we reached out to multiple moving companies in every major metro in the country. It wasn't efficient, but we did build some momentum as word started to spread between associated moving labor companies across different states, and helpers started coming to us.

Since then I've heard that companies like Uber and Airbnb did the same thing - starting by signing up a couple new helpers/vendors in each major city. We were pretty proud when we found out that we accidentally did it right.

As a side-note, what's more interesting (and no one ever asks about) is how we got reviews to start off. Helpers were really easy to sign up, but convincing customers to book these companies that we had very little information on was extremely difficult. My co-founder, Pete Johnson, was the one who told me one day, "*If we had 10 reviews for all these companies, our conversion rate would HAVE to double*." I told him those would come, but there wasn't really a way to speed up that process. (We weren't going to scrape what could be fake reviews from yelp or Google. We were committed to 100% real reviews from real customers.) Pete proved me wrong. Pete proceeded to call thousands of our past customers over the next year and get them to give him a review - good or bad - even if it meant transcribing what they said verbatim over the phone if they were too lazy to go online. He was right, within a month our conversion rates started increasing drastically.

Patrick DeAmorim | www.decate.no
The two main things about getting traction on a social network is that you need a relatively large influx of users to begin with, and you also need those initial users to stay. There is no single way to tackle this; it's more of a combination of things that you can do together to tackle this issue. The first is that your product has to be good, so that people will actually give it a chance. From there, it has to be something which is habitual, a product/service, so that they are inclined to come back.

Once those 2 main criteria are met, they register, and they stay, then it's up to you to find a way to get a large amount of users to your site, so that it can reach critical mass fast enough to "*take off*". This is a very, very simplistic explanation though; a good explanation of all of these concepts could in itself take up a whole book.

Mike Townsend | www.homehero.org / www.flowtab.com
HomeHero has typical supply / demand marketplace dynamics. To solve this problem, we had to acquire a critical mass of supply side caregivers. We did this by promising the long term benefits of creating a

profile on HomeHero, which caregivers can build credibility over time, similar to a LinkedIn profile.

Matt Keiser | www.liveintent.com

First, we had to recognize the problem specifically that it was not as easy to buy and sell ad inventory in the email channel. Everything followed from that. (A quick clarification, LiveIntent is an exchange, not a network.)

Before LiveIntent, publishers trying to monetize their email newsletters were stuck in Groundhog Day. Every day, they had to go into their email template, update it, put in the new ad units, and then send the message. The next day, they had to do it all over again – very laborious and inefficient.

With LiveIntent, publishers create a template one time and then all optimization and targeting happens automatically in the cloud. This saves publishers a lot of time and allows them to delight their readers by providing far more relevant, targeted ads.

Thus, we were able to sign up publishers before we had a list of premium advertisers.

Rob Infantino | www.openbay.com

We started with a small group of providers and vehicle owners. Once we saw deals getting processed on our platform, we carefully added providers and slowly added vehicle owners but always kept focus on our initial target market - a defined territory. We didn't go beyond it in the beginning.

Our initial target market was the surrounding Route 128 beltway just outside of Boston, MA where we had calculated that there was over a billion dollars spent on auto repair annually. This was our testing ground. Our goal was to determine what the recipe for success was in this area before we scaled beyond.

We signed up service providers by phone, email and in-person visits. It was also a good opportunity to establish relationships with this group. We needed them to participate in our marketplace, and invest their time in responding to service requests. Then we had to reach vehicle owners, and we tried many methods, including putting fliers on cars, which didn't impact our sign-ups, but it wound up bringing us one of our biggest service providers in the area. So that turned an otherwise fruitless effort into a worthwhile one.

Fast forward to our national launch (October 28, 2013), which coincided with the launch of our mobile app, and by far the most effective 'marketing' tool for driving new vehicle-owner sign-up has been by investing in PR and getting press -- third party endorsements by widely read outlets have shown an immediate effect.

Aaron Skonnard | www.pluralsight.com

In the early days, my co-founders and I actually taught the lion's share of Pluralsight's tutorials, which helped us stay lean and build a customer base without heavy overhead. Like all start-ups, we had to prove our product initially, but we had the benefit of being highly ingrained in the software developer community, which was our target demographic, so we had some credibility out of the gate. By building Pluralsight on a shoestring, we had the flexibility to add the costs of content development over time as my co-founders and I shifted our focus to the daily demands of managing a growing business.

Our experience highlights a couple of key takeaways for entrepreneurs. First, it's really helpful to master a technical skill. In almost every start-up scenario, there will be a place for that skill, and if you possess it you'll save the cost of acquiring it. Also, it's a huge advantage to build a company that your immediate network would find valuable enough to become paying customers.

Jay Barnett | www.prioritypickup.com.au

I had to think of things from the customer side. If a customer was to view the website and it did not meet their expectations, they would simply move on. In the early stages I had to provide '*the range of drivers*' the customer expected in order to meet their needs. This came at the expense of driver enquiries. In order to keep the drivers interested and give me time to demonstrate the potential of the business concept, I offered them a 3 month free trial. It was a win, win situation, having drivers who were committed for 3 months and customers who instantly had a range of drivers to choose from.

Jeb Blount | www.salesgravy.com

Getting an audience was the most pressing priority when we launched and continues to be our most pressing priority (other than sales) today. There was no "*build it and they will come*" moment for us. Getting an audience was hard, tough work.

We started with a focus on a) good content and b) constant improvement of the site to provide a better user experience and c) Search Engine Optimization

Then we went to work. I attended trade shows where salespeople would be working booths and walked around handing out flyers and cards to those salespeople, I crashed job fairs and handed flyers out to employers, we produced a podcast that got very popular (7 million downloads), I guest lectured at Universities that had sales schools, my books have our website on the front, we leveraged social media, I developed great relationships with sales experts and authors and asked them to talk about us, and I blogged every week. We also built our newsletter from 12 initial subscribers to over 250,000 today. Once we became profitable we were able to invest in SEM. Getting our audience is and was a daily, relentless grind driven by data and sweat equity.

Greg Tseng | www.tagged.com

Social networks are better when more friends participate and users are compelled to invite friends to join them. They could just tell them by word of mouth, or at Tagged, we let people invite friends by email. In today's mobile world, you could also build ways to invite friends by text message.

Chapter 9 : Growth vs. Revenue - What Comes First?

Not all businesses make money from day one. In some cases, you will need to focus on growing the business to a critical mass before building a monetization strategy. However, that's easier said than done since making money is crucial to staying afloat and sustaining the business till it grows big enough. So how did the successful entrepreneurs work this out?

Dan DeLuca recently launched GrownSmall.com. But before that, he successfully sold his start-up ClassChatter.com to a Holdings company. Talking about ClassChatter, Dan tells me that although he focused on growth during the early stages, in hindsight, he believes this was a mistake. "*I wish I had asked for a little money from the beginning but I just gave it away. I had vague notions that advertising would someday make the site money*". As the site grew, the number of bugs and tweaks grew too which meant his focus naturally drifted towards the product enhancement.

Dan says, "*Once I drummed up my small core of users, I basically stopped user acquisition efforts and focused on the site. I would do dozens of small bug fixes and tweaks a week. The site was basic even for the time, but I was able to grow with my user base and refine my niche. At a certain point I did not have to worry about attracting users any more, they just showed up. I received some donations back then, but when you are bootstrapping a company you would be surprised what you can do with a slim budget. Don't waste money on advertising, I have not found it useful in attracting active users. Make sure you choose a hosting service that can grow with you.*"

Mike Glanz | www.hireahelper.com

Our focus was revenue! We only had a little bit of money to start out with and we learned quickly that it goes fast. For the first six days of the business we did everything possible just to generate our first $1 per year in revenue. From there we set out to keep adding zeros. We told ourselves it was only a six-step process to get to $1,000,000 per year in revenue - and it somehow always kept us motivated and focused.

I counsel entrepreneurs all the time, and there's always someone trying to build big, grandiose software products that will make them tens of millions of dollars - despite that they are currently only doing $500 a month in sales. I tell them to focus. If your end goal is $5,000 a month, what is the fastest way to get there? It's amazing how clear the path is for people when you give them smaller attainable targets. I'm currently helping a friend with a start-up and the hardest thing to do is to keep him laser focused on making that first $1.

Be scrappy. Use hacks, shortcuts, whatever you can to get to your first $1 in sales. It's much harder to go from zero to one dollar in revenue, than from one dollar to one million dollars in revenue.

Aaron Skonnard | www.pluralsight.com

Right out of the gate, we just wanted people to use our product, so we didn't focus on revenue, but we also couldn't enter a true growth mode until we had established a replicable revenue model. Every company enters a phase where growth trumps everything, but putting growth ahead of revenue in the nascent stages of building a business establishes the wrong foundation and sets the company up for fundamental problems down the road. The entrepreneurial world is littered with examples of failed companies that sprinted out of the gate only to find that they never really proved the basic economics of their business. I think it's always better to build the fire before throwing on the gas.

Chris Thierry | www.etelesolv.com

In my case, there was no VC, so it was all about revenue. Those early years I call my AFM years, anything for money. To fund the growth and my dream of building a product, I needed to create a cash engine, which was my web consulting business. The revenue and profits generated from this allowed me to bootstrap my transformation into a product company.

Audrius Jankauskas | www.impresspages.org

We say it unanimously – growth. There's no real way of combining growth and revenue (if you know one, fill us in!). That is why we collected investment from a venture capital as we couldn't sustain the growth from our day job revenues. We spent quite some time and energy to find the suitable investors and to be fair, it's not always the best way to go with seed funds. Even if you get the investment, you still have to find ways to generate a positive cash flow - if you can't find any, your business model is wrong. To add up, two important things when focusing on growth are: to avoid all unnecessary expenses; and to avoid creating anything that requires constant maintenance.

Courtney Ilarrazza | www.babybodyguards.com

Our first goal was growth. We wanted to quickly capture as much market share as possible. We also wanted to create a large network of customers to be salespeople in terms of referrals. Customers that love you will never refer anyone to you. It is only the customers that are fanatical about your company that refer new customers. It is our goal to turn each and every customer into that fanatical super satisfied customer. In the beginning it was really hard but it is an investment in building the brand. Those first few months of tightening the belt helped shoot us into being the dominant company in our market.

Bas Beerens | www.wetransfer.com

In all honesty, user experience has been the main focus (and the main driver) for us. We've found that if you get this right, growth and revenue will come in droves.

Nalden and I always shared the dream of the internet being free and easy to use. We've incorporated a paid 'Plus account' subscription for WeTransfer users that have the funds and would like extra services, but the core service has always remained free. And we also don't share or sell our users data to third parties.

This *'freemium'* model relies heavily on quality user experience. It is the reason why many *'file receivers'* become *'file uploaders'* on WeTransfer shortly after their first experience with the service. It is also the reason why we have an extremely high level of user retention and have grown to over 50 million monthly users. And, ultimately, it is the reason why so many of our users have seen value in upgrading to *'Plus'* accounts.

Blake Smith | www.cladwell.com

We are in fashion e-commerce, so a revenue model is pretty inherent. We're really focusing more on engagement right now, which I think is a form of revenue in terms of the life-time-value of the user. We are looking for growth, but given that we are very transactional, we don't mind paying for our customers with funding from a later round of funding.

Matt Barrie | www.freelancer.com

For Freelancer.com, growth equals revenue. There is no differentiating the two. The more our user base and number of projects grow, the more revenue we generate. We bootstrapped the business and continue to reinvest into the company.

Myke Nahorniak | www.localist.com

It comes down to what makes the most sense for the business. It's imperative to decide early on what your goals are. Otherwise you'll be taking lots of meetings with investors that don't make sense. If you think the business has a chance to (realistically) do $1bn per year one day, venture capital can get you to the "*hockey stick*" growth very quickly. The downside of this: less control of the company, and more inefficiency. It's almost impossible to hire fifty new employees overnight and need 100% of every single one of them.

If you think you can achieve sustainability relatively quickly, and still grow year over year while retaining control of the company, a small seed round is a smart move. In our case, we chose revenue first. We intentionally decided to not pursue venture capital, so we knew we had to become sustainable from our initial seed round. This translated to lower salaries for founders and lean operations until we knew we had a repeatable sales strategy.

Iftach Orr | www.pix.do

When looking into growing your audience, you should make sure you pick the tools that suit the characteristics of your product and your current financial state. For example if you create a consumer app, you should probably focus on getting viral growth by testing out what messaging attracts people from social networks and incentivize your existing users to share your product using this optimized messaging.

John Brady | www.protempartners.com

I focused on growth first, but briefly and to a defined set of metrics. I did not want to keep growing just for the sake of growing. I also could not afford to keep growing without revenue pretty early on since this was a full-time endeavour for me. So I closed clients at my early discounted rates to accelerate not only account acquisition, but word-of-mouth. It also created a little bit of an early rush, as prospective clients knew that the lower rates were not going to stick around very long. Once I had a full calendar, I moved to more of a revenue focus. My growth in those first months was funded entirely by my initial investment in my business and in current revenue. Luckily, the necessity of switching to a revenue focus to pay my personal bills aligned with the point where the business was stable enough to maintain continuity. As my personal and business finances strengthen, I will be balancing revenue and growth as seems appropriate.

Blaine Vess | www.studymode.com

In the beginning of StudyMode, we focused primarily on growing a solid base of users. We knew that we needed to build awareness and demand for the product before we could charge people for it. We sold ad space, which brought in enough money to make two college kids happy, but we didn't begin to monetize in any meaningful way for several years.

In fact, for the first several years of the company my co-founder and I both maintained day jobs. We did freelance computer programming and I also held a consulting job with New Line Cinema.

We kept expenses minimal by working out of my dorm room and then my house. It was mostly just the two of us and a few contract computer programmers.

Scott Perkins & Shawn Boday | www.vube.com

We wanted growth. Always growth. Monetizing at critical mass is much easier. It is the growth that is difficult and holds the real value.
Focusing on profits is a short term play that never yields the best long term results.

Jason Richelson | www.shopkeep.com

I was just trying to get the software working and get any customers using it. I'm not a sales person, I'm a product person, so getting the product right and getting a good group of people using it was more important than revenue at that point.

Chapter 10 : What Do You Charge Your Customers?

What do you charge your customers? What is the rationale behind choosing a price for your product or service? If you price them too high, then it becomes a tough job finding customers. But if you are going to price your product too low, then you could be fighting on volumes which are never easy. Also, pricing is just one part of the puzzle. In a lot of businesses, especially those online, lead generations are done through free trials and freemium services (where the basic service is free but you need to pay for additional features). How do entrepreneurs make a sense of what is good for their business?

Rob Walling runs GetDrip.com, an online service that helps businesses increase their conversion rate. Before launching his business, Rob approached a number of potential clients with the product concept and offered them at a price of $99/month. But an informal consent is never a good way to gauge the optimal pricing point. He says, *"My first 11 purchase commitments agreed to try it out at that price. But as I got closer to launch and started emailing with people on my email launch list, realized that $99/mo is past the "no brainer" price point for most small businesses to try. So at the last minute I lowered it to $49/mo."*

Rob's plan worked. He has a golden piece of advice for entrepreneurs working on a price point for their product - *"Always try to overprice rather than under-price an early product. Because if you try to come into a market as the low price leader you're inevitably going to get the most price sensitive customers, who are typically also the most demanding. The race to the bottom is never pretty."*

Today, Rob is working on building additional features for Drip so that he can create enough value for customers to justify a price rise in future. *"It's easier to grow a business with higher prices, and easier to provide amazing service to customers when you have the margin to do so."*

Michael Lindell | www.mypillow.com

Finding the right price point for MyPillow was also a very difficult part of our business. Typically in the show market your product cost needs to be 1/5th of what the retail price is - that's the formula. If it costs MyPillow $20 to make our pillow then the ending price should be $100. I made a huge mistake with MyPillow in the beginning. I priced it too low and it almost caused me to declare bankruptcy. I wanted to increase MyPillow awareness so badly that I ended up having a negative cash flow. If you have your product priced too low, you can wreck you own market. Remember it is harder to go up but easy to come down

Before you set the price, examine your costs. Your own margin is KING for a sustainable business. It's important to have a margin that will not only cover your fixed costs (monthly burn), but will also allow you to promote, grow and cover unforeseen costs To figure out your margin, figure out how much it will cost you to make the product – ingredients, packaging, outer shippers, labor, etc. In calculating your ultimate price on shelf, you will have various margins to figure in – not just your own. You should factor in what a retailer must make on your product and what the distributor must make. Generally, you will be selling to the distributor so the difference between your cost and what you sell to the distributor will be your margin (you will also have wholesale and direct customers, but most supply chain scenarios will have you selling to the distributor).

Then work backwards from shelf and review the products and prices in store in your category. You want to have price parity. You don't want to be the can of beans that sells for $3.00 when your competition is sitting next to you on shelf at $1.59. So create an Excel spreadsheet with your competition, size and retail price. Let's say it costs you $0.10 to make your can of beans and you want your suggested retail price to be $1.49. Is there enough margin in there for you, the distributor and the retailer? If not, adjust the price or noodle with your own cost of making the product to see how you can gain costs efficiencies. Ultimately, the retailer will set the price but if you establish the pricing structure to meet their needs you should have the suggested retail price that works for the retailer.

Regarding our pricing experience, we did not have a good sustainable margin on our beverage business. That pricing structure did not allow us to grow and promote. However, we would not have done ourselves any good by fattening up our margin because our retail pricing would have been out of whack with our competition. For The Perfect SNAQUE business, we have a good, sustainable margin on each of our products. But it's good to note that the first product we tested in the market had a different price point and packaging. We found that product was priced too high due to our packaging. We adjusted these two areas, maintained a good margin and the pricing is on par with consumer's expectations, so it's working.

We began by looking at other similar products in the market to find a range of pricing. If we priced too high our target market couldn't afford the jeans, too low and we give the impression of using inferior materials. We decided to start at a mid-level price point and then offer some UNIQUE features that would enable us to charge a slightly higher price. For example: our 'Traceability' program which allows customers to trace their jean all the way back to the USA farmer who grew the cotton and the ability to add a custom leather patch to the jeans. By focusing our product/marketing on USA made, we greatly reduced the competition from inexpensive, foreign made products. This makes our jean appear very competitively priced when compared to other USA made brands.

Giancarlo Massaro | www.viralsweep.com

We have switched our pricing around many times since we initially launched. Looking back on it, we priced the service way too high in the beginning at $99, so we were struggling to secure paying customers when there were more affordable solutions available. Our product was really bare-bones in the beginning, so when people would ask for certain features; the answer was always *"we don't have that"*, so they would move on to one of our competitors.

After about 8 months of struggling, we cut our pricing in half to $49, introduced a lower tier plan at $19, and kept out agency plan at $399. This definitely helped us secure more customers, however, we found that the $19 customers had a very low LTV, and they were producing a large amount of support tickets compared to our $49 customers.

We worked diligently to continuously improve and build new features into the application that helped us stand out from our competition. About 5 months after changing our pricing, we were getting more and more traffic, emails and phone calls from larger and larger businesses that were finding us either through Google or through the content we were producing. We decided it was time to change our pricing again, so we dropped our $19 plan, and introduced a $99 plan that sat in between our $49 and $399 plans. This has immediately helped us increase our revenue month over month, and we're currently doing very well.

Bryan Knowlton | www.appraiseallrealestate.com

I knew from the beginning that I did not want to compete on price with companies offering similar products and services. I wanted to become known for providing the most up to date information and services that were targeted directly to my audience. Where other companies were offering directories and resource lists for as little as $25.00, I made sure my products were the highest quality and added additional value by ranking the companies in my directories and providing additional information on them. Another service I offered was to create websites for real estate appraisers. A million companies sell websites, but I made sure that my websites were hyper targeted just for real estate appraisers and contained the information they needed to make more money using them.

Edward DeSalle | www.netirrigate.com

The biggest dilemma we faced was that there was a big gap between what the customer was willing to pay and what we thought the economic value of the product was delivering. At the end of the day, all the economic analysis didn't matter. The product is worth what a substantial customer base is simply willing to pay. You can either strive to change their perceptions or work with their existing perceptions. Accordingly, we had to re-engineer to make a cheaper product such that we could hit our gross margin goals.

Michael Wayne | www.deca.tv

Personally I've worked in the ad driven content business throughout my career, so as a company we have always been focused on the intersection of advertising and content. We've executed every type of content/ad deal you can think of: brand-funded content, integration, media, online/offline, etc. While our brand advertisers have served us well over the years, we want to expand monetization opportunities to include e-commerce, books, TV and more this year.

Mike Townsend | www.homehero.org / www.flowtab.com

The HomeHero transaction fee is low relative to the incumbent agencies, whose transaction fee remains at 40-60%! A typical caregiver through an agency will cost the family $22-$25/hour, of which the caregiver goes home with $8-11/hour. We can afford to take such a low transaction fee because our local marketing and operational costs are so much lower. Typical marketplace dynamics find transaction fee sweet spots around 15% to 25%. We also learned a lot from the success of DogVacay, a marketplace to connect dog owners and dog boarders.

Debra Cohen | www.homeownersreferral.com

I conducted a lot of interviews with local contractors to get their opinion on what commission structures they thought would be fair. I also set up a Board of Advisers and invited a few contractors to participate so that I could consult with them on customary industry charges for different home improvement services.

Kevin Lavelle | www.mizzenandmain.com

Deciding on a price for your product or service comes down ultimately to the type of company you are building including quality, perception, sales targets, profitability needs, and longevity. Pricing is a reflection of who you are rather than a driver of who you are.

Rob Infantino | www.openbay.com

The fee we charge, which is paid by the service provider not the vehicle owner, has to be mutually beneficial and reasonable. By studying other marketplaces, the fee we arrived at was essentially market rate.

Peter Mann | www.oransi.com

At Oransi we introduced the first high performance air purifier made in the USA. The dilemma was that while we offered a superior product the costs are significantly higher than other air purifiers that are made in China so to arrive at a price we had to balance our customers' ability to pay and the costs to manufacture. This resulted in us making lower margin percentages but sufficient enough profits to meet our objectives. To get to this point we had to completely change how we viewed pricing as well as the costs in using the best components available.

Adi Bittan | www.ownerlistens.com

We had two reasons for choosing freemium over a free trial model: We have a two sided marketplace: Consumers send messages to businesses and businesses get the privilege of replying to them privately and directly. We want every consumer to get a response whether the business is signed up for our service or not. That's why replying to customers is always free on the OwnerListens platform. To really see results from our platform you have to deploy it for a long time. Our mission is to create a long term cultural change in the way consumers engage with businesses. It requires commitment for the long term which is the opposite of a free trial model.

Aaron Skonnard | www.pluralsight.com

We completely restructured pricing model a couple of years back because a boom in e-learning overhauled our industry. Originally, we charged thousands of dollars to give in-person tutorials in physical classrooms, but we saw the writing on the wall. We overhauled our model to a modest subscription to access a library of online tutorials, hoping the smaller margins would be offset by the scalability potential of the interactive Web.

Like us, most entrepreneurs will face a brutal reality that upsets your master plan. In these instances, you have two choices: stick with the status-quo or adjust to the times. It's never an easy decision, and hardly ever an obvious one, but the key is to understand the difference between what makes your business fundamentally relevant (which shouldn't be tinkered with) and what's open for negotiation.

Jeff Kuo | www.ragic.com

Pricing is tricky for us and took a lot of trial and error. Basically the thought process is that we don't want to make up new pricing models, we don't want the pricing to raise any questions. Changing buying behavior is a very difficult thing to do, let alone for a start-up to accomplish. And we want to price our product in a scalable way so that small companies can pay a small fee to use Ragic, while still getting reasonable revenue from bigger customers.

We also listened to a lot of advices from other people and our clients on how to price our product. One interesting thing we learned is that customer feedback on pricing usually makes a lot more sense than some expert who has never used your product. Customers always want to pay less, but we can ask those questions and listen to their reasons why they think a certain price is more reasonable in their situation.

Andrew Gazdecki | www.biznessapps.com

Being as we were a "*first to market*" type of company we did not have too many dilemmas in setting initial pricing. If you can find the point between where users will complain about the price but still pay, you've found the sweet spot. However where there is gold there will be miners. Once competitors enter the market it's extremely important to stay on top of the competitive landscape, understand where you're offering and pricing place you in the eyes on a potential client.

There is a reason we chose free trial over the freemium model. Bizness Apps currently offers iPhone, iPad, Android, Tablet and HTML5 apps as well as full websites. However initially we only provided iPhone Apps. This put a huge road block in the freemium model as iPhone apps require a lot of client touches to get up to par and then a 30-45min manual upload and update process. Being that this was so time consuming freemium was simply not an option and we chose to allow users to sign up for free trials until they want to take the app live.

Chandler Crouch | www.chandlercrouch.com

I really started growing a passion for real estate when I learned about the investment opportunities that were possible. So I began trying to buy and sell properties from day one. When I was completely broke. I tried everything I learned from courses I ordered off of late night real estate infomercials. I tried everything they taught and learned a lot. In the beginning I figured out how to buy houses without using any of my own money or credit (because I didn't have either one). So I would get a house, then I would count on getting my immediate income from selling the house on a lease/option (rent to own) or owner finance deal. Setting the price for the "down payment" wasn't always easy because I needed money now, so I wanted to price it low just to get it filled asap, but I also knew I needed to begin to build some reserve capital for future investments and to prepare for the inevitability that a property would someday go vacant and need to be fixed up.

My solution was to come up with a sliding scale that offered several options. The lower the down payment, the more the monthly expense. I held an open house to attract buyers and this created a kind of auction style atmosphere, which drove the price up. I remember several of my first houses were $4-$8,000 "*down payments.*" It was an exciting time. In hindsight what I was doing was pretty irresponsible. I recommend raising capital by acting as a real estate agent first, then moving to investments. The path can go just as quick, but this way if there is a setback, you wouldn't risk breaking a commitment or going into further debt and backsliding too much. I got lucky in many ways.

Jay Barnett | www.prioritypickup.com.au

I am constantly having pricing dilemmas. My market is price sensitive and it is competitive. In a market such as mine, I either have to reduce prices to win more business, or ad value. I choose to add value to my service, because you never really win a price war.

Robert Livingstone | www.royaltext.com

We didn't really have dilemmas when it comes to pricing. Our pricing is mid-range when it comes to the industry, but our focus on ROI (Return on Investment) gives us our competitive edge. Many of our competitors are focused on the short-term of collecting fees, whereas our goal is to show the client the ROI required to maintain the relationship for the long term.

Jeb Blount | www.salesgravy.com

The truth is, when I started the company I did not have a sound monetization strategy and I realized very early on that selling books, sales training products, and banner advertising was not a viable strategy. My niche was not big enough to turn those endeavors into real money makers. That got me thinking about where the money was in my niche – that was jobs. Virtually every company needs to hire salespeople and almost all of them complain that they are unable to find good sales people. That is when we shifted our focus to becoming the hub for sales jobs on the web. That strategy has paid off for us and has allowed us to expand to provide offer sales on-boarding automation software and on-site sales training programs.

Jason Richelson | www.shopkeep.com

We looked what other companies were charging and used that as a starting point, but the main goal was to keep our pricing simple and understandable, just like our product. We went for a $49 per month subscription model with all customer support included, which was a big differentiator because support from the traditional players can be really expensive.

Don't worry about deciding on one, absolute price or monetization strategy from the outset. Split test. For Speedhatch, we created several different landing pages with different one-time prices and monthly prices. We went with the one that converted the most paying customers, while also providing us with the highest acceptable stream of revenue. Be comfortable with the uncertainty and don't be afraid to test different things. For example, we're looking at reexamining our pricing strategy to actually make Speedhatch free and charge users for back-end types of services and add-ons. Get creative. Remember that getting that first dollar is the most important form of validation, then figure out a way to scale it.

Joel Simkhai | www.grindr.com

I decided early on I that I did not want to rely on VC funding so having a revenue model was important for me. Once I realized that Grindr was providing real value to our users, we started to develop Grindr Xtra, a premium subscription service. Grindr Xtra allows users to see more guys around them, add filters to see specific types of guys and really heightens the Grindr experience.

Since we're a location-based app, having targeted advertising by local businesses makes sense so we started to sell local advertising on our free app. We are networked business – having as many users as possible is vital. The free ad supported users are key in giving us the largest all male network in the world. Without them the Grindr experience wouldn't be as powerful. And since we monetize those users – it's a win-win situation.

Mike Niederquell | www.quell.com

What to charge for services has been the subject of many articles, books and commentary. When setting our pricing we surveyed what other firms were charging for services. Pricing information on specific services can also be found online. We set our prices to be very competitive with similar services. We constantly monitor what the prevailing rates are for our services – hourly rates, design costs, etc. When it comes to hard, outside costs we get three estimates from vendors to ensure the client is getting the right deal.

We always consider our cost to deliver the product or service and then factor in a fair and reasonable profit. In the consulting business this impacts hourly rates. Our product offering is fairly unique so we can get a better rate for our services. If you fall into a commodity, then your only leverage is to beat the competition on price.

Raj Sheth | www.recruiterbox.com

When you are not in front of your customer to explain why they should spend time on your product, let alone pay for it, it helps to have a low barrier way for them to see your product and use your product. Hence, we have a completely free plan. Some folks are not ready to make the commitment of using it in 14 or 30 days, so we have a completely free plan. Without this plan we would obtain less than 20% of current day sign-ups. It gives customers comfort to fill the form fast and see if the product will actually help them. This is the main reason we have a freemium model.

Eren Bali | www.udemy.com

Our biggest aim is to help our instructors teach millions of students every day. In order to do this, we employed a revenue-share structure that is based on the source of the student. When Udemy brings a student to a course, the revenue split is 50/50 and when an instructor brings a student to his/her course, the instructor keeps 100% of the revenue.

Our focus has always been on our instructors. We have many different types of instructors on our platform. Some are great course creators who look to Udemy to help them with marketing their courses. Other instructors are amazing teachers and course creators, and are also great marketers. To be able to reward these instructors fairly, we wanted a model that would give them 100% of the revenue.

Bas Beerens | www.wetransfer.com

With the goal of maintaining a quality user experience, we decided to take the long road in terms of monetization, eschewing intrusive banners ads for a '*freemium*' strategy that kept WeTransfer simple, highly-designed and accessible to everybody.

Essentially we developed two key revenue streams for WeTransfer: advertising and subscription '*Plus accounts*'. Our full-screen advertising model was revolutionary and questioned by many, but it has without doubt resonated with brands looking to showcase highly impactful and creative imagery from their campaigns. Now you see other brands copying the full screen model and being successful with it.

Very quickly, we had the likes of Google, Nikon, Red Bull, Vodafone and Mercedes-Benz knocking on our door, wanting to tap into the advertising model and the audience we were developing on WeTransfer, particularly from the creative community. For advertisers the numbers spoke – and continue to speak – for themselves: our click-through rates have been as high as 3 or 4%, compared with an industry average for online advertising of around 0.014%.

We have also seen a huge rise in the numbers of people using our *'Plus'* service. It's a simple model: $10 a month gives you a sharing platform that is entirely self-branded, offers 50GB of cloud storage, even bigger transfers and password protection.

Blake Smith | www.cladwell.com

We saw Mint.com doing the same business model in finance, and we asked, what if we could do the same business model only with a different intimidating world fashion? So the monetization strategy came hand-in-hand with the idea initially.

Dan DeLuca | www.grownsmall.com / www.classchatter.com

This may be embarrassing, but I never have come up with a monetization strategy that worked. I placed a lot of time energy and money into a premium version of ClassChatter, called ClassChatterLive I created an upgrade path for users of the free site. I honestly have never heard the term "*freemium*" at that point, but that was the basic strategy I was using. In the end it was a push. ClassChatterLive, our premium version paid the operational bills, it even won an fairly important industry award but it did not turn much of a profit. Now that I have sold ClassChatter I am working with the new owners to use ClassChatter to develop quality leads for some of our other education sector products.

Sam Tarantino | www.grooveshark.com

Monetization had always been advertising-driven given how we were seeing start-ups like YouTube, Facebook, Tumblr, etc. grow. For us, though, we realized the consumer, especially young consumers, were shifting their investment in music from buying the music itself towards spending even more on live events. This added to our long-term monetization strategy to take advantage of this new trend.

Rob Biederman | www.hourlynerd.com

Since we were a marketplace, we wondered about the right level at which we'd maximize profit, where we'd collect the largest amount but not so high that folks had a deep incentive to dis-intermediate us (e.g. conduct the transaction off the platform). One driving force in our decision (15% fee on businesses) is we are priced at an incredible discount (literally, 90-99% off McKinsey and Co.), that we could afford to charge a slightly higher market than other competing sites like Odesk (10%) whose products are priced more closely with substitutes.

John Brady | www.protempartners.com

In our case we had a benchmark which was market rate for related and/or similar services. So we discounted beneath that benchmark rate during account acquisition in the beginning, and then raised rates from there as we built a brand and became better known. The important part of the exercise was sitting with a spreadsheet and being realistic about costs, possible unexpected personal expenses, research about business expenses, and then determining how much we could afford to charge or not charge and for how long.

Chapter 11 : Challenges With Increasing Demand

When Betsy started her small shop on Etsy in 2008, little did she expect to grow the betsy & iya brand of handmade jewelry to over 100 shops nationwide within a matter of few years. However, the popularity of her brand (www.betsyandiya.com) threw open a challenge she was not ready for – as demand increased, Betsy realized that she could herself design only so many pieces in a day. She had to quickly hire in order to cater to the increasing demand.

It was not easy to let go off responsibilities to another person. She explains, "*I had been hand bending the wires with my own two hands, for so long, it was hard to trust that anyone could do it just like me. I started with one employee in a very informal arrangement. Slowly, driven by her interest, I was able to teach her to make my designs at a level that I felt satisfied by. As each new maker has come on, I'm just as exacting and specific about how I want the pieces made*". Betsy also ensured that the growth happened in a controlled manner so that they could finance the growth themselves without having to secure external funding.

What Betsy experienced is not something unique. Every business goes through a phase when the growth starts to happen but you are not sure how to handle the challenges that this growth brings. I asked this question to multiple entrepreneurs. The challenges they faced and the way they tackled it makes for an interesting read. Here are some great responses.

Matthew Griffin | www.bakersedge.com

It's a good problem, but it's still a problem. Our first production run was made overseas. That meant we had lead times of 12-14 weeks between shipments. This was incredibly frustrating. Once our sales would start to heat up – we would be out of supply – and then 12 weeks later when we had more inventory demand would be cooled off. It was this constant start and stop that really held us back. We eventually moved the production to the USA to reduce these lead times to 7-10 days.

Another HUGE challenge presented itself at tax time. We were growing and reinvesting in inventory to keep up with demand – and then discovered that we were inventory rich and cash poor. You can't pay taxes with your inventory. Most of our margin was being used to pay off debt, buy equipment, and buy more inventories. For the first few years it felt like we were just working to pay taxes. There were times we had to empty our personal savings just to cover the tax bill the business sales were generating. Adding that to our already tired and stressed life was really a tough blow.

Philip Masiello | www.800razors.com

As we began to scale the business, one of our problem areas was something we had never even thought about: packaging. We had developed a package to highlight our product and protect it during shipping, so our branded packaging doubled as our shipping box. It took 16 man-hours for our people to fold 1,000 boxes and only 2 hours to fill those 1,000 boxes. We decided to change the package to a simpler mechanism in order to scale greater numbers.

Michelle MacDonald | www.sweetnotebakery.com

At all stages of my business from the beginning and now I always know based on my production capabilities what my maximum output is. I would base these numbers on how fast I could currently make the product and how much I could store based on the specifics of my product. After I got my first buyer and knew what other potential buyers may order so I was able to say, for example, if one shop orders 4 cases a week and my current capacity to make my product is 20 cases then I can take on 5 more places before I would need to expand.

Once I was getting close to my 4th account I found a helper to make my product with me. I also started looking into manufacturing alternatives for making my product (with the possibility of having someone else make them, common in my industry). I also looked at machinery from the very beginning to know what options were out there to automate my production process and increase my output. I knew how much my facility could handle and projected when I would need to expand to something bigger and purchase equipment and more people to help.

Being prepared ahead with a least the strategy you will use to scale up is important, that way you know what is realistic to tackle. Some challenges I faced with needing to scale up are the funds to do that, especially just starting out. Payment plans and leasing options for machinery is a great option to help minimize the upfront expensive necessary to scale up.

I was also presented with the challenge of finding help in the daily tasks as my demand increased and I spent more time making the product. Making the product is crucial but there are so many other tasks that are important for the growth of a business (marketing, getting the product to buyers, accounting and financial, sales, etc.). The first solution I tried was using a manufacturer to make my product, so that it would allow me the time to continue to expand and meet the demand based on their larger facility and production capabilities.

I spent a few months with the manufacturer and found sales decreasing due to the decreased quality of the product. I decided I needed to take it back in house, expand and manufacture this product myself, so I found some part time helpers to slowly increase the production output. We are still growing and still face the obstacle of up-scaling today. We have our plan in place for our next step in growth (what machinery we need, space, and how many more employees to do the job).

Jojo Hedaya | www.unroll.me

I think the biggest misconception people have about start-ups is that once you have users, it's easy sailing. Being able to support thousands of users is one thing; hundreds of thousands of users is another. I wouldn't necessarily say it gets harder either, it's just becomes a different kind of hard. There's certainly an added motivation factor to it though since you know that all these people love your product and now you want to make sure that they get the most out of it and that it's working for as many people as possible.

Prioritizing is so important. There's always a million and one things you can do and figuring out which one of those things is number one is huge. For example, we had thousands of users on a waiting list for email providers we didn't support. We couldn't just support every provider at once; it wouldn't have worked as well. We had to decide which email providers Unroll.Me would support first so that eventually each user would receive optimal service for whichever email provider their using.

Another thing that I cannot stress enough is the importance of learning from others. We're two really smart twenty somethings that have achieved a lot for our age. But we're still only twenty somethings. Thankfully, there are so many people especially in the start-up world who are ready, willing, and able to lend you their time and give you advice and moral support. Having these people on our side throughout all of this has been invaluable - everyone should go out and find these people.

Tracey Noonan | www.wickedgoodcupcakes.com

Wicked Good Cupcakes was literally started in my kitchen. As awareness of our brand increased, so did the orders. My kitchen couldn't hold all products we needed to keep on hand so we invested in a handful of commercial grade kitchen racks. In the beginning, we used to stockpile extra supply in a bedroom and ran an air conditioner round the clock to keep the room cool. As demand continued to escalate, we soon realized that we were not able to turn around the volume in demand in our current conditions. If we had a large order, it would take hours and hours to complete. Yeah, fun times.

At that point, we decided it was time to go big or go home. We built a 1,200 square foot commercial kitchen and storefront in Cohasset, Ma. Once we heard the news that we had been accepted to appear on ABC's Shark Tank, we knew the expansion must continue. We obtained a second larger location allowing ample space for us to hire and train employees. Shark Tank opened endless doors for my business. We would not be as successful as we are today if it hadn't been for Kevin O'Leary and Shark Tank. The elements that most surprised about Shark Tank was the onslaught of correspondence we received after the show aired. We immediately started receiving thousands of calls and emails. Many all-nighters were spent trying to respond to all the questions. We were riding a giant wave. Our options were to sink or swim. We chose to swim faster than we ever knew we could. It was awesome!

Stacey Lindenberg | www.growyourtalent.com

I was told by others in my industry that when demand increased, it would all hit at the same time. They were right! I chose to outsource smaller tasks that could safely be handled by friends and contacts that could help. I gave myself permission to not pretend to be "supermom". There were nights where picking up a pizza and salad were more than "good enough". It saved me the time, and my family still ate dinner together. You can't do it all. Stick to your core values and resist the temptation to be perfect.

Julie Busha | www.slawsa.com

I have needed to scale my business faster than most start-up food companies ever will, and with that comes more challenges than had it been a slower progression. I launched the brand in late, 2011 and by the time we made our national television debut just two years later, our efforts, without the benefit of having that publicity, had Slawsa placed in nearly 5,200 retail locations in the US & Canada. Please know this is not normal. I would not recommend such an aggressive approach unless you have something so unique and different to the market that requires you gain presence to establish your brand as the first.

There are two major challenges when you need to scale so fast: financial and growing awareness. Shelf stable food products require that you work off of an inventory system, as it is more cost effective to create product in bulk, ship as needed and then project your needs to manufacture in bulk again. Knowing that, I've always had a set amount of savings that I earmarked specifically to fund production and that number grows as sales do. Likewise, I was in a position where I created so many retailer relationships, yet I know a product sitting on the shelf does not sell itself.

Therefore, I made a commitment to my retail partners to actively market

Slawsa by using our profits in various ways. In the beginning, you have to know what your numbers are. Your goal should be to at least break even on your investment when you spend marketing dollars so exactly how many units do you need to sell for every $1, $10 or $100 invested into a specific marketing program? If you're not selling a specific amount for the money you're putting in, you're going to find that you'll soon be out of money to spend. When you know your numbers and what you have to spend on marketing, you'll make wiser decisions to scale your growth as efficiently as possible.

Kathy Crifasi | www.hipzbag.com

The largest challenge we faced when we had to scale up is quality control. As we ordered more and more bags we kept seeing issues of crooked stitching, stained material and other small defects. In response, we put in new processes to make sure that each bag that left our warehouse was as perfect as humanly possible.

Michael Lindell | www.mypillow.com

When demand increased is when MyPillow saw some of our biggest challenges. When you grow as fast as MyPillow did, going from 10 employees to 500 in two months (which is an extreme case), you now need money for everything at the same time. If you don't have credit, it also becomes challenging. If you don't have the money to go to the next level it becomes even more challenging. For MyPillow, we got more investors or we did more shows and worked more hours.

Peter Mann | www.oransi.com

The biggest issues were related to delays from our manufacturers in shipping and stock-outs. This created huge issues for us and our customers as they expected prompt shipping and at times we weren't sure when the product would be shipped. Problems like this are magnified with a strong sales increase. Eventually we set up a warehouse and stocked the product so we could control the distribution and better serve our customers. This required securing a bank line of credit to purchase the inventory and that was critical to moving the business forward.

Matt Shoup | www.mandepainting.com

Delegating responsibility and hiring an amazing team was the hardest part for me. I'm a bit of a control freak, especially in the beginning, so learning to delegate responsibilities to my team members was very difficult. I knew it needed to be done because I wasn't capable of doing everything myself, but finding exactly WHAT to delegate was difficult. Making sure we had enough high quality paint crews to fulfill the demand we had was a struggle as well. There are a lot of painters out there and very few of them live up to our standard of quality both personally and professionally.

Mary Apple | www.prettypushers.com

Inventory shortage was the main reason for our search for funding on a bigger scale. I think it feels worse to have a demand and no supply, then to have supply but no demand. It can be extremely stressful! However, anyone will tell you "*this is a good problem*", hence how we received funding. Once you can prove you've got a demand and simply need to beef up your supply, you will find money.

Rick Martinez | www.senorsangria.com

The challenges haven't been all that hard because we've focused on a slow and steady approach so we've had a good feel for supplies. I think if we would have taken in a ton of investment and have pushed really fast the scale up would have been a lot harder and more pressure related because we won't have had the sales data to truly help us make decisions. That's one thing we pride ourselves on - we are not perfect at all but we do pour over the sales data a TON to understand buying patterns and project out not only next month's sales but sales for the next 4-5 years. This allows us to think through future problems now

Heidi Lamar | www.spalamar.com

In the first three years, our business tripled, so when the other two tenants moved out, we spread out. The build out was exhausting and expensive but we negotiated an early buyout with the tenants who moved out and used the money to help fund our expansion. At 14,000 sf we are now the largest privately owned resort-style spa in the area.

Cricket Allen | www.theperfectsnaque.com

Good question. Early on everything has to do with cash flow. Not everyone pays on time so this can be a challenge and leave you strapped when you need to go buy raw materials. Then when you are buying larger quantities of raw materials, you want credit or increased credit. This is a symbiotic relationship that challenges many start-ups. While you may not have control of when your customers pay you, it is important for you to remember to pay on time – that gives way to better credit opportunities that may alleviate cash flow issues.

Nick Paradise | www.threadbuds.com

The challenge here was meeting the minimum manufacturing requirement for our factory. We had to start at a minimum piece creation number and that's what we went with. It was still a substantial investment in machinery, parts and labor to do this but luckily, we have a stock that has allowed us to keep up with increased demand. So far, we have been pretty lucky in having the supply to meet the demand without having more supply than we can sell.

Beth Shaw | www.yogafit.com

After running YogaFit for a few years, I realized I could not do all of the work by myself. I had to expand my team and hire someone for PR, marketing, etc. It was a difficult time, because I was not well trained in hiring people. I didn't want to just hire anyone – I wanted to make sure that I hired someone who would be the best fit for my company. There was so much interest in YogaFit after the first few years that I couldn't keep up with it. I was constantly missing meetings and different appointments. That's the thing about starting your own business -- you try to do everything yourself. And so I knew I had to get people to help me. It was not easy, because I didn't want to give up my responsibilities. I think it is one of the most difficult aspects of starting a business. Hiring people is like dating. You have to try them out and see if you can trust them. Luckily, I was able to build a good team and meet a lot of amazing and hardworking people.

Chris Grant | www.grantfamilyfarm.com

Our very first farmers market we were accepted to attend was in Salem Massachusetts. Farmers markets are competitive to get into in Massachusetts. We went with a new tent, nice display, and matching shirts. We looked the part, but were severely under prepared that season. We had not planted enough, staffed enough, or had enough products to offer. We had to scramble to fill our display each week, without buying another farm's products to sell. We take pride in selling only what we grow. The following year we had a much better pulse of what people wanted, how much to grow and what to charge. We built a system for each farmers market we attend to know what products other farms bring to sell, and we grow the opposite. We have found a niche growing unique vegetables, cut flowers, and eggs.

Akbar Chisti | www.seamusgolf.com

The demand for our product has grown very quickly over the past couple of years, and our method for scaling is a bit different than our advisors might have suggested. We decided to add contract sewers that worked out of their house, and retained contracts with our vendors to pay them on terms so that we could squeeze every drop out of our working capital. In situations, like when going to international markets, where we needed to sell our product at lower prices we forced them to pay up front at the risk of losing their business such that we wouldn't need to take loans. No bank was willing to give us a line of credit early, and we didn't have the liquidity needed to bank roll our customers.

Michael Folkes | www.mafolkes.com

You must realize that your customers' business needs change for different reasons such as market fluctuation, different seasons of the year or natural disasters, emergencies from their customer base. There are numerous reasons for business fluctuation that can drive scaling up. If you're not willing to work seven days a week, sometimes 14-16 hrs. a day especially when just starting up. I have had situations where I had to work through Thanksgiving, through Christmas, Saturdays and Sundays; seven days a week, 14-16hrs a day to keep my business and my customers' business prosperous.

Danny Maloney | www.tailwindapp.com

If you're successful, you'll constantly face scaling issues. The very first one we ran into was me. Before we had an online dashboard users could log-in to, I would update a spreadsheet by hand for each client every Monday. Soon it took all day Monday, then Monday and most of Tuesday. Building an automated analytics dashboard became an urgent priority to save that lost time. That first version worked well for 4-5 months, but hit limits as we grew. So, we built a more robust version that could scale better. In parallel, we evolved and improved the product. Today, 15,000 brands and agencies use Tailwind and we're prepared to serve many more. Had we built to scale initially though, we would've wasted a lot of time and effort building the wrong product to scale.

Monica Wreede | accessoryconnectz.com

This scares me every day! It seems as if everything is an investment and very important to say the least! I remember ordering 1000 sell sheets for a trade show and have more than half sitting here! I cannot use them anymore due to my price change! It devastates me every time I look at them! It is money down the drain! Currently I am almost out of supplies! As the orders flood in, it scares me because I never know if I will have the $$ to purchase more supplies that are needed to fulfill orders, etc. All of the $$ I do make goes right back into the business!

Eren Bali | www.udemy.com

After we had proven that people would actually pay for online learning content, we had to work at increasing our supply of courses. "*Teaching online*" isn't something in most people's vocabularies, so we had to create tools and resources to help everyday experts believe they had the expertise and technical skills to teach online. We had to show that people "*just like them*" were able to teach online successfully.

Chapter 12 : Strategies To Retain Your Customers

As if acquiring new customers wasn't hard enough, start-ups also have to deal with the churn that happens with customers who drop out. The reason why customers drop out could be due to a wide number of reasons. That's why it is important to listen to them and understand the exact reason they are dropping out. Maybe you are no longer relevant or maybe you under-delivered on your product. Getting an idea of the reason could help you bring them back as well establish a more loyal clientele in future.

While most of the entrepreneurs I talked to mentioned listening to customer feedback and offering fantastic customer service as the key factors to retaining customers, others had pretty interesting stories and advices to share. Read on.

Alex Brola | www.checkmaid.com

To this day, this is our primary struggle. You can't achieve any kind of real growth without retaining customers, and this has to be the most irritating business in the world to retain them for. I was a marketing consultant for SMBs, so I have seen a really wide array of products and services, and cleaning is, I'm afraid to say, the absolute pits. The advantage is that the really smart girls and guys know that and wouldn't waste their time with it in a million years. The downside is there are a million sole proprietors charging nothing that provide amazing service (their lives depend on keeping each and every client). I could drone on all day about the numerous reasons retention is difficult for this business.

Getting unhappy customers back is really something I love doing though. Even though we have a call center now with customer service reps and sales agents (whom are all great at what they do) abstracting me out of a lot of it, I still go through the queue and call people from time to time. The feeling of getting a client back is awesome, even when it's fairly insignificant in a vacuum.

This queue I speak of is a specific list of clients that have used us but didn't recur. So we send automated follow-ups via email, have sales reps call, etc. A lot of big corporations have abused the notion of following up and it can feel a bit spammy to do it if you never have before, but if you make sure not to do it too often, make everything very personalized (i.e. automated emails personally written from the person that the reply-to is going to, plain-text/no HTML, personalized title, etc.), it can work incredibly well. We offer $ or % discounts some of the time as well, but not always. In cleaning specifically, people immediately go to another service if they didn't like the team they got from us, and so it's a bit of an ordeal for them to give us another shot even if they wanted--they'd have to cancel with the current folks, reschedule with us, blah, blah, blah. It's not even close to as simple as I'd like it to be, but even then the simple system we have implemented for following up does give us a second shot a decent amount of the time.

Chris Thierry | www.etelesolv.com

For us, the technological integration is a powerful link we have with customers. However simply having good technology isn't enough, as competitors are there and pitching themselves to get the business from you.

In the early days I'd often physically go see my clients. Despite email, video conferencing etc. I wanted to get face time. It got to be so comfortable going to their offices; they would often let me camp out there anytime I was in town. The upside was that I was a part of their water cooler talk and got to meet new people in other departments, further expanding my network within our clients' organizations.

We don't have any specific tactic per say, as I've always felt that a customer needs to see the value of the solution to stay with is. One of the ways we make sure customers are not at risk is to monitor system usage of each client. If for some reason we don't see any logins for 2 weeks, we highlight this and make calls in to the customer. It could be that the customer is extremely busy and doesn't have time to use our system, or it could be that the person has left. In some of those cases it may be an opportunity to propose a managed service whereby we take over the day to day management.

Zeb Couch | www.offmarketformula.com & www.speedhatch.com

Churn (the number of people opting out or canceling) is to be expected. Of course, you want to make sure you're adding more new (paying) users than losing users. Keeping retention high is all about providing a great product, doing what you say you'll do, solving important problems quickly, and understanding the fact that you can't please everyone. The latter is what a lot of people forget. There will be people who you just can't please. Accept it and forget about them.

Feature creep is another pitfall to be avoided. Feature creep happens when users or customers request additional features or services that you build or provide to the detriment of your business. Before building that new requested feature or service, ask yourself three questions: 1) Are a large number of customers or users requesting this feature or service? 2) Do the benefits of this new feature or service outweigh the costs and time spent to build or offer it? 3) Will this new feature or service significantly benefit your business (differentiate you from competitors, increase revenue, grow user base)?

Andrew Stanten | www.altitudemarketing.com

We are relentlessly focused on results and accountability, which strikes a chord with our clients. We measure. We test. We spend our clients' budgets like it's our own. We are entrepreneurial to the core and have a well-established sweet spot with technology-oriented companies who know that we understand the technology behind what they're selling and who appreciate the kind of analytics we provide to them.

We have been fortunate that many of the clients who left us have parted ways because they reached their ultimate goal – acquisition. Others simply outgrow us. But it's still difficult. And on the occasion where a client doesn't readily renew their contract, we do all that we can to present them with fresh new ideas to implement – with our help – to continue to build their brand and place in the market. We remain flexible, versatile and highly responsive.

Jay Barnett | www.prioritypickup.com.au

I retain customers by communicating with them. I give customers the opportunity to provide feedback. I do this early in the booking, and I have come across times when enquiries have been missed. Because I communicate directly with my customers, at key moments, I am able to intervene and get customers back which might have otherwise been lost. Because I keep my finger on the pulse in regards to customer enquiries, my drivers respond by lifting their standards.

They know if they miss something, I will pick it up, and I will follow it up. So keeping in touch and in tune with your customer is the best way to retain them. You don't ever want to lose a customer, because customers are fickle. Remember, customers don't really care about you or your business. If you can't do what you say you can do, they will just go somewhere else. And that will cost you money because every customer has a dollar value.

Andrew Gazdecki | www.biznessapps.com

Our retainment strategy was simple at first; provide top-notch customer service and really listen to our customer base. By doing that we were able to tailor a solution that solved a problem for a lot of people even when our product was still a bit ruff around the edges. Having the mindset that our customers know what they needed better than we do really benefited both parties.

Nellie Akalp | www.corpnet.com

We retain our clients by constantly engaging with them, listening to them, and making the business building and maintenance process easy for them. Our mission is to provide the most comprehensive cost-effective services when it comes to starting, protecting, and managing a business. So we believe in providing that 'wow' service to our clients from beginning to end to set ourselves apart from our competition!

Every business from time to time will encounter an unhappy customer and our strategy we use to retain an unhappy customer is to make them happy no matter what it takes until they are satisfied. It's a culture that I wanted to be sure I built within the business. We want to make the process for entrepreneurs starting a business as stress-free as possible and if they are stressed and unhappy we do whatever we can to make it right - even if it's giving them the service for free.

Eric Schiffer | www.digitalmarketing.com

If you want to retain customers you must follow these 5 different points:

- You must be relevant to them.

- Align yourself to their worldview.

- Give them a great VIP service! Make their experience memorable, inspiring, and performance driven. You should be focused on solving the problem[s] in their life.

- If issues arise, apologize immediately. Get all the facts, understand their stance, and solve the issue in the timeliest matter.

- Listen to your customers and what matters most to them. You can find ways to grow your brand by solving their other issues and problems or enhancing the quality of their lives.

Matt Shoup | www.mandepainting.com

Honesty, ownership, accountability and responsibility. We take great pride in always being 100% honest with our customers no matter what situation we are in. A huge part of our company credo is that we are humans serving humans and, as humans, we aren't perfect and will make mistakes sometimes. When a mistake is made, we own up to the mistake, account for how to fix it and take full responsibility for not only fixing the mistake, but ensuring the customer has a legendary service experience with us after the fact. That strategy has kept us in business and kept customers coming back to us, even if they try another company. There is no other company in Northern Colorado that is as honest, reliable and hard-working as we are.

Rob Biederman | www.hourlynerd.com

In almost every case of a customer dispute (we've only had 3 despite completing hundreds of projects), we've done whatever was required to keep both the customer and the supplier happy. For these few unsatisfied customers, we've had senior members of our founding team intervene directly. Word-of-mouth and reputation are too precious to ever have a customer be less than completely satisfied.

Matt Keiser | www.liveintent.com

We retain customers by delighting them. We joke that we're the Burger King of advertising, "*Have it your way.*" We try not to impose our will on our clients, we try to execute against their goals. That's our secret. You can't always win. In our case our technology is designed to be transparent. So customer knows our margin. As such, we believe we can hit their goals. If we can't hit their goals, we go our own way.

But on the publisher side of our business nobody leaves. We've created enough value both in the monetization and work-flow optimization.

On the advertiser side, sometimes you can't hit their goals or their goals are unrealistic. For example, if an advertiser compares performance of email ads to paid search, they're always going to be unhappy because paid search targets users that are already aware of your product versus email ads which are trying to create that awareness. And sometimes advertisers aren't a good fit for our publishers. Often it's more about the product than the media mix.

Adi Bittan | www.ownerlistens.com

We listen! When someone leaves we ask them to tell us why and listen closely. We ask what we could've done better. What would have made them stay? What they loved and hated about the service? We can often address those issues immediately and actually keep them. Sometimes, we don't but at least we always learn something.

John Brady | www.protempartners.com

Most of our business model is about helping clients through a transitional period, so retention is not really ideal, but referrals certainly are. Current and past clients are our marketing department. So we remain laser focused on the details, on deadlines, on being a step ahead of what the client may request. This may sound clichéd, but I have found it to be true: provide at least good output and nothing short of outstanding client service. I treat every client and prospective client like my ability to pay my mortgage relies on them...because it does!

Jeff Kuo | www.ragic.com

There's no specific strategy to retain customers for us. We don't want to lock customers in when they don't like us. We try our best to make the best product, and very few customers have left us. A good portion of them even comes back after a few months because there is simply no better solution.

We retain clients by showing them a valuable return on investment. They will see more profit than the cost of our service. Most of our cancellation calls we have received have been due to a misunderstanding including the client not doing their part to succeed, thinking they found a similar product at a better price, management turnover, marketing agency relationship changes or a lack of tracking the results in-store. Once we take a few minutes to isolate and clarify the real issue, the client almost always rescinds their cancellation. We've had a couple of clients leave thinking that they would find a better deal elsewhere. What these clients might have saved in pennies on the monthly fee, they lost in hundreds or thousands of dollars in Return on Investment. Once they realized it, they came back quickly.

Mike Niederquell | www.quell.com

Communications is absolutely paramount to keeping customers. They want to "*feel the love*" and they do want to be surprised. The Quell Group places customer communications as its number one priority. Our account people are in touch with clients every day. Moreover, we send out a "*newsletter*" to keep clients informed of what the agency is doing, we provide a written description each month of the work that was performed along with results, we send cookies at Christmas, candy on Valentine's Day, card's on their birthday and more.

Secondly, our mantra is to "*delight the client*" at all times from delivering work that exceeds their expectations to how we greet them. Because of open communications and delivering great service our client turnover is extremely low. Some things you cannot control such as the purchase of your client company by another firm, budget slashes, or you client going out of business.

Morris Miller | www.xenex.com & www.rackspace.com

I believe communicating to your customers about how much they matter to you is critical to a business's success. At Rackspace, we wanted customers to have a world class customer service experience similar to the Ritz Carlton, Lexus or Federal Express. We called it "*Fanatical Support*"

However, not every company has to strive for a high level of customer service as its differentiator. There are hugely successful restaurant chains that offer something inexpensive, ubiquitous or savory, that have good customer service but differentiate themselves on something other than customer service. I think it's imperative to establish what differentiates you – and make sure you are communicating that to customers, prospects and investors loud and clear.

At Xenex, our mission is to destroy the deadly pathogens that cause infections and kill people. Every day my team wakes up and thinks about our mission and what they can do to save lives. In the U.S., 278 people die every day from an infection they acquired in the hospital – our robots are proven to destroy the superbugs that make people sick and cause these infections. We want to make patients safer by putting our robots in every hospital in the world.

Audrius Jankauskas | www.impresspages.org

Best practice of retaining a customer is providing him the product/service that stands out in the market. Show him your true strengths, be honest, let him decide. If your customer will see the true benefits of your product, he will never leave.

If he does, okay, but try to find out why he did it. Get in contact, sacrifice your time, get as much feedback as you can: if it's the product, you can fix it; if it's their needs, you can find ways to adapt; but sometimes they simply move to the other direction so there's no point in worrying. Just remember, retaining loyal clients is always cheaper than getting new ones on board.

Heidi Lamar | www.spalamar.com

We seldom have an unhappy customer but when we do, we try to turn things around. Sometimes we just need to give a guest another chance to love us with a discount or free service. More often, they just want to know that we are going to use their feedback to improve our training. Often the unhappy customer is that way because they are used to being disappointed. When they see our commitment to making things right, they become a believer and a crusader for our cause.

Chapter 13 : Handling Negative Press & Reviews

In the initial days, every bit of press and review is critical and could potentially make or break your business. But what happens if you get bad press? Do you dismiss this off as *"there is no such thing as bad publicity"* or should you actually panic? What if the negative reviews are made over websites like Yelp by one of your own competitors? How do you recover from that?

Some of the entrepreneurs I talked to had wonderful stories to share from their initial days. These are some really valuable lessons about how other entrepreneurs could tackle challenges as these and show a more positive side of theirs to their customers.

Alex Brola | www.checkmaid.com

I have a lot of really silly stories about reviews. When we first expanded to Miami, we had a competitor post a 1 star on our Yelp page. This was back when we were fairly small and we were paying close attention to any kind of negative feedback. We ended up calling him and asking him to remove it - nicely of course! And he did. He didn't even try to deny it. That was a pretty funny one. We do have clients use Yelp and Angie's List and BBB and whatever else as leverage to get what they want though all the time. We have had people call us and demand service at half off or they would leave a negative Yelp review. These are people we never serviced that came out of the blue. They know what they can get away with and they're not afraid to do it. I'd have to think really hard to fully recall all of the review threats we have gotten.

Our response to all of it was (and generally still is) to give in. Almost every single time. The fact is that the internet has changed business forever and the consumer is in command. While you have the initial urge to fight the injustice being brought against you and your business, you have to realize that it is, in fact, just business. Staying calm is crucial. You can either make the best of it or the worst of it. All said and done, these occurrences don't happen that often, but they can leave a larger-than-normal impact if you don't have a strategy and aren't prepared.

Dianne Crowley | www.wildwingcafe.com

In our first week of business, we ran out of food. We couldn't get items out of the window. Our inexperience was apparent from the get-go.

To resolve this issue, we ran an advertisement in the local paper commenting on our struggles. The ad showed a graphic of us *"In the Weeds"* with the text, *"Thank you for trying our fabulous wings...We are working on the other pieces of the puzzle. Come back soon and we will show you all the improvements that we have made.*" In short, we made fun of ourselves and the community responded positively.

It's so important to address your mistakes. We earned our customers respect by asking for another chance and admitting our faults. From there, they watched us improve, meet and exceed their expectations.

It's critical to treat people how you would want to be treated. If you do that, people will understand when you make a mistake and they will learn to forgive you.

Again, soon after 9/11, we had a group of service men come into our restaurant. One of the men was under the age of 21. We refused to serve the underage patron. Soon after, news began to spread that we refused to serve the service men because we were against the war.

We responded by creating open lines of communication with every media outlet in town. We stood up for ourselves. We didn't bury our head in the sand. We emphasized the truth.

A collegiate tennis coach in the area caught wind of the story and began sharing the news with his network. We contacted him and asked him why he was spreading this awful news about us. He reconnected with his original source and came to the realization that the story was totally inaccurate. To show his apology, he wrote a beautiful letter about how harmful it is to spread lies, gossip and hurt others. His apology touched all of us.

Looking back, I am glad we protected ourselves. Because, you know, It's not just your reputation that suffers, the reputation of your business and everyone that works for you is comprised.

Tracey Noonan | www.wickedgoodcupcakes.com

After our appearance on Shark Tank we were subject to some horrendous commentary. Being told you're fat, ugly, stupid or that someone wishes you would choke on your product isn't worth a second thought although it can be tough to read. The story I will never forget was my twitter exchange with a man named "*George*" from Texas. George constantly told us we were stupid. We ended our twitter battle after this tweet: *That's okay little girl, go back to baking and leave real business to the men.*

I wake up every day and strive to prove him wrong. Having grown from our kitchen to a two million dollar company in two years with projections to do three million in year three, I'd say these *"little girls"* have done okay George.

I no longer read online reviews of Wicked Good Cupcakes and instead leave it up to my staff to monitor our digital perception. The useless negativity was taking my focus away from my dream to build my company. At the same time, it is extremely important to listen to your customers, analyze their feedback and do everything you can do to improve your product and/or business. Use the negativity as a form of motivation.

Alicia Weaver | www.prestigeestateservices.com

This is a HUGE problem for small business. Once we started taking significant market-share from the competition things got nasty. We had one competitor post 5 negative reviews against us in one day. Google did agree to take the posts down, we believe this was due to the malicious content and not about the fact they were fake. Yelp on the other hand doesn't verify the legitimacy and filters good reviews.

This is an ongoing battle that small businesses face and it discouraging that one or two irritated clients (or competitors) can be so harmful to small business. Small businesses need to get ahead of this in every way possible. Do whatever you can to have your customers post reviews on your services. They always have to create a profile with these sites which is unfortunate, but you can't emphasize enough how critical it is to small business success. Beg if you have to, it will be worth it down the road to protect yourself.

Heidi Lamar | www.spalamar.com

We respond to every online review, thanking those who were positive and apologizing and explaining to those who complain. This is very important because so many people are using review sites like YELP to make their purchasing decisions. The owner's feedback shows potential customers that we are involved and really do care about our guests experience. There is no way to stop every negative and/or fake review, but we can outweigh them with the number and quality of great reviews our happy guests post.

Zalmi Duchman | www.freshdiet.com

Yes we did experience negative reviews on Yelp. We overcame them but staying on top of them & reaching out to the clients who posted a negative review. We were successful in turning some of the negative experiences into positive ones by fixing the issues & handling the customers with extra care. We also used free days to show the customers that we do care & wanted to make it better for them.

Chapter 14 : Achieving Work-Life Balance

As your start-up journey begins, life can get quite hectic. When Raj Sheth and his team launched RecruiterBox.com, he had to do as many as 1100 Skype calls and demos over the first 12-16 months. As a company based in Bangalore, India, Sheth had to stay awake till 2 AM every night simply to talk to potential customers from the different time zones. Raj sums his initial days up in one line - *"There was no work-life balance!"*

Things are not too different for other entrepreneurs I talked to. Some of them had full time jobs and had to work long hours in the evening to simply see their dream come true. Others had kids to take care of. Let's hear from them.

Patrick DeAmorim | www.decate.no

I never did. I have barely spent time with my daughter. When my girlfriend and I were together, I barely spent time with her. I had no friends, no time for family, nothing. When I went to parties of her family, I always had a laptop with me so I could work. I worked non-stop. The main reason I believe I will be successful is because I am willing to sacrifice so much to get there. I know 99.9% of people will disagree with the choices I have made, but I know that the harder I work, the sooner I will get to a good financial spot, and I would much rather sacrifice nearly everything today, so that in 7, no 20 years, I can slow down, spend time with my kids, find a wife, enjoy a nice sunny day on the beach.

Business is extremely competitive. If you want to work 3 hours a day on your business, work another 8 hours, spend time with friends, family, enjoy life - can you really compete against those who, like me, are willing to sacrifice everything today and give business our 100% focus?

I'm not telling anyone what to do or not do, I'm simply saying that the more you are willing to sacrifice, the bigger the chances that you will get where you want to be.

Do I wish I could have been more active when my daughter was smaller? Of course.

Do I miss those times? Of course I do.

Do I wish that I have spent more time with family, friends, relaxed more, enjoyed life more - and perhaps be 25% of where I am today? No.

Will I always be like this? Of course not, as I see the business growing, then I'll hire people, expand, and give bigger and bigger tasks to other people. My dream is to be wealthy so I can spend time with my loved ones, but also enjoy the fruit of my work, but I know that to get where I want to be, if I let go of the gas pedal now, perhaps next month I could be at 0 again.

Micha Kaufman | www.fiverr.com

Working from home requires two main things: self-discipline and support from your family. It is hard for you and your family to respect the fact that when you are working from home you are not available. You should adopt a daily schedule that fits into your home routine.

The term 'work-life balance' is overused. It assumes that your work and life are distinct and need to be weighted differently. I think that work -certainly if you are passionate about what you are doing-is a part of life. Work is not something you need to balance against the rest of your life. As adults, we spend two-thirds of our waking hours at work, and roughly 15% of our entire life working. We don't think about sport-life balance. Why should we think of work as something which is not life?

I suspect that the term was invented by someone who was unhappy at work. Someone who saw work simply as a means to provide for financial security. I know that this is a reality for many people. For people who have been fortunate to embark on an entrepreneurial journey and attempt to achieve financial independence on their own terms, work is, in fact, life. At the very least, it is an integral part of life - the part in which you feel accomplished and fulfilled.

Joshua Dorkin | www.biggerpockets.com

I started my company while I was teaching full-time. I worked nights and weekends on the business until I was able to quit my job and go full time. As an entrepreneur, taking work home is part of the job. Not a day goes by where I don't take work home with me. I work at nights after putting my kids to bed, and on weekends when I'm free.

The balance I've found has been to prioritize my family. Instead of waking up and going to work, I focus completely on the family until the kids leave for school; then I get into work mode. The same applies after work as well. I stop working and spend the next few hours completely dedicated to my family. It is easy to get caught up in the business during these down times, but you have to force yourself not to. I don't take business calls, don't go online, and dedicate myself to the people that matter most to me. They see it and we're all better for it.

Monica Wreede | accessoryconnectz.com

My youngest in kindergarten and my oldest in 8th grade! Anyhow I work from 8a.m-2:30p.m. Every week day! It is awesome & of course still challenging at the same time (especially summer months)!

Chapter 15 : Entrepreneur Couples And Finance Planning

There is a growing number of small businesses that are started by married couples. While the operational aspect of business is not too different from any other business, entrepreneur couples face unique challenges. Unlike others, these entrepreneurs cannot expect to live off their spouses' income when they start up. So how did the entrepreneur couples featured in this book handle this challenge? Let us start with the story from Nellie Akalp who is the co-founder of CorpNet, an online legal document filing service.

Nellie Akalp | www.corpnet.com

We really did not have much to lose with the first start-up because we did not have a penny to our name, other than hundreds of thousands of dollars in student loans. The idea of taking a risk was very attractive to both of us and we initially invested only $100 to purchase the domain name. We grew that business day-to-day ourselves without feeling too overwhelmed with high costs at first but grew the business and our team when the time was right and everything worked out!

Today, with our latest business CorpNet.com, the risk is still just as high, but our finances are extremely different from the acquisition of our first company. My advice to other entrepreneurial couples is to really just go for it. Don't let fear hold you back, if you take the leap and see what happened you may be pleasantly surprised that with some hard work and time investment you could be set for the rest of your life!

Courtney Ilarrazza | www.babybodyguards.com

We started Baby Bodyguards in 2007 during the collapse of the real estate market in NYC. My husband owned a successful Title Insurance company that went bust overnight. The phones just stopped ringing. It was a terrible time; I remember feeling desperate to figure out a plan. I had a job as an attorney that was barely paying the bills. We had just had our first child, and the financial stress we were under was overwhelming.

We didn't have money socked away to go big with our new venture immediately. We started small and part time. Starting lean with very little overhead allows you to test the waters with less pressure. It also allows you to test the market to see what works and what doesn't. Once you grab a foot hold, it's much easier to expand on that.

Matthew Griffin | www.bakersedge.com

First and foremost – any team that has mutual finances at stake needs to be on the same page in regards to how much risk is acceptable. It's like a marriage (and in my case – it was a marriage). This requires communication to the point of being redundant. Any start-up should run as lean as possible until it begins to prove itself. Once the cash starts to flow – it is also crucial to be in agreement on how much gets reinvested. We specifically earmarked some savings and credit capacity as our "fund".

We knew we had to achieve cash flow before those funds ran out – and knowing that made us work smart. A no brainer for us was to keep our day jobs deep into the start-up and operating phases. For us – quitting the jobs that paid us to survive to follow an idea in its infancy seemed insane – and it still does. We are just normal people with bills to pay. Without steady incomes during the start-up phase desperation can come into play – and that is a very dangerous decision driver.

Alicia Weaver | www.prestigeestateservices.com

Be ready to live like no other so you can live like no other. I don't remember who said this, but it's a great mindset. Assume that you won't make money the first few years. You'll have enough to pay bills and feed yourself but that's about it. Going into business with your spouse is a great idea, both of you having the visibility to what's going on and you're both engaged in the process. Much easier than one of you trying to communicate to the other one how poor you are now.

Set goals, that way it doesn't seem like you're just continually struggling. Don't take out debt, at least in the beginning. Don't buy fancy stationary, uniforms etc. Keep your overhead LOW. The goal is to survive; you're in it for the long haul. Don't get caught up in the short-term fantasy of being an entrepreneur.

Nick Paradise | www.threadbuds.com

It was really up to me to make sure our finances were alright. I've always handled and worried about our finances. She is always in the loop and has access to all our financial data whenever she wants but she defers to me. We had saved enough on the side to where I felt comfortable investing what we had saved and still being in a good personal financial situation. I had failed with some start-ups before and some of that had to do with wasted money and so I was very careful this time to think more broadly and not make the same mistakes I did in other start-ups.

This really helped me to be more successful in the forecasting of our new venture. My advice would be to have one person handle the finances of the business but to be open and come up with a plan together on what money will be spent on what things and why. Buy-in from both parties is essential to the success. We also have a policy of "*both must say yes to proceed*" so if I want to spend money on something and my wife doesn't, we don't. Likewise, if there's an idea she wants to pursue but I disagree, we don't move on it.

Dianne Crowley | www.wildwingcafe.com

We had money set aside to open the business. However, when we opened Wild Wing Cafe, banks were unwilling to finance a restaurant so we had to use our personal income to finance the project.

Cecil and I underestimated the costs. I would recommend anyone opening a business; add 10% to the anticipated cost of launching the project. You will always spend more than you originally anticipate. For one, labor is expensive. You don't want to be understaffed. It also takes time and money to train your employees.

In terms of expansion, It is always better to have one thriving business than two businesses sucking you dry. I recommend waiting until you have amassed the savings from the first business, before you launch the second business. For instance, we expanded to a bigger location across the street from our original location and became worried that the higher rent cost would inhibit profits. However, the added space gave us room to purchase a commercial washer and dryer so that we no longer had to outsource a linen service to clean our napkins, aprons, towels and other items. We offset the expense.

Chapter 16 : Female Entrepreneurs' Challenges

We may tend to believe that the world is a much fairer place today than it was a few decades back. But the truth remains that challenges do exist for women at the work place; more so when they are the business owners. Not only are women expected by default to own up family responsibilities, there are other challenges like not being taken seriously by investors, suppliers, banks and even the customers.

If you are a woman aspiring to start your own business, these are definitely hindering thoughts that are likely to crop up. So is it true that women face greater challenges in entrepreneurship? Apparently they do, quite often – be it Monique Tatum who was not taken seriously for having a *"baby face"* or Adi Bittan who was constantly asked for her marital status by VCs apprehensive about her ability to run a business - female entrepreneurs I talked to have seen it all. Here are a few experiences they shared.

Michelle MacDonald | www.sweetnotebakery.com

I am continually not taken seriously and to be honest even by some men and women that are close to me and do truly want to see me do well. I guess it's because it's still a very male dominated thing to do. All the risk and guts involved, the hours you put in and the knowledge you need to obtain are all things more well aligned with what men are *"supposed"* to do but not women. I listened to many male entrepreneurs who believe in female entrepreneurship and some of their advice was to *"be ready to get your nose bloody and your teeth kicked in; this isn't for the faint of heart"*. I have so many experiences where this has happened.

Here are a few of the most memorable: When I first started out I rented a facility to start experimenting with my product. It was an existing business. He was very helpful in the beginning stages and we had talked about the idea of continuing to work together as I grew and needed my own facility. As my business grew I realized he wasn't the right fit and if I was going to team up with anyone when it came to manufacturing my product it needed to be someone with experience in that area and that fit with my style and future goals. He got very envious that I was growing and no longer needed his help and actually bombarded me with his attorneys making claims that were untrue. I was surprised and hurt that something like that could even happen. The stress was unbelievable, and I remember questioning why I was even doing this. Once things settled down, I found a new place to use and he and the attorney went away, I was determined to not let that stop me.

A few months later I met another man who was looking to do some manufacturing in my industry. I was hesitant to work with anyone else and proceeded with caution. In conversations I often caught some condescending undertones in the things he would say and ultimately I backed away. I knew he didn't see women as equals and there was no way a partnership would work with him. Another time on 3 separate occasions I went to 3 different big companies that I could potentially team up with get my product to more people where we all make some money. All 3 male owners tried to mentor me and give me advice the whole time. I was trying to sell to them and they would almost discredit everything I said. The 3rd time this happened I knew I had to break the pattern, I knew I needed to get more bold and make my stance louder.

I found a female business coach who taught me how to stand my ground and boldly but politely and in MY own way take back the control in these meetings. I am now able to use my femininity as a strategy. I am now a voice of empowerment and handle the meetings with control and grace at the same time. I am not a man and I don't have the same traits as some of the men I met in business, but I have other traits and can use them to approach situations differently. I am not rude or nasty to get what I want; I am confident. Confidence in yourself and your product is the best way to prepare for these challenges you will face. I started wearing red lipstick, I know it may sound strange at first but hear me out.

I think many women can agree, when you wear red lipstick you stand out, it brings attention to you, it is bold and it is passionate. I never felt confident enough in myself to wear red lipstick; to bring that much attention to myself. I stepped out of my comfort zone and the first time I put it on I could feel the kind of confidence I needed start to grow. Many women come up to me and the other women in my team when we are wearing red lipstick at business events and say they wish they could "*pull that off*" too. My company is actually in the process of planning a non-profit division for female entrepreneur empowerment because of this very reason. We need to believe in ourselves first, confidence in you is the first step to being taken seriously in the male business world. So I say if you are an aspiring female entrepreneur, step one- rock that red lipstick!

Julie Busha | www.slawsa.com

I've never felt I was not taken seriously as a woman because my experience has told me that you are treated in a manner that is based off of the way you present yourself to others. If you tell people you are super crazy with two small children as you start your business, you'll certainly be treated as such. Having been a college athlete and worked in a male-dominated industry before becoming an entrepreneur, I've always been extremely competitive and I am not afraid to negotiate. I always knew I had to prove myself with intelligence and work ethic to offset my youthful appearance (which honestly has been a bigger hurdle for me than being a woman).

I keep my business life separate from my personal life and having that separation, for me, is key. I've found women entrepreneurs to have more of an open dialog with each other, as we are more willing to help each other out. Likewise, I highly recommend that women take advantage of programs that will give them an advantage in their industry. For example, many major retailers have supplier diversity programs where women-owned businesses can get doors opened quicker to buyers or avoid entry fees to the marketplace. Why would we not take advantage of those opportunities if they exist? Being a woman can be quite powerful.

Adi Bittan | www.ownerlistens.com

Of course it's harder. I definitely faced this problem. I don't think VCs ask or look up male entrepreneurs' marital status for example but they will for women. Some VCs were at least honest about it, some made excuses but I could tell. Again, I do not take this personally, I just move on. I knew I needed to prove myself more than a male entrepreneur with similar credentials. I came into meetings with lots of answers prepared and I addressed potential objections head on.

For example, being female and not an engineer a VC is automatically thinking "*will she be able to hire a great technical team?*" That's a fair concern. I'd come in with the slide in my deck ready about my male team of engineers that have already committed to working with me. Since I knew leadership is an issue I'd mention in the beginning that I had been a Captain in the Israeli military. Nothing says leadership more than that. After over 100 meetings I had heard all possible objections and had an answer ready for them.

I ended up having more meetings than perhaps a male entrepreneur would have but I succeeded in raising my round and in the end, it was oversubscribed.

Tracey Noonan | www.wickedgoodcupcakes.com

Before Shark Tank, I definitely got those patronizing smiles as I introduced myself to other professionals. It was frustrating to get the proverbial pat on the head from the old boys club. I don't ever let being a female be my excuse for not getting the job done. Embrace being a woman and use it to your advantage! As women, we can sometimes be our own worst enemies. We need to support one another and not feel threatened by each other. My suggestion for dealing with this is simple - ignore what others do think or say. Believe in yourself 100% and surround yourself with positive people.

Fashion and retail is different, I'd say, in terms of women in the workplace. And handmade products are dominated by women. I'm sure it's not a fair reversal, but Will has had to work to be taken seriously by female wholesale buyers and retail shoppers. The trust and rapport that I experience quite naturally when working with a woman buyer comes for Will only after he's proven himself to them as an equal, as a resource. Again, the power dynamics are completely, different, I'm sure. In general, my biggest lesson has always been to jump. Just do it. Work tirelessly and take big risks. I'm sure that is cold comfort for a woman entrepreneur in Silicon Valley who is doing those things already.

One thing I will say: as much as is financially possible, we try to work with wholesale accounts where there's mutual respect, mutual benefit, a common interest in establishing a relationship that works for both sides. It's more fun, certainly, but there's also a level of self-preservation in running with a pack like this. I believe this is part of the answer. Find clients, colleagues, suppliers, etc., who want this type of relationship with you and distance yourself as much as possible from the others. Grow big in this environment. When you become big, the sexism will either change to court you and for their own self-preservation or you won't need them in your business anyway.

The last thing I'll say is to embrace it, know your strengths, and find a partner with complementary ones. Gender aside, Will and I are always asking each other for help, advice, perspective, and we definitely trade tasks and duties based on our strengths. Sometimes that means I make the phone call, or sometimes Will does. Gender can absolutely play a part in these decisions, but it works both ways: I can do things Will can't (or couldn't do as easily) and vice versa.

Even after being in business for 6 years, my kindness and 'woman's touch' is sometimes mistaken for weakness. I use it to my advantage though. Let the vendor think I don't know about cotton prices or let the VC think I don't know what a balance sheet is; and then I just hit them with the surprise left hook in business talk and it puts them on their back foot every time.

Especially when starting out in my own business, how I was perceived could make the difference in obtaining or sustaining business relationships. Experts say that we make opinions about a person's character within 17 seconds of meeting them. I have to admit that although I try very hard not to do this myself, I find myself sizing people up with very little information as well. What do they really know about me in 17 seconds? What they really know is how I look and how I present myself. So when I first started out, I put a lot of thought in how I looked and how I spoke. I actively and thoughtfully decided how I wanted to be perceived then modeled my dress, manner and interactions accordingly.

Being effective has been a big topic for me as I like to be super casual – I mean holes in the jeans – casual. My verbal communication is very similar. I can complain about just wanting to be me, or I can work on being effective. Once my business became successful, people would seek out me to work with rather than the other way around. Now, I can show more of who I am because my reputation precedes me and I have an opportunity to be influential /helpful to others pursuing their dreams which is even more exciting!

Myra Roldan | herbanluxe.etsy.com

I've faced all kinds of challenges but the hardest challenges have been when I've been dismissed as just another little lady wanting to play with the big dogs. It is completely infuriating. I've stopped counting the incidents where I've been made to feel that I'm incapable of running a successful business because I'm a woman. I don't think there is any properly to prepare for these situations except to remember that you have to keep you calm - hold those tears back until you are alone in your car.

As women we have to grow tough skin. There is still this archaic belief that women who are successful don't have children or families to hold them back. It is a big challenge to juggle family and business but it doesn't make us any less destined for success.

Stacey Lindenberg | www.growyourtalent.com

I have found that female business owners are more likely to refer one another, send leads and contacts, and support one another. Finding a network of like-minded women in your community, volunteering with them, and building friendships helps to create a network of people encouraging one another. The majority of my clients have been male, and I haven't experienced any gender bias. Only encouragement and respect.

Aditi Kapur | www.deliverychef.in

In some cases, this is true, but in some cases, being female also has its advantages. This depends upon the country/ city/ industry you operate in. Hospitality in India is male dominated. VCs too are more skeptical of female entrepreneurs – how long will they stick with the business, how much time they will devote to it, etc. To these people, you need to prove you are serious and credible – show your passion and your resolve.

However, sometimes, men are more polite towards women entrepreneurs – more open to giving them a chance to prove themselves, correct themselves if they are wrong and help them when needed, so in that case, it is great!

J'Amy Owens | www.billthebutcher.com

We have to get past talking about gender. I happen to be female, but what on earth does that have to do with anything related to me being an entrepreneur? If you are a female and think you have to prepare for being a woman who has to face sexism, misogyny, and ignorance then you should come out from living under that rock.

Monique Tatum | www.beautifulplanning.com

There was one particular challenge. I am a young entrepreneur with a baby face. Around 26, I began to notice that when clients had issues they would not take me as seriously as they would my colleagues. For instance, they would think it was OK to not pay their invoices and one woman even took it so far as to call me little girl in an email. I never conducted myself like a little girl and didn't think that I should then either. I calmly sent the email to my lawyer who drafted a letter and mailed it to her. I had my payment 4 days later. I have not run in to that problem a lot but it's happened a few times. On the flip side, I found it a bit more difficult to close larger deals. I did combat that by offering prospects a month trial without long term contracts in the beginning. If their fear was that I could not work to the standard of someone more seasoned, then I would quickly squash that fear through my performance. Now we are one of the top, most reputable PR firms, with clients based worldwide.

Debra Cohen | www.homeownersreferral.com

Well, I'm a female in a male dominated industry (construction) and I have no home improvement experience whatsoever. Ultimately I realized that I should embrace the differences. I wasn't expected to be an expert in construction, my business offered sales and marketing expertise. And, many of my contractors even tell me it's a pleasure to work with a woman after dealing with sweaty men all day.

Beth Shaw | www.yogafit.com

Luckily in the field of yoga and meditation, there isn't so much sexism. But sometimes sexism does come up. There have been times when men don't think women can successfully run a business. It is frustrating and demeaning. I overcome this by – interestingly enough – exercising, meditating, and practicing yoga. It is a great stress reliever, and has helped me get through a number of tough spots.

Chapter 17 : Raising Kids While Starting Up

Starting up can be extremely hard, and doing so when you have kids to raise is even harder. I asked a few entrepreneurs who had small kids to take care of while they managed their business to understand what the experience is like. Here are their responses.

Matthew Griffin | www.bakersedge.com

To borrow from the comedian Jim Gaffigan "*It's like your drowning...and then someone hands you ...a baby*". We were pretty extreme in our approach. We actually tried to be parents first and foremost. We tried to not work on business stuff unless the kids were asleep. We wanted to be "*in the moment*" and giving them our full attention.

This was not a good plan. We had many late nights – like a few years' worth. We were always half asleep – and in the end everything suffered a little. My wife did A LOT of extra work – especially when I traveled for trade shows or TV stuff. It was a strain. The best advice I can give is "*be realistic*". If you have little kids, and want to grow a start-up – know that you are going to give up most of your free time for a long stretch. Vacations and socializing will likely be non-existent. Be patient with your business, kids, and spouse. It's still something I'm figuring out.

Nellie Akalp | www.corpnet.com

When we launched our first company back in 1997, Phil and I did not have any children yet. A few years into owning that business, in 2001, we had our first children, a set of boy and girl twins! Then in 2004 we had our third child before the business was acquired. By the time we had children, our first business was running smoothly so it was not too challenging. However, when we started my current company in 2009, we were in the midst of raising the three children who were back then 8 and 6 so much tougher as all three are very different from one another and each have their own set of activities and personalities. On top of that, we had our fourth, and final, child after CorpNet.com launched so that was quite challenging.

We handled it by dividing and conquering to the best of our abilities. We co-parented together and were each other's support system while not only running a business and having a career, but also tending to the children. My advice to other entrepreneurial couples with kids is to realize that not everything will be perfect. There will be times when you have an issue with the kids while at work, or an issue with the business when at home. Just handle the situations as they come to you and try not to let the stress overwhelm you.

Monica Wreede | accessoryconnectz.com

Oh goodness, where do I start? Honestly I would have given anything to be home with my children when they were growing up and my husband knew that! It was my ambition & inspiration to get into girly accessories when our daughter was born! I did not intend at all to start of business, but it just happened! I thought, *"why not make some extra $$ doing what I love to do?!"* I think it was my calling back in 2004 which lead to where I am today!

While my children were younger, I did what I could. I listed accessories when I could, etc. I LOVED every moment of being a mother while having a hobby and small business on the side. Things changed when I filed my first patent in Aug. of 2011. I had invested a lot of $$ and was certain that my product would sell like hot cakes! I knew I had to make something out of this since my hubby was pretty much my investor and still is to this day! While being a stay at home mom and trying to run a business is challenging and honestly very overwhelming!! Always stay true to yourself and your children!

Jeb Blount | www.salesgravy.com

I have a son who was eight at the time. Fortunately I also have a supportive spouse who took on much of the responsibility for him during the years where we were starting up. There was no work/life balance. I was working at my day job to keep the lights on and working on Sales Gravy until 2 or 3 each morning. I'd get three, maybe four hours of sleep and start all over again. I did this for four years until I was able to leave my job and could afford to hire people to help me grow the business. It is easier these days to manage the business but as we continue to grow the company, balancing work and life continues to be a struggle. Last year, for example, I spent more than 250 days on the road traveling all over the world speaking to and training sales professionals and sales leaders.

Nick Paradise | www.threadbuds.com

We weren't raising kids and I would say this definitely makes starting the business easier, especially when it comes to finances. Having said that, we have two dogs and while I'm not comparing them to raising kids, we still have the time and costs associated with those dogs. We still have to balance the vet bills, food, toys, etc. and when one of your dogs is allergic to everything under the sun, a special diet is a must and we end up spending $120 every month just for her food.

Our best advice in starting the business is to have balance. You're always going to have other responsibilities, costs and activities to tie up your time, you have to find a balance and be willing to both pitch in. I would also recommend that you not keep score. If you keep score on who helps more with something or does more in one area than the other person, you'll fail.

Mary Apple | www.prettypushers.com

In the beginning, I tried to separate myself and my time between being a mother and a business owner. I somehow thought that it wasn't *"professional"* to have a baby cry in the background or to roll into a meeting with a stroller. But guess what – I wouldn't have come up with this crazy idea had I not gone through birth itself.

I realized that in the case of Pretty Pushers, my children ARE my business plan. They were the idea and they are what I look forward to going home to. Many mompreneurs will find that there is not only tolerance but support from their business community for mothers of young children. And if anyone isn't supportive, you don't need to do business with them!

Courtney Ilarrazza | www.babybodyguards.com

The birth of our first child was partly what inspired us to start Baby Bodyguards. For us, the biggest challenge of having children while starting a company was time management. The benefit of being your own boss, is that we were able to make our schedule fit around the needs of our family, and still do to this day. I love that I don't have to consult my boss if I have to pick a sick child up from school. Once I became a mother, my goal was to become my own boss and be able to spend more quality time with my kids. Having my husband as my business partner helps as we can offload responsibilities and shares the workload.

Stacey Lindenberg | www.growyourtalent.com

The challenges of being a mom while starting up motivated me even more to be successful. I talked with my child about the changes they would see in our household (the home office, my being around more, etc.). This would have been more difficult if I had younger children who were not in school.

Kathy Crifasi | www.hipzbag.com

I made a decision for myself that when I began my business, I would be conscious of how it affected who I say I am: I am a Mom, Wife, Sister, Friend, worker, and now business owner. Since I had a full-time job that paid the bills until my Hipzbag business could do so, I chose to work on the business while the kids were in bed or at school – that was my rule back then. I was lucky I could function on just a few hours of sleep. I would do all research, emails, business planning, etc. at night so that I would have time for meetings/phone calls during the couple of hours in the day I had open outside my regular job. I consider it time management at its best.

Debra Cohen | www.homeownersreferral.com

I had a newborn and then gave birth to my second daughter while I was working. I planned my work day around their schedules--I worked in the early morning hours before they woke up, nap times, after dinner and on weekends. I also set my office up in our basement which was a playroom at the time so that I could watch them play while I worked.

I always tried to carve out an hour or two each day when I left the office to take them to a park, gymnastics, play a game or some other fun activity to try and keep everyone happy. My husband is also very helpful.

Alicia Weaver | www.prestigeestateservices.com

We had our first kid in the very beginning of year two. Our agreement was to start a family when the business was profitable. That was motivation for both of us, especially for me. I also had the flexibility of having my kid with me for the first 1.5 years. One of the many perks of being your own boss. As mortifying as it was, most people these days are often very understanding of having crackers in the backseat or an occasional kid squeal on the phone when they sneak into your office.

Chapter 18 : Tech Startups Outside USA

As someone who has been associated with tech start-ups in India for a while, one of the overwhelming gripes expressed by tech entrepreneurs here is that the opportunities that are available to you in the United States (read Silicon Valley) is unlike anywhere else. It's no wonder then that a number of tech entrepreneurs choose to move to the US once they gain a little traction. I asked all the non-American tech entrepreneurs I talked to about their experience working outside the United States. Does it make a difference staying outside the US? Here are their responses.

Micha Kaufman | www.fiverr.com

I split my time between the US and Israel. When we started Fiverr we acknowledged that in today's world it's important to be open minded about the work environment, which is a topic I frequently write about. I believe in measuring team members not on the hours they put in at a physical office, but rather based on performance. At Fiverr, we don't care if employees work from the office or home, if they come late or leave early. It's all about getting things done, and we have a team that does that exceptionally well.

We always saw Fiverr as an international company - a global organization that hires the most talented people --wherever they are. This is what led to the opening of the office in NYC. We hired fantastic people and they needed a space to operate. The US was (and is) our biggest market--over 50% of our business--long before we opened the first office here.

Matt Barrie | www.freelancer.com

The beauty of the internet is that you can start a business from anywhere! An entrepreneur in India, Romania or Paraguay can come up with a great idea and start a successful global business. With sites like Freelancer.com, you can also start up a business off the back of a credit card! A challenge I guess would be time zones which often sees me work around the clock and chasing the business hour.

Patrick DeAmorim | www.decate.no

While I have never lived in the US, I would NEVER base my business out of there. There is the advantage of talent, but the tax rate is crippling (compared to what I pay in Bulgaria), the cost of hiring good people is also far, far, far higher than in Bulgaria, which would have made it a lot harder for me to scale in the future.

I'm sure the US has a lot of unique opportunities, especially in networking, but I would not be willing to cripple myself economically just for that. In that case, it's far better to have money, and then just take trips to the US for events/networking. If you live in the US though, depending on how extreme you want to take things and depending on your situation/business, I would honestly suggest for you to move to a low tax, cheaper state and run things from there. This might be an awful idea if you have family, or need talent, of course, but having low personal and business costs means more money in the bank, which means more opportunities for your money to be reinvested and compounded.

Jeff Kuo | www.ragic.com

I believe being in the US is a pretty big advantage as far as the infrastructure and community goes. What we can do is to always stay up-to-date with the latest Silicon Valley trends, and target US market early on. The product design would be pretty different when you target different regions, changing it later on can be pretty difficult. If we intend to go for the bigger market, I think we should do it from the get go.

Raj Sheth | www.recruiterbox.com

For a business like ours, most people meet us on their browser screen. Whether you are based in New York or Bangalore, the first impression is your website and your work-flow when someone signs into your software. So while it is difficult being based out of the US, getting a lot of small companies to solve their problems quickly is a low-touch process. Many of our customers do not want complicated tools that need training. They need something that works, like their Gmail inbox. With that in mind, as of this year, we are adding more people to our US office to cater to companies with larger hiring requirements.

Chapter 19 : Hiring – Mistakes & Lessons Learned

Hiring your first employee can be quite daunting. What is the right time to hire? Do you hire someone simply because you like them? Or do you hire someone with strong credentials even if you dislike them for their attitude? What if your new hire is not what you expected them to be? These are questions that run through your mind as you are about to hire your first person.

When Greg Tseng, the founder of Tagged.com first went about hiring people for his social network start-up, he was a little desperate to find someone who could take over the role of the Vice President. With very little time on hand, Tseng hired a candidate he was not completely happy with, but assumed the person could do justice to the role once hired. He was wrong – Tagged.com had to let go of the person just four weeks later and had to resume the search all over again. It was a waste of time and money. Looking back at the blunder, Tseng tells me that the best hiring advice he could give is to "*set a bar and only hire people above that bar. It can be very tempting to hire a marginal candidate because you are so desperate to fill the position, but that almost never works out.*"

One thing I realized after hearing from these various entrepreneurs is that there is no one rule when it comes to hiring for start-ups – some believe you should only hire when it hurts while others believe you should hire when things are still comfortable. While some advocate hiring based on personality alignment, others are completely against it. Ultimately, I believe it is all about what business you do and what your own ground realities are.

Blaine Vess | www.studymode.com

I have two pieces of advice. The first is: hire when it hurts. The last thing anyone wants to do is hire a bunch of people and then have to lay them off when you realize you didn't really need those roles. At StudyMode, we employ a hire when it hurts philosophy. This means we don't go searching for a new employee until we know that the work we need done cannot be supported by the current team – either because we don't have enough people or because we don't yet have a person with the right skill set.

The second piece of advice is to hire within your company culture. StudyMode is a small team of people who truly are experts in their fields. When you have 25 people in an office, making sure employees are a cultural fit is crucial for ensuring that the work gets done, the office runs smoothly and people are happy. I'm proud to say that since we started building our team, we've only ever had one person leave us. We have, however, had to let a few people go – and more often than not, it was due to a culture clash. Twice we hired people who had great experience, but my gut told me they weren't a cultural fit for the company – neither of them worked out. I've learned now to really go with my gut on those things.

Michelle MacDonald | www.sweetnotebakery.com

Hiring when you absolutely need someone is not a good idea. It makes for a rushed decision without finding the best fit. I made a mistake in doing so but fortunately the employee also realized it was not the right fit for them either. I think it's important to always be looking for your next employee before you need them. This is a great way to find some great people and plan how they can fit into your company.

Whenever I come across someone that I think is a great fit I bring them in to start helping out and just get a feel for the job. I found our President of Sales and Marketing when I wasn't in need of that position yet. I met Brittany and invited her to come see the operation and as i grew we began working together and now she handles most of the sales. Someone I knew seemed like a great fit for the team; Alison currently works another job, but helps Sweet Note out whenever she can. Once the operations position is necessary she will be the likely addition. Both of these are examples of how to build a staff that is a great fit for your company and what you are trying to achieve. They need to have a passion and aligned goal with what you are trying to do, especially your first few employees, as they are the most helpful and involved in the growing and building process.

Aditi Kapur | www.deliverychef.in

I had never hired anyone before I made my first hire for DeliveryChef.in – somehow, I lucked out and hired a person who is very senior with the company even today (four years later). He's stuck around through all the ups and downs and is a pillar of strength for the company. That said, initially, I really struggled with hiring. Didn't know what positions I needed to fill, how to fill them, how to interview candidates, judge whether they are capable, what salary to offer, how to train and so on.

After all these years, I've learnt – referrals are one of the best sources of hires. You get people who are more dependable and qualified (if the person referring them has done a good job). You can look on online portals as well, in India; we have naukri.com or others which are more specialized to the post you are filling. I would recommend having questions prepared in advance – and digging deep to see if the candidate can actually do what you need him for. It's not enough if he just says he can do it – most people think they can do more than they actually can. So getting into the details of situations they might face, understanding how they would tackle them, what systems they would bring in place, etc., helps.

Dianne Crowley | www.wildwingcafe.com

The most important thing to keep in mind when hiring is finding people that share your vision. I want my staff to believe in the concept. I want them to believe the way I believe. We all play together and we all win together. I can teach anybody to wait tables. However, I can't teach people how to treat people the way I would want to be treated. I can't teach them how to genuinely care about every customer that they serve–How to express empathy, care and concern.

Here is a great example of a hiring mistake that I made in the past: We hired a hot shot manager from a neighboring chain restaurant to bring his expertise to Wild Wing. He was rule driven. He knew the rules and he knew how to enforce them. So, one day, one of our hostesses showed up to her shift with open toed shoes. He immediately sent her home, despite the restaurant being on a two-hour wait. Without a hostess, things became very chaotic. He put everyone in a comprising position because he was so hyper focused on a minute detail. He missed the big picture.

We want employees that share our vision. Although this manager was a great fit for another restaurant, it didn't translate to our concept. We need the right players for our team.

Giancarlo Massaro | www.viralsweep.com

I have yet to hire an employee, but I have hired several contractors over the past 10 years. The first thing I would suggest is ALWAYS give the potential candidate a trial to see how they work with you and your teams before you decide to hire them. This will save you hours and hours of headaches and lost money. Someone may sound amazing in the interview and you may want to hire them on the spot, but you really should give them a trial first to see exactly how they work, if the quality of their work is good, and how their communication skills are. You'll often find that a week or two of working with someone, you'll know right off the bat if things are going to work out or not.

Mark McClain | www.sailpoint.com

Hiring based on "*personality*" is dangerous, because you tend to overlook issues. I've always tried to hire based on aptitude and attitude, but skill and experience were pretty critical in our early days, as we didn't have time to "*bring someone up to speed*". Everyone had to contribute and hit the ground running. Because of our past success in a larger company, my co-founders and I did have a network of people to connect with. The main thing to keep in mind with early stage hiring is to ensure you bring in people who complement you as the leader – skills, aptitude, temperament, etc, - rather than focus on people who feel comfortable, because they're probably too much like you, and won't bring enough additional value.

Joshua Dorkin | www.biggerpockets.com

I've made many of these mistakes, and ultimately, could have avoided doing so by better screening. I hired one guy who, had I done a criminal or drug test on, I would have never brought on board. In the end, it caught up with me and I had to fire him after he was locked in jail for more bad behavior.

I hired a developer once who told me that my ideas were all crap. He literally told me that I needed to do as he told me in terms of the project and wouldn't build what I was asking him to build. He believed that he was in charge and quickly learned otherwise. He was promptly fired, but astoundingly, for the next few years, would send me his resume and ask that I bring him back on board.

In the end, I think that the key in finding good hires is to make sure you've got a good personality match. My best hires have been those people who I get along with best. Do keep in mind that these people do have strong personalities and are quite outspoken, but there is a level of mutual respect that is essential.

Philip Masiello | www.800razors.com

When hiring someone in a start-up, it's important to look for candidates with versatility. I want people who can juggle many different tasks and don't mind change. If you are hiring for the first time for a start-up and were looking at a candidate who only performed one job for the last few years, chances are good that they won't make it in an evolving start-up environment. I have made the mistake of hiring people who I got along with well, but could not perform the range of tasks I needed.

Jason Schultz | www.jason.me

Every single personnel problem I've experienced at one of my companies had stemmed from either hiring skills over values, or, not realistically managing people's expectations about job security. When hiring people, always look for values over skill. You can train just about anyone to do anything better, however it's nearly impossible to teach someone how to have more integrity. Don't hire people who impress you with their dazzling skills and give you all sorts of unsettling feelings regarding their honesty. Also, be sure to realistically manage people's expectations honestly from the start. Make sure they understand what risk there is with their job with your start-up company and keep them informed.

Dan DeLuca | www.grownsmall.com / www.classchatter.com

I never was in the role of employer. If you are talking about hiring developers or contractors, I have a little advice. When you go to hire a developer or contractor the communication of your idea is critical. It is a great time to try your elevator pitch. If you are having a hard time finding someone who *"gets it"* you might need to refine your pitch and message. I know money can be tight when you are first starting, but look for people who understand the product. You will have a lot easier time getting out of them when you need. Even if it is for relatively short term freelance work.

Nellie Akalp | www.corpnet.com

So I have a ton of input here specifically because I started a company after selling my first one. When you start all over again, old employees will definitely want to come and work for you again and although there are exceptions to this rule, you should in general shy away from hiring old blood. Times have changed, you have grown yourself as a business owner, and sometimes hiring old blood can complicate things and work against your success in growing your new company. So that is one mistake I made and learned from quickly. Others would be in trying to do the recruiting yourself instead of having a recruiter do the work for you which is much easier, less complicated and lends itself to hiring the best talent.

Chris Thierry | www.etelesolv.com

Hire people with the same core values you have. Before I knew what my core values were or had them on my walls, I was always looking for people who had the entrepreneurial attitude. Remember in start-up mode, everyone is a key employee, so the old adage of hire slow and fire fast works. In the early days I was guilty of hiring people based on my gut feel, however that was only about 50% effective and it cost me time and money. Today we make prospective employees interview with multiple people multiple times and include skills test for technical people. Never take someone's CV at face value. CV's are like a dating profile of a person, so spend some time and get to know the real individual before you 'get married' and bring them into your business.

Mike Matousek | www.flashnotes.com

Some of the toughest lessons I have learned have been through hiring. You need to make difficult decisions as a boss. When I hire someone now, I have learned to never hire for a specific role. At a startup, roles change and need to be molded, which means you need to hire great people who are passionate about your idea. With a tight budget, you will most likely never pay someone the highest wage or give them the most equity, so you need to find someone who believes in your business. It's also important to be honest with the people you've hired – the good, the bad, and the ugly. If you are not, and it comes time to make a move, they will be blindsided and it could potentially make the situation worse.

Ashok Subramanian | www.liazon.com

Many people love to say they want to work for a start-up, but few really have the right mindset and drive. Be selective and rigorous when interviewing. Find the people who really believe in not only what you do and their role, but in the start-up process. Are they committed to the long haul? Are they willing to make sacrifices right alongside you? One of our first hires spent an entire flight to a meeting across the country reprogramming almost our entire product! Those are the types of people you need to find. He's still here by the way – although we give him a bit more time to work.

Michael Folkes | www.mafolkes.com

Never hire your best friend, or family members. You should think twice about the consequences should the business relationship fail. Try to find employees that are passionate about the work they will be doing for you. It's like the old cliché goes 'don't try to fit a square peg into a round hole'. Naturally it's just not going to work.

Mike Niederquell | www.quell.com

Everyone looks great on his or her resume. Mistakes are made by not really understanding a prospective candidate's previous work experience. For example, we often look at portfolios of young writers who show samples of their work. Only upon probing do we find out that the samples were the product of the candidate but also someone else that edited or rewrote the article. Too often the work claimed by an individual is the outcome of a group of people they worked with.

You need a good job description for the position you want to fill and use the description as part of the interview process. Not aligning the skills with your needs will create problems down the road. If at all possible, engage the employee on a trial basis, perhaps 30 or 60 days. If performance is good, make the position permanent. A big mistake is hanging onto folks who don't perform well. This impacts moral, quality of work, profitability, and relationships with your customers.

Christy Ferer | www.vidicom.com

I have had so many bad hires over 30 years I am embarrassed. First do not be gullible and always trust your instincts. Don't hire anyone who has skipped around for short periods of time. If you are hiring someone you want to be a revenue generator make sure they can sell you on themselves. Ask for a list of prospects and examples of what they have sold before. Look for the honest and proactive. I hired someone so smooth once that even I couldn't have detected the fact that he had two jobs at once. We found communication from his "*second job*" in the fax machine. I had to fire him.

Tracey Noonan | www.wickedgoodcupcakes.com

All in all we've have been fortunate to find a talented group of people who love and thrive in our company culture. We have unbelievably dedicated staffs who are inspired each day to be part of a business that has gone through 600% growth literally before their eyes.

One of my biggest mistakes as a manager has been maintaining that fine line of management vs. staff. I would strongly recommend all start-ups launch a strong internship program. We've had tremendous success in finding talented, eager and hardworking interns. Our track record shows, we have a distinct pattern for hiring our interns upon graduation. Talented individuals more often than not can be right at your fingertips so remember to prospect out of your direct industry. I hire talented art students to do our decorating. A mentor once told me, "*be slow to hire and quick to fire*". Boy was he right. Don't hire for the moment, put together a team of talented & dedicated individuals who want to help build your company, not collect a pay check.

Hill Ferguson | www.zong.com (Chief Product Officer, Paypal)

Early in my career, I hired a person without checking any references. Big mistake. Checking references is such a simple, yet critical, step in the hiring process. Hiring is one of the hardest and most important things you will have to do when building your company. Gather as many data points as possible on the candidates you are considering for the job. Pay attention to the types of referrers a candidate offers up - Are they successful? Are they passionate in their support of this candidate? Good people always have good support from former colleagues. People who can summon their own fans quickly should be avoided.

Adam Simpson | www.easyofficephone.com

Instinct is everything. I've hired staff that had outstanding resumes despite the fact that their personality or demeanor seemed a little "*off*" during the interview. That might mean a salesperson who wasn't as outgoing as you'd expect, or a developer who had a great attitude but glossed over the more detailed technical questions. Never ignore those gut feelings; they're your best indicator of a fit or lack thereof. You need to be quick to cut when you don't believe someone will share the vision and perform accordingly. In a start-up, you don't have time to try to turn someone around – you have to move on.

Eric Schiffer | www.digitalmarketing.com

The most important thing in hiring anyone is to validate facts and not get influenced in a way causes you to buy a lemon. There are a lot of lemons out there that are dressed up like Ferraris'. The more questions you ask and the more facts you uncover, the easier it is to determine what's real and what's fake. I look for integrity in a person. You can never go wrong with someone who is honest and keeps his or her integrity. They might not have all the skill-sets you're looking for, but that can be taught. Look for someone who has a keen mind and is willing to give you their best. Being genuine and nice person on top of all that makes working with them that much better.

Matt Keiser | www.liveintent.com

Hiring too fast. It's everyone's problem. It's easy to hire and it's hard to fire. So at the end of the day, you can get ahead of yourself. The most important thing is to make smart decisions – no need to rush or act impulsively. Additionally, interviews are of very limited value. Almost anyone can perform well in an interview for 30 minutes. So, you have to do a lot of background checks. And you have to do them with someone you have a relationship with.

The team and players that are right when you're a start-up aren't necessarily the same team that are right when you've found product-market fit and you're at the execution and scaling stage. Often people think to themselves, "*How do I hire people that scale with me from here to my IPO?*" And it's often just not possible. You need to be realistic that you're going to have to re-jigger your team as it grows. The guy that helps you get from 0 to 20 people, isn't necessarily the guy that helps you get from 20 to 100. That's because in the early days of a start-up you have to be willing to wear many hats- not be a specialist, and be willing to run into walls.

Chapter 20 : How Important Is A Co-Founder?

Finding a business partner who shares the same dreams and work ethics as you is no easy feat. When Julie Busha of Slawsa (www.slawsa.com) walked into the sets of Shark Tank, her request for funding was rejected by the investors who said it was too risky for them to invest in a one-person company. *"What if you get run over by a bus?"*, was the question she was asked.

Having a co-founder is seen as an advantage for more than one reason. But there are a number of solopreneurs who have done exceedingly well for themselves. I asked several entrepreneurs from both sides for their views on the importance of a co-founder. Would things have changed if they were a solopreneur instead? Here are the answers I received.

Jojo Hedaya | www.unroll.me

Having a co-founder can be a huge advantage. Everybody works and thinks differently and for a start-up to be successful, you often have to combine ideas or have a "*plan B*" when your idea doesn't work. For example, my co-founder Josh is a big picture thinker. He's the one who knows the certainty what Unroll.Me should be 10 years down the line. Me, I'm a details guy and way more focused on what's going on with Unroll.Me today and this week or this month. Together we make such a great team because we're able to bounce ideas off of each other and get the input of someone who thinks differently than either of us does on our own.

I've also found that having a co-founder helps you stay motivated. Creating a company, let alone a successful one, is hard work and there have been times when it would've been so easy to give it up especially if I were a solopreneur. I'm sure Josh would agree. We definitely motivate each other to keep going and keep getting better - and clearly it's been paying off; we're 700K users strong after just two years. I don't know if either one of us would've achieved that as quickly as a solopreneur.

Whether you're a solopreneur or a co-founder, I think having great mentors and advisors are extremely important. These aren't just people with good names you can throw around. A good mentor, a good advisor is someone who will speak with you regularly and someone you can trust wholeheartedly and receive great advice from and bounce ideas off of.

Iftach Orr | www.pix.do

As a solopreneur myself, I think there are workarounds to having a co-founder. One way to succeed as a solopreneur is to create an active community of users on social networks and discussion websites who can help you in gathering feedback, testing QA and developing marketing that you'd normally do with a co-founder (it also happens to be cheaper this way). In order to do so requires the right incentives, such as a referral program, and being highly communicative with your users. One way to attract these devoted users is to understand your market audience and be active in the forums they themselves gather in in order to communicate with one another, be that a Facebook group, chat room or a professional conference.

It's important to remember that the nature of your co-founder arrangement needn't be a traditional 50/50 split. For instance, it's possible to bring on a co-founder that is less experienced than you and share a small portion of the equity with them, where the tradeoff would be you serving as a kind of mentor teaching them how to build a successful start-up.

Bas Beerens | www.wetransfer.com

I believe in surrounding yourself with the right people – good people who you can listen to and who can provide great value in anything you do. At WeTransfer we even consult a psychologist when we brainstorm new strategies.

I'd already developed an online tool at my agency *OY* to share large content with clients via download links. But it wasn't until I met Nalden that we were able to take this service to the next level and create what we now know as WeTransfer. I probably wouldn't have started WeTransfer without being able to incorporate Nalden's business model, as I wasn't comfortable with the common ones, i.e. generating revenue through banner advertising. WeTransfer might have existed without him, but it would have been a very different beast.

Along the way I have benefited greatly from Nalden's ideas around simplicity and design, his unique business model, and his pioneering activities and spirit. His eye for upcoming artists, trends, brands and entrepreneurship has influenced the WeTransfer experience significantly. It's due to Nalden that WeTransfer has the tone of voice that our users appreciate so much.

I always think of David Ogilvy's quote: "*If each of us hires people who are smaller than we are, we shall become a company of dwarfs. But if each of us hires people who are bigger than we are, we shall become a company of giants.*" Having the right people provide more perspectives on your vision will help take you to your shared goal.

Andrew Stanten | www.altitudemarketing.com

In my personal experience, a co-founder was absolutely necessary. Stan Zukowski, who now serves as VP for creative services at Altitude, and I had the idea to start Altitude Marketing together while we were both working at Lehigh University. We previously worked on the purchasing side of outsourced marketing services (PR, web, trade show support, graphic design) for years – and before Lehigh, Stan and I worked together at Rodale – and we knew we could do it better.

Stan brought ideas to the table that I didn't think about. Our strengths complemented one another. We were both honest. So we started on our way. About three years in, we realized we needed another critical thinker at the table to help us refine our messaging, build our brand as a B2B, tech-oriented marketing firm and so we brought Gwen Hoover in as a third partner. So, in my case, yes – I absolutely needed to be able to rely on Stan and Gwen to be all in.

I don't think, however, it's necessary for every entrepreneur to have a co-founder, per-se. But what every entrepreneur does need is an ability to ask themselves hard questions and surround themselves with a team of people who complement and challenge talents and assumptions. Tearing ideas apart, presenting the opposing point of view, asking difficult questions – these are things that make a company stronger. It takes a special kind of person – who can be brutally honest but constructive at the same time – who you can trust implicitly to help you to do what's best for your business.

Jason Schultz | www.jason.me

A co-founder is not absolutely necessary; however it's usually pretty important. Think of things you did in school by yourself and with a partner. Think of things you've done at work yourself and with a partner. Chances are with most people that they were more likely to follow through when someone else was there both counting on them and there for support.

I've founded lots of companies myself, as well as many with co-founders. I think that in the right situation, sometimes a trusted peer group can actually fulfill some of the aspects a co-founder does. Seek out and build a group that you engage with regularly, try to hold other entrepreneurs accountable and help them when possible. Try to get closer with people who hold you accountable and can also pitch in and help when times get tough. Some good places to find peers or even potentially co-founders are: Meetup.com, cofoundersLab.com, and FounderDating.com.

It's not a must to have multiple co-founders. Many companies have succeeded with single entrepreneurs. However, having a founding team that is greater than one has benefits. Entrepreneurship comes with financial, emotional and intellectual burdens and pressures. Having someone to share failure and success, brainstorm ideas and do strategic planning is a huge plus. As you grow a company you realize that no single person-not even the founders- knows all the answers.

It's about the collective wisdom of a group of people who are incredibly passionate about the mission and have a vested interest in its success. On the flip side, picking the wrong co-founder --much like your life partner-- can have a very harmful effect on the business.

If you do start as a solo entrepreneur, I would recommend getting in smart people with complementary skills that you can use as a soundboards to run ideas by. If you are a young entrepreneur, find yourself a mentor that can walk you through the process of starting and scaling a business.

Nellie Akalp | www.corpnet.com

I do not think a co-founder is absolutely necessary, however for us, its works because we come from such different sides of the spectrum. Phil is more the creative/idea guy and I am more the operations gal. It allows us to not only have our careers, but also be there and be present for our 4 children. It's also a plus that we get to see each other all the time, have lunches together, bounce ideas off one another so for me, it's perfect!

If I was a solopreneur I would find mentors and confidants who are willing to help me along my entrepreneurial path. For me, I need to talk things out and run ideas by people which I can't do alone. So that would be the most important thing, finding people to just listen and provide feedback so I can feel confident about the decisions I would make to grow the business.

Aditi Kapur | www.deliverychef.in

I am a solopreneur. Planning your team and hires then becomes critical. Delegating tasks well to your team, giving them authority to take decisions and incentivizing them to grow the business is the way to go. That said, I think it is a good idea to have a co-founder. Investors (if you need them), will value one, you will value one when you have no one to turn to for brainstorming or support when you need it.

Philip Masiello | www.800razors.com

A co-founder is not necessary, especially if you both have the same skill sets. However, some entrepreneurs find it helpful to work with one or more co-founders. Successful co-founders should have complimentary skill sets, compatible personalities and effective communication skills for smart decision-making.

Ryan Wallace | www.iphoneantidote.com

A co-founder isn't absolutely necessary, and in some cases I think it might hurt productivity. It really depends. I am the kind of person that can work 12 hours straight as long as I am by myself, but I think sometimes working with a partner can make you slow down. There could be a mentality of *"hey, he's not working; I can take a break too"*. But if you can make it work, so that both of you are proud to show how much work you've gotten done that day, I think it can work out for the better. Long story short, I don't think you need a co-founder, but depending on your personality, I am not sure if I would go out of my way to avoid a partner.

Michael Kawula | www.selfemployedking.com

Knowing what I know today I would have outsourced more verse bringing on a partner in an online business I started in late 2008. I had a strong marketing and sales background, but lacked the technical knowledge to put together a website. I decided to partner with someone who could do the technical work while I'd build handle the marketing and sales. The company outgrew my partner's technical background fast and this caused me to learn the power of outsourcing. I quickly realized how much more affordable it was verse giving up ownership in a company.

I don't think a co-founder is needed; though do believe participating in Mastermind groups of other owners can provide you the benefits without sacrificing ownership.

Betsy | www.betsyandiya.com

betsy & iya would not be where it is without Will coming on as a partner, end of story. In our case, our partnership makes the business stronger, because we make each other better. We believe our constant dialog on business decisions drives the company potential up.

Jay Barnett | www.prioritypickup.com.au

One of the most important lessons I got in life was to not go into a partnership with anyone. No matter what else you may do wrong or right, friends and money don't mix. It may seem like it is a heavy load to carry all yourself at first, but you will be better off in the long run. Get advice from as many people as you can (qualified people with proven results), but don't go into partnership with anyone.

Alex Brola | www.checkmaid.com

If you don't have a successful history and/or connections to guarantee that you can raise, then yes I think it's necessary. There's too much work to go around, on top of the mountains of issues you can never foresee (and the associated stress that comes with them).

And it really depends if you have someone else that's a match for you. When I do something, I do it to win and everything else come 2nd, 3rd, and 10th, in line. I don't really enjoy most things unless it's very competitive. It has been nearly impossible finding someone else like that who also shares the dream of being a successful entrepreneur. The few people I know who are like that are already successful (duh!)

Patrick DeAmorim | www.decate.no

It's hard to say as I've never done any business with a co-founder who was also very active as I was, so I can't imagine what that is like. But for me it has been quite nice being alone in managing, learning, and doing everything. The reason for that is because I got to learn so much - everything about running the business, I know. So I have an extreme amount of knowledge which I can apply to a wide array of businesses, simply because I had to learn everything myself.

It's also nice being the sole decision maker, I'm not always right, but I trust myself extremely much to make the right decisions, so while it would be good to have someone to discuss things with, I would not like it if I had to get them to either agree to something, or it would not be done. I also know that I give my 100%, and I trust myself to really focus on quality in everything that I do. If I had a co-founder who was exactly as I am, the business would have been far, far larger than it is now - but finding that "unicorn" partner can't be easy.

Lastly, I like responsibility. I don't like to rely on other people as I have been let down by "potential partners", or "clients" so much, that if something HAS to be done, I only trust myself to do it. I also understand that this is something I will have to change a bit, as I can't scale like this.

The downsides of being alone though, the 2 main that I can think of are that you're quite limited in how fast you can grow, as you're one person and not two, and secondly, some people may not be built to handle all of the stress and "being alone" in everything.

Blake Smith | www.cladwell.com

My co-founders were absolutely necessary. They have knowledge that I don't possess and we've kept each other sane when things got crazy. It has pushed our relationship to the limit, and has taught us more about grace, forgiveness, and friendship than any endeavor I've ever done. What if I was a solopreneur? I don't know how to answer this question – Cladwell wouldn't exist without my co-founders and if it could, I wouldn't want it to.

Mike Mataousek | www.flashnotes.com

I would not say anything is absolutely necessary because every entrepreneur takes a different path. However, I can say that it's certainly nice to have the support of a co-founder when going through the ups and downs of starting your own business. There are many long nights where you question everything around you, and it's nice to be able to lean on someone during those times for support.

If I had chosen to be a solo entrepreneur, I would make sure that the people closest to me are able to lend similar support during difficult times. With any journey, there are both good and bad days – you need to have someone who can help you celebrate the highs and survive the lows, even if it is not as a founder. Entrepreneurs always say that you need to have passion to make your company successful, and that's 100% true – putting your heart and soul into your work is the only way your business will truly take off.

Audrius Jankauskas | www.impresspages.org

It's without doubt a big plus to have co-founders but the number has to be limited. Try to avoid too many people on company's board. From our experience the ultimate number is three: you get three people with expertise in three different areas – this makes your product versatile. Co-founders also ensure that you work with as passionate people as you are, this helps to drive your product to success and not get stuck on the way.

Solopreneur approach is possible if you have enough funds to hire the best people right from the start. Otherwise you can end up with a really sloppy team or doing everything on your own which is really too much of a hassle.

Ashok Subramanian | www.liazon.com

I do. Having other people believing in the company early on was a real boost. It was incredibly helpful to have someone to bounce ideas off of and to help fight through the tough days. I truly believe we wouldn't be here today without my co-founders.

Arnon Rose | www.localmaven.com

I don't think that co-founders are necessary but it is nice to have someone to lean on and toss ideas around with. Starting a business is a lonely ordeal and it's nice to have someone to talk to. I have a co-founder with LocalMaven.com and it's been a very rewarding experience. We often debate issues for ours and having a different point of view has been helpful. This doesn't necessarily have to come in the form of a co-founder but it is a benefit of sharing the journey with someone else. The other benefit of a co-founder or partner is that you have someone to put you in check when you are on a path that may not be productive. As founders we are on missions and often have blinders on and it's good to have someone who can stop you and say *"hey, this isn't going to work, it's time to change your direction"*.

Kevin Lavelle | www.mizzenandmain.com

In our view, doing this alone would be foolish. It's an excruciatingly difficult process, and from having each other to vent to and lean on in the hard times, to sharing the overwhelming joy when something goes right, having a co-founder makes the process of building a company emotionally more tolerable. This is, of course, not to mention the fundamental importance of rounding out skill sets and capabilities. You cannot be all things. Finding a co-founder whose skills complement yours dramatically improves your chances of success. That is what Web and I have found in each other. Were either of us to do this as solo founders, rather than co-founders, we both know we'd have to build a great team around us very quickly.

Adi Bittan | www.ownerlistens.com

There is of course the time argument: There's just so much to do that doing out alone is going to take you longer. The other argument which I think is more important is that there are so many decisions to make; you need to talk them out with someone. Yes, you have advisers and mentors and investors but that's not the same perspective as being in the trenches together. There is risk of course. Many companies fail because founders don't get along, disagree on strategy or fall out somehow. Make sure you and your co-founder work together for a while before committing and go through some crises or challenges together.

John Brady | www.protempartners.com

I am a solopreneur, and about 4-5 months in I hired a coach who had experience building a business closest in structure and offering to mine. He was also experienced as a coach and came highly recommended. Initially I put this off because I was concerned about the expense. Moreover, I had experience in sales and am much disciplined about how I approach my work, so I was hesitant to spend any money I didn't have to. It seemed like a luxury to me. Once I realized that I was hitting a wall, and I needed an outside perspective, I hired him. While you should do your homework before hiring a coach, this turned out to be one of the best decisions I made and money I spent. So if I could start over again, I would have hired my coach in the beginning as I might have gotten traction earlier.

Mike Niederquell | www.quell.com

A co-founder would not have been absolutely necessary to achieve the same results, but some kind of assistance would have been needed to allow the required focus on sales. The advantage of two of us starting the business was the complementary skill set and a broader network. We both worked at public relations and advertising firms. Most important we were married, had similar talents and wanted to start a business together. By working together we immediately had a staff of two that could write, plan and service clients. If I were the solopreneur, my first hire would be my partner who had the needed skills and networking opportunities to accelerate success.

Raj Sheth | www.recruiterbox.com

Yes, a co-founder is super necessary. I failed as a solopreneur the first two times I attempted an internet venture (a classifieds portal and a commerce site). When it came to Recruiterbox, we were all missing some skills and experience that the other had to get it off the ground. Raghu and Girish could code and design, but their bandwidth was tapped out when it came to thinking of how they would get users for this. I didn't have any perspective of how to develop business software, but when I saw Recruiterbox. I wanted to market the site and sell it in a lot of different places.

This is just one primary example. There are countless more that evolved when the three of us worked together. If I now found myself in a situation of being a solo founder, I would hire very early on and make sure the core team had a good amount of equity in the company.

Michelle MacDonald | www.sweetnotebakery.com

I feel pretty strongly that a co-founder is not necessary. I started my business for me and my goals for myself and my company. As selfish as that may sound this is my journey to do what I want. I have been lucky to have found people who share that goal, but at the end of the day I get to decide what that looks like and how it's done. It's still important to listen to other ideas and thoughts and make a well-rounded decision. Maybe it's from seeing how other partnerships have ended or the struggles as growth happens and the partners aren't on the same page that makes me feel strongly about not having a co-founder.

On the same foot that I say a co-founder isn't necessary and certainly isn't for me, it has some great benefits. It was extremely lonely starting this business on my own with no one who was really right there doing it with me. It's amazing what you can do with others and how you can feed off each other. Your first few key employees can be just that, it has been that way for me. My first 2 employees are the ones that are "*down in the trenches*" with me helping to grow the business. They take on things even outside their position because they want to and believe it in, they have made it their "*baby*" too. With the right precautions (aligned goals, open communication, clear expectations and more) a co-founder could be just the thing you need to get your business off the ground, only you can decide that.

Greg Tseng | www.tagged.com

I don't think having a co-founder is absolutely necessary, but having a co-founder will increase your chance of success. That said, having too many co-founders can be counterproductive, possibly due to internal conflicts. There's a reason most successful companies were started by two or three co-founders. The best co-founder relationships, like all human relationships, are founded on open and honest communication, which builds connection and trust.

Morris Miller | www.xenex.com & www.rackspace.com

I think it's important to have a team of people – the more founders the better. You need to trust and respect them to make decisions when starting a company. It's important to be able to bounce ideas off of someone – and to have someone who's got your back on the days when things aren't going your way (you don't get a deal, you get turned down by an investor, etc.). Being a successful entrepreneur means being able to look at a situation from many different angles, and to keep trying different tactics and messages on your marketplace.

At Xenex, we know that hospitals save money when they use our robots. We hear from customers that they have a 20:1 ROI because of fewer infections, fewer deaths, lower re-admissions, better reimbursement, etc. We're working hard to communicate that to decision makers in the healthcare community.

Matt Barrie | www.freelancer.com

Running Freelancer.com is the hardest but most rewarding thing I have ever done. It is extremely difficult to run a successful business if you do not have a proven track record. So get experience, learn to start and fail and pave your way for success. But most importantly, you need to have the willpower to overcome any obstacle that will, without doubt, be thrown your way.

Chapter 21 : Rejected By VCs. Are VCs Necessary?

Most websites and blogs targeted at startups glorify VC funding as some sort of ultimate validation of your business. A lot of entrepreneurs see VC funding as an end rather than the means to a new beginning. I wanted to ask two things to the successful entrepreneurs I talked to – One, have you ever been rejected by VCs? And two, do you think VC funding is absolutely important?

Let's start with their answers to the first question. An overwhelming majority of start-ups that seek VC funding get rejected by the investors. How did these entrepreneurs process this information and how did they take it? Why do they get rejected? Here are their answers.

George Burciaga | www.elevatedigital.com

I've been rejected by VCs more often than not. Just about everyone has – it's the natural course of entrepreneurship. VCs are always looking for the proper fit – and so are we – which is the most common reason we've been rejected. I've found that there are three primary factors that determine a proper fit – the industry or technology you're developing, the size of the investment and the team dynamic.

Most VCs have an agenda or specific idea of the technology they are looking to invest in. Oftentimes this is focused on a specific industry or current trend, and your product just might not fit into their portfolio.

Rejection is just a part of entrepreneurship. There are going to be a lot of people who say no, and a lot of people who say yes, but really mean no. Even if someone isn't on board, you've still created a relationship. Many entrepreneurs get frustrated and stop following up after getting rejected, but you should continue to build on that relationship. Every meeting could turn into a resource down the line.

You also have to stay focused on your goals and determine what you are looking for in an investment partner. Don't undersell yourself. Many entrepreneurs believe that if they don't take this chance, it won't happen again, and that's absolutely incorrect. It's critically important to find "smart money," meaning a firm, fund or group that could be instrumental beyond just financing - teams that can share knowledge, expertise and even relationships.

Mike Townsend | www.homehero.org / www.flowtab.com

Most VCs I've met with are genuinely nice people, and are in the business of helping entrepreneurs grow their businesses. That said, there are multiple stages in a relationship with an investor where the deal can fall apart. Having experience and relationships with investors is ideal, but if that were the case, you wouldn't be reading this, so here are some tips.

First - Identify. Identify a list of (10-15) investors that have made investments in your industry who can bring value to your business.

Second - Connect. Check Linkedin, Angellist, Facebook, Twitter, etc to find someone you know personally who can help you get in touch. For first time entrepreneurs, this is the grind that will test your persistence and hustle, but it will pay off. Only send extremely short emails with a 3 sentence limit.

Third - Pitch. If they like your idea and accept a meeting, come prepared with your presentation deck and a demo of the product. Remember that you are the prize; make them feel lucky to invest in your company.

Arnon Rose | www.localmaven.com

I have been rejected by many VC's and investors over the course of my life. There are so many reasons why a VC might reject an investment in one's new business and many of them have nothing to do with the business idea or the entrepreneur. The investment size might not fit with their charter, the industry segment may not be one they invest in, they may be at the tail end of a fund, or they might just be having a bad day. I don't really let such rejections throw me off and there's always another investor or VC out there who may have the absolute opposite opinion of your business than the one who just rejected you.

Daniel Kahneman, a behavioral economist who I admire once said that a key trait of entrepreneurs is that they have delusional optimism. I would agree with that but don't ever lose that delusional optimism. As we were raising money for LocalMaven, I found that it gets much easier when you have a good chunk of your capital raise already locked down. I don't know if it's your own attitude that changes or people feel more comfortable getting behind ideas that others have backed but it's important to work towards those first few anchor investors and the rest comes much more easily. Just remember, your job as a founder is to build your business, show traction, and the rest will inevitably follow.

Edward DeSalle | www.netirrigate.com

We were rejected by a number of VCs. There are all kinds of reasons why a VC might reject a deal: management experience, industry expertise, competitive landscape, market size, etc. It's important to understand that VC funds are all different and might utilize different criteria for evaluating deals. There is no magic formula. One VC told us the market was too small and another told us the market was plenty big enough.

I think the most important thing to do when pitching to VCs is to understand what type of deals they typically do. For example, how big, what industry, are they looking for synergies with other portfolio companies? Use a rifle approach rather than a shotgun approach when choosing a venture partner. Also, learn to be succinct as most people in the VC community don't have a lot of free time. Try to figure out what's most important to the particular firm you might be pitching to and present those pieces of data about your company as succinctly as possible.

Jordan Eisenberg | www.urgentrx.com

I have been rejected by every type of investor out there – VC's, angels, PE investors, and beyond. The reasons are myriad: my pitch was bad, my projections too aggressive, they simply didn't get or buy into the business, didn't agree with my strategy, possibly just didn't like me - the list goes on. I have yet to meet a single entrepreneur who has successfully funded a business that hasn't been rejected by a potential investor. It is simply a reality that when you go out to pitch your idea not everyone will say yes. You need to have thick skin and not take it personally.

More people will pass than will invest, and it's more important to keep pushing forward than to lick your wounds. That said, I believe that there are always reasons why you were rejected – and I am a fan of asking a potential investor why they passed (in a very polite way). By removing your ego from the equation and truly being open to feedback, you have an incredible opportunity to get honest feedback on how you can improve your pitch, product, plan, etc. If you don't push too hard on attempting to change their mind, I think people are generally willing to share this feedback. Importantly, you can – and should - bake these nuggets of feedback into your future pitches and make it better by anticipating and addressing these questions / issues before the next potential investor brings them up.

Sam Tarantino | www.grooveshark.com

To say 'yes' would be an understatement. I joke with colleagues that I can't watch "Shark Tank" because I get PTSD after how many rejections I've gotten. Here I was, a 20-year old college dropout with a team of other 20-year old college dropouts based in Florida, a state not known for start-ups, and having no real business or start-up experience entering an industry where every start-up gets sued, shutdown, or forced to run out of money. I have a spreadsheet of VC meetings I've had over the years that is over 120 people. All it took was one 'yes', one influential believer to get us to the next 'yes' and so forth, until we got to where we are today. My main lesson out of that experience was you leave no stone unturned because you never know when the person who clears the path for you is right under the next stone you turn over.

Adi Bittan | www.ownerlistens.com

I've been rejected many many times. That's just part of the game. There are numerous reasons VCs can and will reject you and you can never really tell the exact reason why. They don't like you, they don't like the idea, they don't like that industry, and they don't think it's the right time. The list is endless. Rarely will you get the true answer out of VCs but it's worth asking. I learned a lot from reflecting on VC meetings and analyzing how I could do better.

There is a topic that comes up a lot when dealing with VC rejection but people are often afraid to talk about it. I don't mind saying outright that VCs are less likely to invest in entrepreneurs that don't fit a pattern they've seen work before. That pattern typically involves a white, male, engineer, Ivy League grad (if B2B can also be Indian or Asian). It's true that VCs are more likely to fund entrepreneurs that fit the pattern but that's not something to take personally. It's a VC's job to invest in what s/he thinks will get the highest returns and that assessment is naturally based on patterns. It's unfortunate but that's the current reality. As a more diverse set of people turn to entrepreneurship, there will be other patterns and entrepreneurs who don't fit the 'classic' pattern will become successful and pave the way for others like them. It just takes time and it's already starting. For example, fashion tech start-up founded by women can get funded as VCs note the success of great companies like Gilt Group and Rent the Runway.

I'm female and I'm not an engineer and my start-up is not in fashion tech / ecommerce, yet I got funding eventually. You can still get funded if you don't fit the pattern exactly; you just have to work harder to prove to VCs that you can be successful and make them successful.

Better than all of that, my best advice and something I wish I had done is work on an idea that has revenues from the get go. If you have growing revenues, VCs will follow, regardless of you fit with any pattern. Especially with first start-ups, I'd go with ideas that have revenues up front.

Philip Masiello | www.800razors.com

Yes, I've been rejected more times than I can count. The key is to find the VC group that is interested in the channel or industry you are working in and has experience that will be helpful to scaling the business. You want money as well as expertise.

Jason Schultz | www.jason.me
Forget about the word rejection and the negative feelings surrounding getting a VC deal. People so often treat a VC deal as the ultimate validation of their business or worse, themselves. Don't be that person. If you're business requires VC, then create a way of thinking about getting a "no" answer that empowers your or at least doesn't slow you down. In my opinion most start-ups who think they "need" VC really just need to figure out how to start smaller and grow more organically.

Joshua Dorkin | www.biggerpockets.com
To this day I've never formally pitched a VC for funding (we bootstrapped from day 1 and today fund growth through profits), but I've had meetings with high-profile VCs who flat out told me to stop doing what I was doing. Their belief was that there wasn't a market for our company, but they didn't have a good enough understanding of the marketplace themselves, I believe.

While I think that there are many fantastic VCs out there, do keep in mind that everyone has an opinion. Each VC has their own standard of what an investable company is, and if your company isn't in line, then there just won't be a match. I always encourage entrepreneurs to go on their own instead of taking outside money if they can. Not only do you have more control of your own destiny, but you won't suffer the same fate that many start-up CEOs do and lose your company when you don't multiply revenues 10x in short time.

Don't get me wrong, I'm not opposed to raising money, but I see many entrepreneurs take money with terrible terms for them because they are desperate and that never seems to pan out.

Julien Smith | www.breather.com
Everyone has been rejected by VCs. Absolutely everyone, no matter how cool or amazing your product is. People need to stop focusing on trying to sell to everyone, and start focusing on trying to find the right partner for the right deal.

Nellie Akalp | www.corpnet.com
I've never been rejected! In fact I have one every week knocking at my door, sending me emails, leaving me voicemails, interested in investing in my company and I normally delete them as it's not what I am interested in right now. So really the only nugget I can share is beware of VC's and only do it if you are ready as an entrepreneur to answer to a bunch of other people!

If you have ever undertaken a fund-raising process, then you have been rejected by a VC! During our Series B, we kept track of all of the funds we met with and how many meetings we had with each. We met with over 30. We had first meetings with all of them, probably second meetings with half of those, then third meetings with half of those, and so on. You hear this a lot while fund-raising: "*it's a numbers game*" and "*all it takes is one*". If you can find one VC who is really passionate about you and your business, you will (probably) have a successful fund-raise. Anything can happen however. It is a fragile process. We started our Series B in the summer of 2008. We were about to sign a term-sheet the day Lehman Bros. went out of business. Needless to say, we didn't that day and the VC bolted. Ultimately we stayed the course and closed the round 3 months later. The key take away: stay focused on closing the deal. Even if the building is on fire and about the collapse, stay focused on getting out the door. Don't worry about everything else around you.

Aditi Kapur | www.deliverychef.in

We have been rejected by several VCs before we actually raised a round of funding, and in the process, we learnt a lot. You should not raise money too early. Understand the market, understand the business and obtain some traction. Face challenges. Struggle. Bootstrap. Become tight on costs. That's when you'll know where you REALLY need to invest your money. How much you really need to invest for the results you want. Be fully ready to deploy the funds. Get your ground work done. E.g.: If your plan is to expand your geographical presence, identify the markets you want to go next to before approaching a VC. Be able to show why those markets, show how you will expand – so if it involves hiring someone, who will you hire, how will you reach the person, train them, what are you expecting out of them – all this needs to be thought through before approaching the VCs; not after the money has come into your account and their clocks for return are already ticking.

Mike Matousek | www.flashnotes.com

Like most start-ups, I have been rejected time and time again by VC firms. When I first started, I got great advice -- look at it as a free throw percentage, not a batting average.

You will get a lot of no's before a yes comes along. To find the right VC firm, all of the stars need to align -- the firm needs to have capital, be interested in your space, have the bandwidth to join another board, be actively writing checks, and love your idea and team. Do not take it personally if you get a no. Instead, let it fuel you.

After walking away from pitching a VC, you will know in your gut whether it's a fit or not. A VC will never tell you no, but instead drag things out. Instead of hearing *"no,"* you will hear things like, *"it's not a fit right now"* or *"we are not sure how this business will scale,"* etc. These are *"no's,"* and do not waste your time trying to convince them otherwise.

Rob Biederman | www.hourlynerd.com

We were rejected by dozens of VCs! It's critical (even if you have a good idea, with traction) to have a specific plan for how you'll spend the money and the team you need to realize your vision. In our early fund-raising we were insufficiently specific on how we'd grow demand in our marketplace, we weren't sure of future team needs, and hadn't gathered enough data to make a compelling case that we could plan for the future. Investors don't want to fund ideas, willy-nilly: they want to see that you have a concrete set of actions to get to the next level.

Ashok Subramanian | www.liazon.com

We were rejected by lots of VCs for lots of reasons. Some didn't believe in our product. Some didn't believe in the market. Some didn't even believe in me! In fact, the first VC who funded us actually cut their funding later on. The best advice I can give really applies to any aspect of entrepreneurship – don't give up.

Jake Sigal | www.livioconnect.com

So many investors rejected me that I can't even think about what the total number is. They rejected me for all sorts of reasons. There are way too many to list or even try to count. It's easy to find a reason no to invest in a business. My advice is to bootstrap your business, and use crowd-sourcing and other grants available for start-ups to get going. Pitching VCs is a big waste of time. Don't do it. When you have a real product with customers, they will find you. Trust me.

Myke Nahorniak | www.localist.com

Back when we were still a destination site, we knew we had to acquire venture capital to scale Localist to a point of sustainability by launching in over one hundred cities.

Ultimately, VCs want to see a direct path to their return on investment in as short a window as possible. The more believable it is the better. In our case, as a destination site, we were a big unknown with a questionable event horizon on being acquired, going public, etc.

Before going into any VC (or angel) meeting, make sure you know the answer to: *"what's in it for them?"* Many entrepreneurs look at investors as banks that they have to beg for money, or as accountants who are lucky to be at your table. In reality, they're partners. You have to prove you understand their perspective before they'll be willing to understand yours.

Rob Infantino | www.openbay.com

Each VC has its own lingo on how they communicate that they're not interested in your deal. I call it "*VC Speak.*" The challenge becomes is how to correctly decipher their language so you don't set false expectations for yourself. Some examples are, "*We are very interested, we'll get back to you,*" "*Reach back out to us when you find a lead investor,*" "*We are in the middle of wrapping up a new deal and need some time to think about your deal,*" "*Call me next week to discuss next steps,*" etc. VCs or investors typically don't want to deliver a flat "No" to an entrepreneur, because in the event you gain traction with other VCs they can always pull themselves back into the deal.

Aaron Skonnard | www.pluralsight.com

Fortunately, we had the opposite experience — we actually rejected VCs for nearly a decade. My co-founders and I decided that we would only take private investment if we had a very specific purpose for it. We built the company organically for nearly a decade to prove the model and put ourselves in the position to grow exponentially via acquisitions. When we finally decided to take a Series A in 2012 to stoke our growth plans, we had the luxury of choosing between several VC partners and select the right one for us instead of being relegated to partnering with whichever group would agree to spend money on us.

Jeb Blount | www.salesgravy.com

I never sought VC money or outside investment. Early on I had enough cash to fund the start-up. I ran lean and focused on the fundamentals that would make us profitable. It took a little more than two years to get profitable and we've continued to run lean and invest back into the business since then. We have had a couple of VCs contact us but we've kept them at arm's length because we like having control of our own destiny. There is no doubt that with VC money might have grown faster and been more formidable. Sometimes I think that an infusion of cash would help us build a much stronger brand. On the other hand we have to answer to no one about the decisions we make and that is often a blessing that allows us to take calculated risk.

Julie Busha | www.slawsa.com

My rejection happened on national television! To be honest, I am fortunate that I received nothing but compliments from the investors on ABC's "*Shark Tank*," which is rare, and their comments supported the fact that I am indeed on the right path.

I think it is important for business owners to realize that the best investors or partners will want to bring something of value to the table beyond financial support. They should bring value of equal proportion to their ownership, otherwise it becomes a partnership that does not work or lined with disdain. Perhaps the Sharks I presented to didn't understand my industry well or didn't feel they could bring that additional value they ethically would feel obligated to. I respect that. Also, a one-hour pitch made for television isn't realistic with what would occur in a meeting with an investor. Bottom line: Never let someone else's inability to see your value determine your worth. My deal with the Sharks was never meant to be but perhaps that was for the best.

Zeb Couch | www.offmarketformula.com / www.speedhatch.com

It's always been important for us to retain complete control over our own destinies and the destiny of our company. We've bootstrapped from the beginning and continue to be. If you're considering VC money, make sure you have a trusted advisor with experience raising money from VCs. Also read *"Venture Deals"* by Brad Feld. Remember that VCs look for huge scale. They may invest in 10 or so companies in a year, with the hopes that 1 of them will be worth tens or hundreds of millions. Not all business fit that mold, and that's okay.

Justyn Howard | www.sproutsocial.com

When we were getting started, not everyone was convinced we were on to anything significant. Twitter itself had less than 30 employees when we started and Facebook wasn't used commercially the way it is today, so it wasn't clear what the commercial utility of social would be long-term. The best opportunities won't make sense to everyone; if they did you'd be too late. For early stage start-ups, the key is to work with investors who light up the first time you pitch the idea and see the world through a similar lens.

Greg Tseng | www.tagged.com

We have been rejected by dozens of VCs, the vast majority of VCs we've ever met with. It's hard to get an offer from a VC firm because all their partners have to unanimously support you. There are tons of reasons a partner does not vote *"yes,"* which could include: didn't feel personal chemistry with you, other concerns about you or your team, not interested in your product or market, already invested in a competing company, differences in the valuation assigned to your company, or just don't understand your company. That's fine because you're looking for a partner for the next 5+ years so it has to be a situation where you are both excited about starting a multi-year relationship together. Tagged's relationship with our VC firm, Mayfield, is a perfect example of this type of long-term, two-way partnership.

Danny Maloney | www.tailwindapp.com

Thankfully, we were rejected by every VC we spoke to for our first product, BridesView. Some gave idiotic reasons, e.g. *"you can't build a meaningful tech company outside of the Valley,"* which are being disproven by thousands of companies every day. Others had valid concerns. The most common was that in a market with the same number of customers every year and high turnover, we hadn't proven we could monetize our users deeply. We listened, tried to monetize and failed. In failing, we stumbled on a better business altogether. VC rejection saved us years of time we'd never get back.

Joel Simkhai | www.grindr.com

We've been approached by many VCs and angels but it never made sense for us to take their capital. I'm fortunate that Grindr has remained self-funded by offering both a free ad-supported app and a subscription based app early on. This has given me the autonomy to run my own company and not have to answer to VCs or other outside investors. If you can avoid raising outside capital – do it.

Raj Sheth | www.recruiterbox.com

We never did pursue funding; however, we applied to Y-Combinator in 2011 and received an invitation for the in-person interviews (Round 2). We were finally rejected because they didn't see us leaping into a large company. In hindsight, I understand why they would say that. There are different players in our market and we were not a net new concept like some consumer businesses are. Plus, they had to pick 60 out of a shortlist of 200 (we made it to 200 out of 3000), so it's pretty much a gamble. We learned more about our business and moved on with our execution.

Eren Bali | www.udemy.com

When my co-founder, Oktay Caglar, and I first set out to raise money, the online education space wasn't as super-hot as it is today. Over 50 investors initially rejected us, but that didn't stop us from launching the platform in May 2010. By July, we had over 2,000 courses and 10,000 registered users on Udemy.

Less than a year after we faced universal rejection, we raised a $1 million seed round, led by influential investors, including Yelp CEO Jeremy Stoppelman and Square COO Keith Rabois. That was a turning point for us. We were able to go full time with Udemy.

I think investors were initially hesitant to offer us funding because the education space wasn't popular. Many had a hard time believing that there was a market of people who would pay for online courses; few companies were successful. Another factor that contributed to our initial rejection was the fact that we didn't have enough traction to validate the business. To get traction we worked really hard on bringing additional 10,000-15,000 users onto the platform.

It also helps to have a lead investor that other folks will look to for validation. When we brought Keith Rabois on board, we were able to use his reputation in the industry to convince other investors about our idea.

Josh Rosenwald | www.unroll.me

Of course - well not flat out. Venture capitalists never give you a straight "*no.*" They're the ultimate teasers. Talking to VCs is a phenomenon like no other. Unless you have a vast amount of experience, it's so hard to tell what they're thinking. VCs never want to miss out on "*the next big thing.*" But it's so hard to tell what that thing actually is so they string you along forever while they try and figure it out. Like with everything else in a start-up, speaking with and pitching to VCs is a learning process. The more you do it, the better you get at it.

Scott Perkins & Shawn Boday | www.vube.com

Coincidentally, we have had a bigger problem turning the VC's down and convincing them we don't need their money. We have even had a founder of a VC company fly across the country and show up in our office uninvited due to his interest in Vube. Getting money from a VC is like getting a loan from a bank. When you don't need their money, they want to give it to you. However, when you really need the cash, they see it as a risk and aren't nearly as interested.

Jason Cohen | www.wpengine.com

Every single person who has tried to raise money has been rejected by a VC. Including companies like Google, Amazon, Facebook, and Apple. So being rejected by a VC doesn't mean anything. I've raised millions of dollars from VCs, but I've been rejected dozens of times.

The main thing you need to consider before approaching a VC is whether you want to build a billion-dollar company, and whether it's plausible that your product and your marketing could become such a company. If not, VCs are not interested. That's not because VCs are dumb, but because they're their business model.

Morris Miller | www.xenex.com & www.rackspace.com

Absolutely we were turned down by VCs. Every VC firm is different – different management styles, different investment strategies, different areas of focus. It's important to understand their differentiator just like you understand your company's. They may be a great VC firm, but feel that your industry isn't right for them or not agree with your growth strategy. Getting turned down is never fun or easy, but it's going to happen. What's important is how you handle that rejection and turn it into a positive.

Hill Ferguson | www.zong.com (Chief Product Officer, Paypal)

We've been rejected several times. In one company's case, the business simply didn't support the time of "*risk vs reward*" equation. Remember, VCs are always looking for home-runs, not singles and doubles. You need to know what type of company you're building and match the investor profile accordingly.

In my case, this company was more suitable for debt financing than venture capital. Other VC rejections came because I didn't do enough homework on the VC to understand what types of investments they were looking for. Every VC has a "*sweet spot*" for what they like to bet on and they're usually not shy about telling the public about it. Do your homework and try to find a pattern of investments that best resemble what you're trying to build and then chase hard after them.

Mark McClain | www.sailpoint.com

I didn't experience VC rejection, but I've certainly known a lot of folks who did. Many people are rejected because they simply haven't thought through the real market need they're addressing and how they can uniquely solve it. In the tech field, entrepreneurs often get enamored with new technology, and forget to focus on addressing a real need.

Eric Schiffer | www.digitalmarketing.com

No, I have not been rejected by a VC. I have always understood that whenever you're going to raise money, you should always do your homework and research the VC firm's investments. Many, who do fund-raising, don't. You can determine their criteria by just looking at the deals they have rejected and accepted. Do an analysis of what products and services they have invested in. Look at the kind of management they like to invest in. Match that up against your core product and leadership team.

Once you've done this, the decision to go after that VC should be much easier. It isn't a numbers game, it's a focus and target game. You should look at yourself and ask: Have you thought through your market? Have you launched your service/product? Is it just concept at the moment? A VC wants to see you're in the game and already making money. The more traction you have, the better a VC views you. VCs shows less fear about investing when you offer them better odds of future success. Lowering their fears raises their greed to invest in you.

If you haven't been rejected by a VC you haven't met with enough of them. You get rejected a lot many times. It's a numbers game for you and for the VC.

For VCs it's tough. They see dozens of smart people every month with dozens of good ideas that they're really passionate about and the VCs are only able to make a few bets per year.

The most important tip about raising money is you have to be really disciplined about the process. If you aren't, and you just go out and try to get anyone to seed fund you, you'll find that it's very hard to get the first bid. You must condense the period of time that you provide information. Provide all the same info to all of the VCs who are good for you, your stage of business, and target market. Pick a day where you're asking all of them to put in a terms sheet at the same time. That way there's a process that drives that very first investment.

It's important to know that what's in one VC's wheelhouse is not in another's. What's interesting is the reason a VC rejects you is often not as straightforward as you think. Sometimes your business will be doing incredibly well and your expectations are very high and you'll be rejected from a VC because they think you're aiming too high. Other times, you're too early or your business is too much of a contrarian idea. That's why I say if you can't sell yourself and market your ideas, you're out of luck.

A huge piece of raising rounds is personal fit. If the VC doesn't like you, that can be another reason for a "no." If you are able to land an investor you have to live with them for years. It's best if there is a fit for both parties, especially there are going to be hard conversations and you want to make sure you can communicate when things are tough, which is most of the time in an early stage company.

Given that rejections from venture capitalists are so common, is their funding so important? Is there any other way to solve the funding problem than approach the VCs? Here are the responses I received from the entrepreneurs I talked to.

Rick Martinez | www.senorsangria.com

We haven't yet taking funding. Part of the reason we haven't done so is that VC's would take our business in a different direction. I feel we are still teaching who our consumers or and what the strength of the brand would be. Also we are taking a slow and steady approach in the sense of building a market strong before adding more markets. I didn't feel like a VC would care. They would want a return on their money ASAP.

I'm not saying my route was the right way of doing it. I've just been lucky. I feel like we've created our own luck along the way by the success we've had. Though I think our success does come because of the DEEP focus we have within our existing markets. If you are truly dedicated to your cause and have the ability to sacrifice to build your business I would do so. Our sacrifice is that I'm making MUCH less now than I did when I had a real job. For the past 8 years I've made 30%-50% of what I made in my prior job. Our life style has totally changed, we live paycheck to paycheck.

This approach is not for everyone. But it's my personality. People have hobbies. My hobby is my business. If you are not willing to sacrifice for a long period of time; not one year but multiple years, and truly adjust your lifestyle then you aren't ready to be an entrepreneur yet in my opinion.

Chris Thierry | www.etelesolv.com

I never took VC money in the traditional sense. My funding and mentorship came from my former employer. I got my start like a lot of people, not aspiring to be an entrepreneur per say, but almost falling into it. I got a job straight out of university working for a privately owned, medium sized company building and managing their entry into e-commerce. I was young, highly motivated, and was not afraid of a little hard work. I worked directly under the owner who was a well-known entrepreneur and who had started a few businesses. It was 1999, and the internet boom was in full swing so the opportunity to sell web solutions to a growing market seemed to be an easy thing for us, beyond just doing e-commerce for his company.

Like a lot of internet ideas, we wrote up a business plan hoping to land funding. When the internet bubble burst, the funding didn't happen. I then proceeded to go through my AFM years, my Anything For Money years. These years taught me how to hustle, how to make payroll, and how to be responsible for a business.

Later as the business became profitable and I wanted to grow faster, the VCs came looking for me. While I take the calls, as you never know the future, my advice to budding entrepreneurs is to find your mentor first. In my case, my mentor was an angel investor, and had a large network of other entrepreneurs; many are now in my own network of friends.

Alex Brola | www.checkmaid.com

We planned on raising VC once we had 1m+ in sales. Once we beat that mark, we upped the amount again. The plan was to have as much leverage as possible when we finally approached investors. A few did end up approaching us, but so far nothing has been decided.

Mike Matousek | www.flashnotes.com

VC money is not essential, but it will help accelerate the growth of your business and can be important if you want to build a huge business. You will get to where you want faster, however funding does not come without risks. If you do not meet the expected growth, they will replace you with someone who can.

If I did not receive VC funding, I would have needed to focus much more on the unit economics from day one --- to make sure that for every dollar out, I brought a dollar plus in.

Matt Barrie | www.freelancer.com

We bootstrapped the business from the beginning except when we raised a very small amount of money to allow us to buy GetAFreelancer in 2009. I believe by following this route and leading up to our IPO on the Australian Securities Exchange last November (2013), we were able to remain masters of our own destiny and keep the direction of the company following the company mission to give 1 billion people on this planet a job through Freelancer.com.

Raghu Kulkarni | www.idrive.com

We could have taken VC funding at some point in late 90s or early 2000, but that would have been at a huge cost of giving up significant piece of ownership. While it may have been best for companies in other segments, for online backup, it probably was the best decision because most companies who did take funding, did not last long. However, this situation was not the same around 2006 onwards where many successful startups succeeded in the space with VC funding.

Jake Sigal | www.livioconnect.com

It all depends on your industry. It's not about the VC funding; it's about the cash it takes to hire the best people to work on the problem you want to solve. If you make hardware, there's also this thing called working capital you need to buy inventory. Our VC partners were great at Livio, and I'd recommend doing business with them again. However if you can avoid taking other people's money, you will be a lot happier, with more free time.

I sold my lawn business and went to live with my brother to work-off the $2000 he so graciously let me borrow. I saved up about $3000, paid off a 6 month lease (in Waco, TX) to collect my thoughts. I sold my big shiny red truck so I could buy a computer and a Geo Metro (55mgp or so). I worked my way back up to about $2000 in savings and figured out how to get $4000 in available credit (credit cards). I also cut my expenses as much as possible by finding the cheapest rent I could ($365/mo all bills paid). I was in business for 6 months before making my first sale. By this time I was down to $11 or so and all my credit cards were maxed out.

Mark McClain | www.sailpoint.com

VC funding is less important than it used to be, primarily because it's so much more cost-effective to start businesses now (outsourcing, cloud technology, work for hire, etc.). However, for some types of businesses, it's still a great alternative, because it provides "*jet fuel*" that helps you grow fast enough to keep pace with much larger competitors, which is pretty important in the B-to-B market.

Blaine Vess | www.studymode.com

VC funding can be a great source of capital – and if you have a business model that requires a high level of upfront investment or a big cash flow, you pretty much can't avoid taking VC dollars. The problem with taking on investors is that you then have to serve your masters. That is, you have to meet their specific expectations. Not only does this create a lot of pressure on you as you launch your business, but it also means you lose some degree of creative control. And after all, you become an entrepreneur because you want to run the show, right? With StudyMode, I had a business model that scaled well without a large capital infusion. So I opted to retain complete creative control and remain self-funded.

Peter Mann | www.oransi.com

I have always gone to banks for funding. The SBA loan program while still somewhat cumbersome has improved and now that SBA backed loans are available through banks the funding for small businesses has increased greatly. If you have a business bank loan you cannot get an SBA loan so the trick is to secure an SBA backed loan first and then if you need additional funds in the future the bank can write a separate loan or line of credit.

Chapter 22 : Start-up Failure – How Do You Recover?

Start-ups can fail due to a number of reasons and not all of them are due to your mistakes. Before founding Bill The Butcher, J'Amy Owens owned a video rental store. She could not have been more optimistic about her business at that point in time – there was demand and the consumption of video rentals was growing. Nothing could have possibly gone wrong. But just six months later, the first Blockbuster store opened in the neighborhood. Owens failed and with it, she ended up with close to $100K worth of debt. It took a lot of time for her to repay the debts.

I asked entrepreneurs who have had failures in the past to talk about these businesses. Why did they fail? How does one typically recover from the debts? Let us start with the story from Chris Grant who owns the Grant Farms.

Chris Grant | www.grantfamilyfarm.com

When I was 20 years old, my greenhouse business had taken its toll on me. I hit a wall, and couldn't fight the fact that I no longer enjoyed the business anymore. I tried to light my spark again and again by shifting the focus of the business, but in the end, the risk and work was not entirely worth the reward. I chose to end the greenhouse business, and move back to my true passion, vegetable and egg production. The wholesale greenhouse business was no more, but without missing a beat, I rolled the business into what it is today.

From Grant's Plants to Grant Family Farm. Changing the identity of the business, scope, and focus took a lot of energy. It took a lot of cooperation with the family and all involved to make the switch after the greenhouse business failed. I thought that if I failed, everyone would see me walking away from this train wreck like some epic scene in a movie. But at the end of the day, the biggest critic of my failure was me. I was the only one thinking that I had failed. At the age of 21, I formed Grant Family Farm, and my first business was the best business class I could have ever taken. I went to college for agriculture and focused in business, but the best lessons were the ones that cost me time and more importantly money.

Bryan Knowlton | www.appraiseallrealestate.com

I have failed at start-ups in the past and always had an exit strategy in place prior to the time of exit. If I was unable to meet income goals, I always had another business and enough in savings that allowed me to continue to bring in an income. At this time I have 2 primary companies, both require about 10 hours of week. The rest of my time is consumed in production of a podcast called the Daily Blogcast for Internet Marketing where my podcasting partner and I discuss internet marketing related blog posts and do interview with industry experts. This is a recent start-up that was founded in November of 2013 and we are nearing 100 episodes.

Although it is consistently in the top 20 internet marketing podcasts on iTunes, the company has yet to produce a profit. We only have 2 and a half more months until that plug might need to be pulled. You have to set the time-line for success, and when it does not come, you have to have that date set to move on. Although some might term it a failure if we close down the show, there were invaluable lessons learned throughout the process that have helped my other businesses and will definitely springboard the next start-up that is on the project board.

Philip Masiello | www.800razors.com

I started my first business when I was 23 years old and I thought I knew everything. After about 4 years, the value of the business was no greater than when I began and I did not have a concept or a brand. I decided to shut it down, sell off the assets and take whatever I could get out of it and go back to school. Luckily I was debt free, but I used the asset sale proceeds to pay for my MBA and moved on from there.

Nellie Akalp | www.corpnet.com

I have failed many times, I am not done failing, but not I am not done succeeding either. Each of my past failures has lent themselves to each of my successes. You must fail at one point in your life before you can truly be successful. I would not be the driven, passionate, focused small business owner and entrepreneur that I am today if I did not fear failure. Fear of failure drives me to work and push harder for myself, for my kids and as a leader for my company.

Micha Kaufman | www.fiverr.com

One of my previous start-ups reached the point of running out of funding. In hindsight we had plenty of opportunities to raise additional capital to ensure that the company would sustain its livelihood. Instead we elected to continue experimenting while staying very lean, thinking that when we'd run out of money we would raise more.

The reality was that when we ran out of money, it became very hard to raise additional funding and the company was forced to close its doors. Not all failures are big. A typical day of an entrepreneur is made out of a lot of small decisions. Inevitably a lot of them are going to turn out to be wrong.

At Fiverr we encourage people to take risks, knowing that some of them will fail. Having this culture empowers team members to embrace their mistakes and grow from their learning experience. The only thing that we ask in return is that people will not make the same mistake twice.

Mike Townsend | www.homehero.org / www.flowtab.com

Flowtab was not successful, but it gave Kyle and I the tools to build something much bigger. Each project you work on deserved your full 100% dedication, but when you don't find product market fit, leverage your experience and level up to the next thing. At Flowtab, we were lucky enough to convince Mike Jones (CEO of Science-Inc) to be our advisor. He saw our progression and offered to invest in Kyle and I with HomeHero.

Arnon Rose | www.localmaven.com

I have been fortunate to not have a failure yet, but I am not so naïve as to think this is as a result of pure brilliance on my part. There is a lot to timing and luck and perhaps I have had both a little luck and good timing. That said, there were many times in each and every one of my businesses where I thought "*this is it, we are not going to be able to pull it off. We can't make payroll and the gig is up*". Each time this happened, I put my head down and re-doubled my efforts. Ironically, as I look back, I now realize that it's often darkest right before a big breakout is about to occur. I'm not sure why that is, but I would always recommend that an entrepreneur not give up until they absolutely have to. I used to say at one of my prior companies that we "*take it to the mat – every time*" and that we never give up. That is something that has to be part of every start-ups culture and DNA. Besides, if you have outside investor monies, you owe it to them to fight to the last man.

Adi Bittan | www.ownerlistens.com

My first start-up failed after our investor pulled the plug. It was for reasons unrelated to us but it still made it impossible to raise money and recapitalize the company. Even though we were able to salvage some of it and it wasn't a total waste, it was nowhere close to where we envisioned it going. It felt terrible! Thousands of hours of work and hope all go up in smoke. We recovered one step at a time. It's sad but it's not a tragedy. No one died or was harmed. It's important to keep things in perspective. I still had my education, my reputation, the lessons I'd learned. Not all was lost. I was very deliberate about not dwelling on it. Packed everything up and started to think about next steps.

I went back to do some consulting just to get more income through the door. The ecosystem around me did not have any trouble considering me for jobs and in fact people in my network reached out to see if I wanted to join them whether big companies or start-ups. I don't think there's a stigma anymore. In fact I think companies are fine with entrepreneurs coming in for 2-3 years, breathing fresh life into an older company, spreading new practices and thinking and then leaving. Not everyone has to be a lifer. For me, it was clear I really loved entrepreneurship so I started looking for the next idea a few days later.

Michael Kawula | www.selfemployedking.com

Failure only occurs in entrepreneurship when you don't get back up from getting punched in the face. Entrepreneurship, like life, has rounds you win and rounds you get your butt kicked. You have to learn to be comfortable with being uncomfortable for success. You're guaranteed to have set-backs, failure though is a choice.

I've had plenty of set-backs but fortunately I've always validated my businesses beforehand that I was fully prepared and able to avoid disasters. Once I bought a shipment of mops from China and did so well selling them online that I bought a container full of them. They arrived in the USA and 2 days later I got a cease order from "*As Seen On TV*" because the company that sold the mops to us didn't have the rights. Luckily my network helped me think it through and we stripped the mops apart and sold parts making even more. Be comfortable with being uncomfortable as an entrepreneur.

My 2 rules in life that I have made on a T-Shirt:
#1 Don't Quit
#2 Remember Rule #1

Jason Richelson | www.shopkeep.com

I was one of the founders of Internet Cash back in 1999. That company went out of business, but I took a job right away with one of the inventors before I started my first wine store. I've seen tech start-ups grow fast and then go out of business, and it is not a pretty picture. If it does happen you have to recover quickly. Get another job, no matter what it is; to take you mind off it and move on.

Zeb Couch | www.offmarketformula.com / www.speedhatch.com

"*Failure*" is difficult for me to define. Have I been a part of ventures having made little or no money? Yes. They may have "*failed*" financially but the contacts I made and concepts I learned prepared me that much more for the next venture. Every time the probability of success increases, while more and more risk is mitigated.

I was trying to grow a consulting business for real estate investors called DealFlow that completely failed financially. I couldn't get anyone to buy anything. I took what didn't work with that business, learned from it, and launched OffMarketFormula.com which generated revenue within its first month of launch.

Greg Tseng | www.tagged.com

I have failed at start-ups earlier. A good example is Limespot where we raised $100,000 as a group of college students during the dot-com boom and burned through all of it without much to show for it. I was never set back with debt and no job, but I will say that a lot, and perhaps most, of what you learning comes from failures, not successes, and that makes failing worthwhile even though it's tough.

Scott Perkins & Shawn Boday | www.vube.com

No, we have never failed. You fail when you don't try. We've had ideas that didn't pan out, but we tried them and learned from them. Regardless of how good your ideas are, every great product will have challenges. It is your ability to overcome those challenges that will enable you to compete and sustain your business. If you decide to start a company you have to believe in it 110%.

Almost all the entrepreneurs above have quit failed start-ups to only start another company. But as an aspiring entrepreneur, one might be curious about the job prospects after a failed venture. For this, I specifically talked to two entrepreneurs who failed in their respective ventures and had to seek another job. I have produced an excerpt from my interview with them below. The first is from Andy Hart and the second interview is from Robin Ian Turner.

What did you do in your start-up?

Andy : My start-up was a clothing line. I started in 2008. I fully funded, and ran everything myself. Eventually I hired a Public Relations Person to handle the events and twitter and Facebook and such things. Things didn't really go the way I had hoped and eventually I was back to doing everything myself again. I'm a very indecisive person and things like t shirt materials and what designs to print got overwhelming as no one I would show my work to wanted to give me feedback. So I had a few successful runs with printed shirts. Friends and family wanted to support me and they bought them. I still feel like things would be successful having a team of likeminded people to push it like I wanted to. It's my dying dream these days.

What are some reasons you think your business failed?

Andy : When I look back I think some of the reasons that I failed were partially due to my indecisiveness along with not having a team to help me push things. But I guess I can't chalk it up to other people, because I started the business, and I ultimately failed.

How difficult is it to find a job? Are employers open to employ ex-entrepreneurs well knowing that you are prone to quitting and

going back on your own?

Andy : My field is graphic design. I have been trying to find a job in my field for over a year. Employers love my portfolio but when they find out I ran my own business they seem to run the other direction. I don't know if it's because they think I will start another business and leave the company right away. Sometimes I almost think it's better to not tell them I owned a business.

When you put money and time into your start-up, were you ready for a possible failure? What was your backup plan?

Andy : I guess when I think about it I was ready to fail. But I wanted to succeed so badly. I thought the drive and the passion I had would have been enough. But that's what young, naive me had thought. As far as finances go, I was lucky enough to have a "*business*" that provided me with enough income that I didn't have to think twice about dumping money into this clothing line. The bills were paid, and the problems were nonexistent in my life at that time. So I did whatever I wanted. And I lost about 40k trying to make my dream a reality.

And here is a snapshot from my interview with Robin Ian Turner who ran a company called Keyzi.

What did you do in your start-up?

Robin : I've spent the past few years (on and off) working in property development in the UK - basically buying houses for a low price, renovating them completely and selling them on/renting them out. In late spring/early summer 2013 I was looking for a new property to begin work on but was getting frustrated with having to trawl through lists of old and neglected properties that just weren't appealing to me (mostly old, ex-council properties in less desirable areas). I was looking for properties with a bit of character (as I always do). I found it annoying that I had to continually set my criteria (price, bedrooms, bathrooms, area etc) into the same search fields. That's when I came up with the idea for *'Keyzi'*. A property search website that will learn what it is you're looking for and then begin to recommend properties based on your ratings of other results - a sort of Netflix for the property sector.

So I bought a new notebook and began work. I developed the basic premise, the functionality the site should have, did market research, created some mockups and then set out to find somebody who could help me get the thing off the ground (seeing as I have *very* limited coding knowledge). I put a few adverts online and received a few responses, spoke to a few candidates via email, explained the project further and got somebody on board! I went out, bought the domain name, and analyzed the different servers that could be used and all that other technical business whilst my tech guy got to work on the code for the prototype. Together we discussed how to make the best prototype but still leave plenty of room for growth. We finished a prototype and that's where it all ended. I felt I had spent so much time and effort from my initial idea to the prototype that it would be a pain to start the process all over again.

What are some reasons you think your business failed?

Robin : To be completely honest, I feel that the reason the project failed was down to me. The guy who had developed the prototype just wasn't creating what I saw 'Keyzi' to be. This could be because I wasn't clear (even though I think I was seeing as other potential candidates got the idea pretty easily), or it could be that I didn't really test out my techies coding ability - but what could I test him on?! I don't know a thing about coding. I decided to use this guy because he had agreed to everything I had asked of him and I found it easy to persuade him to do things (not in a manipulative way, but in a way to make *my* vision a reality). So I think that's where I fell short - I picked a person who was able to do what I wanted, not what was best for the business.

How difficult is it to find a job? Are employers open to employ ex-entrepreneurs well knowing that you are prone to quitting and going back on your own?

Robin : Finding a job is somewhat difficult at the moment and it's has consistently been down to one of one of 3 different reasons:

1. Employers seem to think that I have a huge load of *'know-how'* when it comes to running a business. Even when I tell them things didn't progress with *'Keyzi'* they assume that because I had researched the property market and other competitors I must have used all different programs and systems to evaluate data or that I know the ins and outs of a sales pitch. I really don't!

2. They don't want to hire me because I don't have *enough* experience in a *'reputable'* business/office environment. Even when I'm applying to internships in other start-ups they always have an interest in my past with 'Keyzi' but don't think there's enough there to warrant a term of employment.

3. More recently I have been turned down from jobs because after reviewing my CV/resume I am viewed as "*too ambitious*". Just two weeks ago I was told that I was unlikely to get a job because the manager thought I would learn everything I could about their business quickly and then go off and do my own thing. In some ways this is quite flattering but at the same time it's a pain to be rejected from a job because they are happy with '*average*' salespeople.

When you put money and time into your start-up, were you ready for a failure? What was your backup plan?
Robin : Luckily, my family were supportive in me trying something for myself. I had also saved a bit of money from my previous job and had money to come in from a property I had developed. I was open to failure. I had read the statistics about how x amount of businesses don't get off the ground and I was willing to accept that. Failure didn't scare me. I knew that I could always go back and make a bit of money in property development, or maybe some other part of the property industry, even though I wasn't passionate about it at that moment in time.

But the problem for me was this: even though I wasn't afraid of failing, when I eventually did '*fail*' and couldn't get a job, it hit me *really* hard. I'm not one to beat myself up over mistakes. I know that I would rather give something a try than to just go through life knowing I didn't try. But to have to stop doing something you are passionate about (even if it is just for the time being) and then to be shot down from working for all sorts of reasons, it really takes its toll on you mentally. To be told that all your positive attributes (ambition, drive, innovative, creative and so on) were not enough to outweigh your negative ones (a lack of formal work in an office environment) really delivers quite a blow. I was not prepared for that. A*t all*.

Chapter 23 : Risk Taking For Starting Up

Entrepreneurship is regarded a pretty risky alternative to a regular 9-5 job. Despite the inherent risks, so many smart people have ventured into starting their own businesses. Do these entrepreneurs understand the risks involved? What was their back-up plan and how did they convince their family about it?

Interestingly, despite what media makes you think about entrepreneurship, most founders I talked to were pretty risk-averse people themselves. They seemed to have their finances and career plans under control while starting up. Take the example of Lawson Nickol from the All American Clothing. He started small and worked two jobs for some time to ensure he had enough capital to get through the first year in business. Lawson tells me that working two jobs not only helped him with income but would have also served as his back-up plan, had his start-up failed.

Michael Folkes | www.mafolkes.com

Within my hardship as a child, I learned from my grandparents the value of hard work and that it could pay off. America is still the land of opportunity and all I ever wanted was for someone to believe in me and give me a chance. I had decided a long time ago. I would never live my life thinking I should have, I could have or I would have. My mind was made up there was no room to conceive risk or failure. It was never an option! However, there are risks in everything that we do, as we go through life each day. Still for me if you plan properly, execute your plan, follow through, not follow up, confirm, and hold yourself and others accountable it's difficult to fail.

I did try the 9-to-5 job. In fact I worked not one, not two but up to three jobs for almost 2 years. I have worked as little as 40 hours per week to as many as 108 hours per week. However after many success and failures, I now call them opportunities. I realize I could start my own company because I was smarter than most of the people I was working under such as my bosses, even though they had college degrees.(I risked everything) I sold everything I had and put it all into starting my own company. I also moved away from the state I lived in for many years, starting anew in a different state that I was not familiar with and had no ties.

I did not have a backup plan. I told myself I'm living in America. I'm young and strong and I have my whole life ahead of me. I can start all over and rebuild myself if I didn't succeed. I guess you could say that was my backup plan. Still I believed in myself and set out to achieving my goals.

Convincing the family about the risks depend on the individual and their current circumstances. My circumstances were different, I came to America to make it and nothing or no one was going to prevent that from happening. However, there is an old cliché I think it goes like this 'no money no honey'. I look at life this way, financial stability is important in many ways for family, as well as community. So I think it's very important to choose a partner that is like minded and is there to support you. You in turn must support your partner as well, through the good times and bad times.

Monique Tatum | www.beautifulplanning.com

In the beginning I started my company as a freelancer on the side of my regular 9-5 job as the Director of PR, Sales and Marketing for an accounting software company. I honestly did not have any idea that 10 years later I would be running a full-fledged PR firm. I did not jump ship from my regular 9-5 until I was thoroughly exhausted and realized that I was going home at 5 and then working from about 7pm to 4am. I literally had two jobs and it was due to the fact that my clients were happy with my work and requested more, and they also referred me out. I would spend hours working because I actually loved what I was doing and didn't want to put it down. I wanted to give them my all.

When I did finally jump ship from my 9-5 job, I was terrified. What if my clients suddenly fell off? How would I pay my rent? I figured it was more of a risk to be unhappy and that if all failed I could go back to a 9-5 and explain that I had taken some time off to try to jump-start a business. My family was supportive, however I remember my mom being a bit nervous for me. She wanted me to remain in the security of a corporate position. After all, I was a young woman that had moved up to my earned position quickly. I took the time to explain to her why I was making my decision and pushed forward with my dream. My start-up costs were relatively low because I started up out of a room in my home and remained there for 2 years. I could fit 3 desks in this room and I hired one part time person and a weekly accountant to come in and we were off and running.

Patrick DeAmorim | www.decate.no

There was no risk in funding, but I had a child and was living with my girlfriend, so there was a LOT of talk about how I'm lazy, irresponsible, how I should "be a man, and just get a job", how I was basically useless as a father, this came from relatives, "friends" and people who knew about us. My parents wanted me to go to school, stop the business nonsense, go to school, and get a job.

Was it easy putting up with all of that? No. There were a lot of fights, tons of arguments; it caused a LOT of stress between me and my girlfriend. So I never convinced anyone, I just did it. And I suppose when it got to the point where I, as a 22 year old was making almost 2 times (almost 3x at one point) as much as any of the people who called me lazy, irresponsible - it made them realize that I was onto something after all.

Chris Grant | www.grantfamilyfarm.com

When I first started, I was only 16 years old. So to finance the business, there were not venture capitalists chasing down my school bus. I used the duct tape and bubblegum budget to get the infrastructure off the ground. To start our farm, I began buying used equipment, fixing old equipment, and borrowing it from other farmers. I took small risks in stride. As each expense came about, we had to calculate where the funds would come from. Primarily, the money came from my own savings, on top of working another job, and going to school.

The risk was so small that if it failed, my back up plan would be to just go back to working for other farms, until I had a chance to try it again. My family was a tough sell on the idea and the risk. I was so young, and they were wary about me getting back into the industry of agriculture in such uncertain times. Each step forward made them believe more and more that I was serious, thinking it through, and taking calculated risks.

Hill Ferguson | www.zong.com (Chief Product Officer, Paypal)

This is a real personal question and the answer will always depend on the person. I have always been comfortable taking risks when it comes to starting new companies and/or creating new products. I believe there is more risk in "*not trying*" something you are passionate about versus trying and failing.

That said, there definitely are pitfalls. I put my family in many risky situations as it relates to our financial future (e.g., quitting a job with one kid and one on the way to start a company), and it strained my personal relationships. But in the long run, I will always be happier and more productive when I am following my passion versus playing it safe. Again, this is a personal choice and may not be right for everyone. You will never know until you try!

Sam Tarantino | www.grooveshark.com

I think many people get into entrepreneurship with the attitude that it is about risk vs. reward or that somehow you are playing a game of chance in the casino of business. I'm sure there are cases where people have succeeded using that approach, but to me the goal of entrepreneurship is purpose. This is not something you can achieve with a 5-year plan, investment, partners, or even profit. It is a state of mind that is completely separated from risk/reward. Purpose brings you happiness and it is a choice from within. It is the magnet that attracts people to what you do and coalesces the synchronicity and coincidences that make the impossible journey possible. I didn't go through everything I just shared because of money or because of fame. I would have almost certainly given up had those been the motivations. I embarked and continue on this Grooveshark journey because it gives my life purpose beyond anything I ever imagined.

Knowing that millions of people every day use something you and your team have created from nothing, and that countless artists and creators now have a piece of technology to get their music exposed worldwide, is the most incredible feeling in the world. People used to tell me "*Aren't you afraid that Grooveshark will fail?*" My answer always is that we fail every day and that failing in the traditional sense (what I call "*giving up*") is a choice. When you make the life choice to have purpose and be happy doing what you love, suddenly you become invincible because no one can take that away from you.

Kyle James | www.rather-be-shopping.com

I handled the financial risk by not quitting my day job until I was making enough money with Rather-Be-Shopping to make the move to full-time. It really took the pressure off my shoulders knowing that I was making enough money to pay my monthly bills. I burned the candle at both ends and worked on the website in the evenings and on weekends. My backup plan was pretty simple; if it didn't work out I'd just scrap the whole idea and continue to work at my 9 to 5 gig.

Andrew Stanten | www.altitudemarketing.com

As a services-based company, our start up needs were modest – maybe $10,000. A couple of computers, cellphones, software, coffee, Cheez-Its and gas. We started out in a back bedroom in my house and stayed there for two years – until my wife was 7 months pregnant and got tired of four people coming over every day. The backup plan was that failure is not an option. I asked my wife to give me three years to either sink or swim. She agreed – with the caveat that when I swam, she'd get her three years to spread her entrepreneurial wings. Ten years later, it worked out great for our entire family.

Myra Roldan | herbanluxe.etsy.com

I tend to jump in with both feet; however, I also like to mitigate my risks. I like to think of myself as a financially savvy person. I did take a big risk – not huge like mortgaging my home, but I did borrow from my 401K. I didn't worry about convincing my family about the risk because as a single mom I make all my own financial decisions. If I failed I would have learned a huge lesson, if I succeeded I'd reap the rewards.

I know that I'd be able to replace the money I borrowed from my 401K eventually and I didn't stress it too much. I used all of my own money and felt that no one else really has an opinion in what I do with my money. I could have been doing worse things than starting a business.

Giancarlo Massaro | www.viralsweep.com

Luckily for myself, I am 2 years out of college, and I do not yet have a family to support. In college, I ran a business where I was promoting products for businesses and creating videos for them, and this allowed me to put a decent chunk of change away in the bank for future ventures.

My co-founder is a few years out of college and does not have a family to support either. He worked for AppSumo when we launched ViralSweep, so I would be working full-time on ViralSweep in the early days, while he would come home from work and squeeze in 4 or 5 hours per night.

We're extremely lean when it comes to spending money and we only invested about $3,000 into the initial development from our own savings. We've never taken any outside funding, nor have we approached any investors, simply because that is not the direction we wanted to take this business. For anyone that says you can't grow a business without funding, they're wrong – it just takes a little longer. We're 14 months in, my partner left his position at AppSumo 8 months ago, and ViralSweep is generating over 5 figures of revenue per month.

There really was no risk for me – I had enough saved to support me for a while and if things didn't work out, I knew I could always get a job. I was 23 when we started the business, so there was no better time to start. For my partner who was 26 at the time, he was taking a risk by leaving a great position and salary at AppSumo, but he believed enough in the product and vision that once it started to grow some legs, he knew it was time to leave and join me full-time.

Jason Schultz | www.jason.me

You have to make sacrifices and work hard for what you really want. No matter how busy you think you are, if you want it bad enough you'll find ways to make time around your day job and personal commitments. If you're going to run a successful company you should probably be able to manage your own time around a job.

So get with it, put things in motion and keep them moving forward. The magic lies in the little day to day improvements that seem irrelevant at the time. It's in the moments when things feel endless that you're making the important gains - keep going.

Courtney Ilarrazza | www.babybodyguards.com

We planned from the beginning to start small. Near us is a restaurant that owns nearly an entire city block. They didn't start like that though. He started with a small food cart. He grew a big following and moved to a tiny store front. He then took over the store next to it. He then bought the building, then the one next to it and so on. There is a lot more room to tinker, to find out what works when you start small. Dream and plan for the day when you own the entire city block but don't open your doors day one with that. Start with the small place and expand as demand grows. Minimize your risk.

J'Amy Owens | www.billthebutcher.com

I personally invested about 100k of seed capital to start the company and also personally purchased the public company. I had about a year of income saved and got lucky that in month 3 of the business found a large investor to provide early seed capital of $500,000. While all of this sounds easy, I did it by having a retail idea in a sector where I am considered an expert. Our early stage strategy was to open our own shops and then buy a public company and conduct a reverse merger and this resonated well with investors. I also kept my consulting practice open to augment my income and then did what all good natural risk taking entrepreneurs do - borrowed money from my family, recruited a generous and loyal management that both invested and did not need an immediate income, maxed out my credit and lived on coffee and the undying hope that I could pull off a big dream.

Alex Brola | www.checkmaid.com

We both took work sporadically on the side (we were/are consultants) as needed to pay bills, and all other time was dedicated to the business. I wouldn't say there was much risk involved, but that's largely because neither of us had many bills to pay, we were both single at the time, our families didn't care, etc. I am sure that I would not have even considered it had I had responsibilities that so many others do. Then again, if you want to be an entrepreneur you have to take those things into account. Finding out you want to be an entrepreneur in your 20s is definitely an advantage.

Matt Shoup | www.mandepainting.com

I busted my butt! Every day I was hitting the streets by handing out fliers, knocking on doors and using every connection I had to book paint jobs. It was definitely a huge financial risk because I didn't have a real back-up plan, but I knew that this was exactly what I needed to be doing. My wife knew how driven I was to make this succeed and she knew I would not rest until I was able to provide for my family.

Prayer. No joke. Everyone on our team has taken some serious risk. We went without pay initially for 9 months. We also had a month where we took out a personal loan to make payroll before closing a round of funding – and we told everyone exactly what was happening as it happened. The backup plan is that we're a really young team. My dad coached my co-founder and I that in this economy, failing as a young person can really help you in the long run. In terms of convincing our families – we're trying to foster a sense of the family being plugged into Cladwell. So before we hire people we hang out with their whole family, answer any questions, and really get to know each other as people. We also eat lunch together as families every Friday. We want the whole family to be jumping on board, because they are the real support system.

Rob Walling | www.getdrip.com

I did not take a huge risk. I'm actually fairly risk averse; never betting more than I'm comfortable to lose. This meant I worked a full-time job until I was able to make enough money to "*buy out*" my time. I had a wife, son and a mortgage while trying to start my business so this was far more difficult than it would have been in my earlier years.

Therefore, my backup plan was simple: shut it down and continue with full-time work. Not my ideal scenario, but at least I wouldn't be losing my house. This also helped show my wife that I was a competent entrepreneur. Going the route I did take a lot longer than quitting your job and living off credit cards, but it gave me time to demonstrate that I was capable of building a sustainable business that could support us. After a few years, many failures, and a few successes, it didn't take a lot of convincing to show my wife that I could hit "*my number*" (what we needed to live on) every month.

Adam Simpson | www.easyofficephone.com

I had some start-up capital on hand from my earlier businesses. The risk was still sizable, and it usually is when doing something worthwhile, but I knew I had a safety buffer of time to ramp up and turn profitable. In terms of backup plans, I'm a serial entrepreneur and tend to have a few projects on the go in various stages at any given moment. In the worst-case scenario, if you have to switch your game plan, you've at least got a head start on another venture rather than scrambling for ideas when you're under financial and emotional strain. My family is accustomed to the peaks and valleys of the entrepreneur's life, but convincing them can be tough when it's your first time out. One good approach is to set goals and hard time limits for them – for example, "*give me a year to work at this, and if I haven't achieved X, I will fall back to my other plan, which is Y.*" In my first business, when I was 18, that meant a year to try my hand at the Internet advertising industry, and if it didn't work out I had my university courses already selected.

Dan DeLuca | www.grownsmall.com / www.classchatter.com

I am a low risk guy. I think that one of the great things about the internet, it allows people to be entrepreneurs without taking large personal risks. My message to aspiring entrepreneurs is don't be afraid to start small. If you are not starting with millions in venture capital don't try and compete with those who are. Define a niche and become an expert while cultivating a loyal following. No matter how prepared you are, you still have a lot to learn. Every new venture is different and it is easier to be flexible with a small start-up footprint.

Chris Thierry | www.etelesolv.com

I rationalized the risk by telling myself if I couldn't take the risk now, while I was living with my parents, no kids, no mortgage, when would I? The big risk for me actually came later on in 2005 when the company was losing money and I needed to make a life decision and re-mortgage my house or cut my losses. At the time I was living in a house with my girlfriend, now wife, and I remember saying to her that if it didn't work I might have to grow up and find a real job.

Matt Barrie | www.freelancer.com

I took an incredible risk with Freelancer.com but you just need to be dogged. You need to have a firm belief in what you are doing and really go for it. If you have a great idea, seize the opportunity. From the very beginning, we used our own product, Freelancer.com, to build a global business using cost efficient and flexible labour.

Stacey Lindenberg | www.growyourtalent.com

Don't over-invest in office space or equipment; don't decide you have to have all of the bells and whistles a successful company would have right out of the box. It is okay to start on a shoestring, live lean, and be creative. When I asked a friend about helping me build a desk, he mentioned his accountant was giving one away. The accountant, who was also a small business owner, held the desk for me until I could pick it up. I still have his desk in my home office, and hos generosity isn't forgotten. I still send clients his way. When your family sees that you are being creative and frugal, they appreciate your concern for the impact your decision has on the household. You have to make this decision with your partner. They need to be on board. As long as you are both on the same page, you are more likely to succeed

Mike Glanz | www.hireahelper.com

I started trying to raise money for HireAHelper.com by going to investors. When they all turned me down, I went to friends and family and showed them what I wanted to do. My former boss, my uncle, and my parents all contributed enough money to allow me to quit my job and work full time on HireAHelper.com.

Literally every start-up owner I've ever talked to have some story of when they were down and out - credit cards maxed, retirement account cashed out, and down to their last penny in their personal and business checking accounts. Pete and I have skipped so many months of paychecks that I couldn't count them if I tried. Risk is part of the equation. It's there, it's very real, and it's daunting if you've had a 9-5 and never dealt with it before - but dealing with it isn't as bad as you'd think. When we were the in middle of tough times, we just crossed each obstacle as they came, usually with a lot of hard work and prayer. Now when I look back I can't believe all the stuff we went through and survived. It's more amazing to me than anybody else.

Debra Cohen | www.homeownersreferral.com

I was terrified. We had a new house and a new baby and taking a loan against our retirement money was a tremendous risk. My husband was very supportive which made my start up much easier. My strategy for dealing with stress is to work so, whenever I started to worry about money, I went to work. And, as I mentioned above, I took a part time job in a local furniture store and tried to cut our household expenses to help close the financial gap a little bit.

Rob Biederman | www.hourlynerd.com

We were fortunate to start the company during business school, when we were already budgeting not to be making any money and had fairly low expense bases. For others considering starting a company, I'd recommend beginning with your idea and demonstrating some serious traction before you quit your job. With a small amount of weekly time (and a small amount of capital), it's often possible to get a sense of whether business ideas are going to gain traction.

Raghu Kulkarni | www.idrive.com

Most of the start-ups in backup and storage space at the time focused on the ad based model. We quickly realized that it wouldn't work for online backup. We stuck to a subscription model. But this also meant that we had to wait for a long time, many years, actually to see impactful revenues trickling in. We had a software consulting business that provided the necessary revenues and cash flow to wait out this period as a backup revenue source.

It was a huge risk, but at the same time, we didn't raise funds. If we had, then we would be under some sort of a time pressure to show results, and almost no other online backup could, at the time. So most online backup that started around this time (90s), folded up quickly within a few years because the internet bandwidth and the market was not ready for online storage. Because we were supported by our alternate business in software consulting, we could withstand the long waiting period until subscription model became significant.

Ryan Wallace | www.iphoneantidote.com

We tried to keep the funding to a minimum, but the real cost was time. The time could have been spent in a "*normal*" job, which would definitely earn money. There was certainly a big risk in starting any company that can range from losing thousands, to simply wasting some time. And really, it is most likely that you will fail before you succeed. We haven't had a backup plan. If you focus on a backup plan, it can really inhibit your ability to take the risks that are needed to start a business. I have heard a quote before, stating that people with high IQ's don't make for good businessmen. They see the possible rewards, and then they realize the risks are too great, and instead play it safe. Luckily, I started iPhone Antidote directly out of college and was able to minimize some risks because of that. If I were to have family/dependents, I would make sure to save up money as a backup, and I would do my best to work on the business while continuing my current work. At the end, it takes money to make money, and you will need to take some risks, but it can definitely be worth it if you've done your homework.

Jake Sigal | www.livioconnect.com

I put my reputation on the line. Also once you become an entrepreneur, it's really hard to get hired (or getting a boss ever again). Once you take the plunge, don't ever look back. I see a lot of entrepreneurs (or wantrapreneurs) trying to moonlight their new start-up. If you want to be successful, you need to put 100% of your energy into it, like anything in life.

The backup plan was finding another great idea. I suppose if there was some sort of family emergency, I could also go back to work for the man. My wife was always supportive of me being an entrepreneur. We don't have any kids right now but I can imagine with a family you'd need to have more money in the bank (more runway), and more importantly more time, to support the family.

Myke Nahorniak | www.localist.com

Having a healthy sense of confidence (or arrogance, whatever works) is helpful. Backup plans are damned. You don't know what you don't know. I embraced not knowing everything instead of being scared that I might miss something. I was used to getting thrown in the proverbial "*pit*," forced to dig my way out. Going into a start-up full-time didn't seem much different.

Before diving into the start-up world full-time, I had a cushy IT job at a newspaper. The pay was great, the benefits were good, and I had an inspiring group of colleagues. On paper, it was "*stable*." Leaving was "*risky*," only because it was unknown. The stress only came when we were building the business plan, as it's an exercise in mapping out the long-term "*what ifs*." Day-to-day, taking things one week at a time allowed me to sleep at night. As time progresses and you gain more confidence, you're able to continually looking to the future without your heart rate going up too much.

The best part is: newspapers have downsized over the years, and the job I had would likely be on the chopping block today. It would have been a bigger long-term risk not to stay.

Arnon Rose | www.localmaven.com

My first full-time business was started out of business school, where I had the luxury of sleeping in my mom's apartment and working out of my dad's office so it didn't feel that risky to me. I had nothing to lose, no-one to answer to, and could always go get a job. Subsequent businesses felt riskier to me because now I had an apartment to pay for, a family to support, and savings to protect.

It's ironic how when you have nothing to lose and practically no net worth its almost easier to take a chance and launch a new business. I remember my mother saying to me when I graduated business school that I should get a job in investment banking. I wanted to try starting my own business and she just couldn't believe I would take such a risk. Now that I have had several successful businesses with successful exits, my family knows that it's the start-up environment that drives me and they aren't so worried about whether I will pull it off with LocalMaven.com. I think everyone believes in the idea but more importantly they believe in my abilities.

Michael Lindell | www.mypillow.com

I didn't have a backup plan with MyPillow. I always believed MyPillow wouldn't fail. When I was convincing my friends and family, they initially thought I was nuts until I had them try the product. I was so passionate about it that they became a support system, but more importantly my original critics. They would suggest what else they wanted to see and feel with a pillow. That's why so many people love MyPillow. It is important as an entrepreneur to show your passion in the product; then it should be easy to convince everyone. If you are passionate enough, you can get investors easily and the support you need. It's hard to sell something you don't believe in. if you have a doubt about the product then you shouldn't be selling it. If you believe in it, go all the way.

Edward DeSalle | www.netirrigate.com

Risk is a very broad term and I find people measure it differently. From a financial standpoint, I consider nothing more risky than letting someone else control your financial future. I worked in the Oil and Gas industry in the early part of my career in Houston right down the street from Enron. I had friends that worked at that company were who bright, talented, and hardworking people. Because of criminal behavior within the leadership of that company, I watched good people suffer a financial hardship. Because most people's income is generated from a business they work at, I decided a great way to eliminate some risk was to make sure I could control the business or at least have a much higher degree of transparency into the business and its underlying decisions than the average employee. At the same time, you create fulfillment by choosing your own path.

As far as starting Net Irrigate was concerned, I really didn't ever consider it a huge risk because of my financial perspective on risk. I've been blessed with unconditional love from my wife and other family members and knew that I'd still have them if the company went down in flames. Likewise, I've been told I'm a pretty good software developer, which fortunately is a skill that's in demand these days. So I convinced myself I could always get by with a programming job and support my family well enough if the ship ever went down.

Peter Mann | www.oransi.com

I started my first business while I worked at Dell. My start-up was my night job and I grew it to where I was able to replace most of my salary and then I moved into the start-up full-time. So rather than taking a huge risk I worked really hard to get the business going. Since the business was producing income it mitigated some of the risks and looking back I was probably naïve because I never spent much time thinking about the possibility of it failing. If the business was not successful I would have to search for another job although was able to build up some savings from my corporate career so that took some of the stress off.

Aaron Skonnard | www.pluralsight.com

Coping with the bootstrap experience is all about setting expectations from the start — both as a company and with family. In founding Pluralsight, my co-founders and I laid out a long-term vision and were honest about the need for patience and discipline. If we hadn't done this, we would have heard the murmurings of doubt and impatience creep in when our start-up didn't become the next Facebook or Amazon overnight.

Regarding backup plans, I think it's important to NOT have one. This might be difficult to swallow for founders and their families, but it changes the start-up psychology. If success is the only option, you find a way to succeed. Again, the key thing here is to be transparent about this from the start. It needs to be clear to all involved that this venture will be long and difficult, but ultimately rewarding — and that there's no Plan B.

John Brady | www.protempartners.com

I'm a worrier, and most entrepreneurs I have come to know will tell you that risk tolerance is a lot lower than you think it is when you go in. Once the bank account starts to drain, the months pass, and it all becomes "*real*" the stress can be overwhelming. The risk was significant in my case, though I figured I was mid-career if I really failed and truly needed to start all over again. All of that said, the sense of accomplishment is equally amazing. I worry about making the math work every month, but I also remember when I worried about making ANY revenue or getting just ONE first client. Then I go a step further and remember that a year ago, none of this enterprise existed. Today, it's always busy, the phones ring, new opportunities present themselves, we get cited in major publications, we create jobs and opportunities, we help people, we operate with the values of the kind of workplace we all wish we had; and that is worth every sleepless night.

Mark McClain | www.sailpoint.com

I left a mid-level management job and took some initial angel funding to start my first company. It was a moderate risk (no danger of losing my house or racking up big credit card debt!), but still a big step away from the corporate safety net. The backup plan was to go back to a "*safe*" corporate job, and since risk-taking is pretty acceptable in the software industry, it didn't seem too daunting. It did take some convincing for my family to give up on the "*safe*" corporate job, including some nice incentives to stay. But, we were young enough to "*give it a shot*".

Jeb Blount | www.salesgravy.com

I funded Sales Gravy's start up from my own savings. It was very big risk because I put almost all of the savings I had accumulated over a twenty year period into the company. I was fortunate to have a spouse who believed in me. That doesn't mean she wasn't skeptical. I am sure it was hard for her to remain supportive when huge amounts of cash were being drawn from our savings account. I think I was able to convince her to trust me because I'd been successful in the past and had not made very many mistakes with money. Additionally we cut our expenses to the bone so that the cash flow from our jobs could be used to cover some of the start-up expenses.

There was no back-up plan. For me there was no option to fail. That is what drove me to work insane hours and to be persistent in the face of fear, doubt, and adversity. I knew that if I focused relentlessly on good business practices and remained lean that we would succeed. Today we have replaced the savings I took to start the company and we have zero debt. We have an office building that is paid for and solid cash flow.

Michael Kawula | www.selfemployedking.com

Initially I tried buying businesses that had cash-flow coming in before I started my first franchise. I remember the night was 9/10/2001 (the day before 9/11) and my wife told me we were having our first child. I traveled for work frequently and we knew that wasn't the way we wanted to raise our children.

I continued to keep my network strong in case my businesses didn't work out, but knew ultimately that to succeed I couldn't keep 1 toe in the water and one on the island. Friends were like crabs in the bucket saying it was risky, but together my wife and I made a decision based on knowing we wanted to both be active with our children as we are today.

Julie Busha | www.slawsa.com

Every entrepreneur takes a huge financial risk and I think it is important to assume that your idea or product won't take off as quickly as you want it to. It never does. Be prepared to make a personal long-term financial sacrifice for many years to come. I came from working for over a decade in the male-dominated industry of sports marketing where I rose up the ranks rather quickly and was fortunately valued more than most men my age by the time I was in my late 20's.

That is rare but that value came as a result of hard work and making me invaluable to my employer and clients. Because my husband and I have always been "*savers*" and never being people who got into debt or lived beyond our means, we were financially prepared for me to leave my professional career in my early 30's, giving up good pay and benefits, in a very down economy. We knew that we could never ask family for money so we had to assume the responsibility to grow it on my shoulders alone (while my husband maintained his job to support the family). We have open conversations about finances with each other and if we got to a point where we saw it wouldn't work, I would probably go back into the workforce. Knowing how important it is for me to put full-time efforts (and when I say full-time, I mean 80+ hours/week) for years to come to launch a brand in the highly competitive grocery industry and to invest profits from sales right back into marketing, sacrificing compensation for myself, is a pretty big risk. Not many people are willing to do that but it's a reality of the efforts needed to start a company.

My husband and I trust one another and have a good understanding of each other's abilities. My husband has as much confidence in me to grow my company as an entrepreneur as much as I have confidence in his abilities to work hard to support our household expenses. While our businesses are separate, we are working toward a shared, common goal.

Zeb Couch | www.offmarketformula.com / www.speedhatch.com

I saved. When I was in college working, I saved. When I was running my residential real estate company, I saved. Start-ups need a financial "runway," a certain amount of cash required to operate pre-revenue. Start-up founders need runways, too. Starting a business is stressful enough. If you have to worry about your own financial well-being while trying to build something, you're destined to fail. If you're working a 9-5 job now, make sure you're saving enough to be able to cover your bills for at least 6 months. If you can begin working on your business on weekends and after hours while still at your job, do it. It'll make things that much easier when you make the leap. Many of the world's most successful entrepreneurs started out working 9-5 jobs. They saved, met key contacts and were prepared to make the leap when the time was right. You can, too. There's no reason why you can't get paid helping build someone else's dream while you prepare and plan to build your own, but never forget the goal is to build your dream, not someone else's.

I'm fortunate enough to have a family that's always been supportive of me. I'm also not married and don't have kids, which definitely makes things easier for me. I have friends who are married, though, and actively planned with their spouse or lived off the spouse's income while building their business.

Justyn Howard | www.sproutsocial.com

I believe the right (and only) time to start a company is when you can't imagine not doing it. There's always a great deal of risk and our early team left lucrative jobs to bet on Sprout Social. Fortunately, we had a good deal of validation early on that we were on the right track. While everyone has doubts, ours were minimal.

Blaine Vess | www.studymode.com

I'm a big advocate of backup plans. I believe that backup plans give you the confidence you need to take risks with your business.

I didn't give up my day job until we were earning well over a million in yearly profits. For years, I grew StudyMode while doing freelance work as a computer programmer and serving as a consultant for New Line Cinema. The fact that I had another source of income, and a backup plan, allowed me to take bigger risks with StudyMode.

Michelle MacDonald | www.sweetnotebakery.com

I knew I wanted to be an entrepreneur when I was 18 and in college, my plan was always to get a degree and a "*good job*" so that I could save up and one day start my own business. I worked a full time job through college and maintained good credit standing as part of my plan to make it less risky. At 21 when I graduated I thought about turning my passion of baking that I had developed since I was 8 into a business.

I spoke with my family and friends about my idea. I noticed I common theme: If I spoke to someone who never started a business their advice was very weary and concerned about how I would do something like that if I never even worked in a bakery or started a business before. If I spoke to someone who had started a business their advice was very strategic and cautioned me to put together a plan before proceeding but encouraged me to do so. I decided to work at a bakery out of college, almost to silence those that thought "*you may not even like it*". I did realize that a retail bakery was not the right path for me and my future and so I learned about the alternatives (wholesale, online). I got scared and also felt like I wouldn't be able to do it. I took job opportunities in Human Resources and continued to just bake as a hobby for the next 5 years. I would create recipes that I was excited about and "*sell*" them to friends and family for small events. I never took on too much and never felt confident enough to just do the baking business completely. I guess it was getting older and wanting this for the past 7 years but I finally stopped talking myself out of it after reading some inspirational books and frequently checking out entrepreneur.com.

Hearing other people's stories about taking that "*leap of faith*", I realized I needed to follow my passion. I started experimenting and planning my business any free chance I could and surrounded myself with enough knowledge so that I could feel confident that I had a good idea that solved a problem (something I learned from reading other entrepreneur's stories). Once I had a product I was passionate and confident about I continued to juggle my regular job where I was making $50,000 a year and trying to sell and get my first customers for my product. I did both until I knew that I couldn't grow my business if I wasn't able to work on it all 7 days a week. My employer fortunately let me slowly phase out of my job until I finally was working solely on my business. For me, especially being on my own with just my income, it felt like a huge risk and I carried that weight on my shoulders for a while. I knew the numbers I needed to be able to replace my income and it was doable, but would take time to get there. I had rent and expenses that I acquired given my past income. I cut expenses where I could. I keep reminding myself that my backup plan would be to go back to the company I worked for, or find another job in that industry.

Several times I questioned my judgment of deciding to quit my job, especially as my income was not as easy as I had hoped to replace and the expenses of starting a business were inevitable. My family was very supportive of my decision to take these risks, they had heard me "*talking*" about it long enough and my father being an entrepreneur himself he knew that working for you was a viable dream. I had some resistance from my friends about the risks I was taking.

The more I expressed how scared I was the more they would suggest that I maybe just go back to working for someone else. I learned that not everyone understands the risks an entrepreneur must take and why someone would want to take such risks. It not for everyone, if it was everyone would do it. I actually started feeling myself being talked out of continuing down this path to see my business through. I knew I needed to do something; I didn't want to talk myself out of it again, so I found a therapist. And for me, especially after not really "*believing*" in therapy it was a big step. It became someone I could talk to about the self-doubt and challenges but would encourage me to keep pushing myself and help me build the confidence and tools I needed to slowly but surely quite that doubting voice in my head.

Greg Tseng | www.tagged.com

My co-founder Johann Schleier-Smith and I first started companies in college, when we were only 19 and 20, and didn't have many expenses. The backup plan was to go to graduate school. We didn't have outside funding so we had to be profitable pretty soon after launch. If you get funding, you can wait much longer to be profitable. No matter what your situation, my mentor Reid Hoffman would say you should have a Plan A (what you want to do), Plan B (backup plan if it doesn't work) and Plan Z (safety net if everything falls apart). Walking your family through all three plans can help alleviate some concerns.

Joel Simkhai | www.grindr.com

There are lots of risks to building a start-up. I come from a family of entrepreneurs so I'm lucky to have parents who helped to instill good business sense in me. I also didn't make any risky financial decisions – I didn't quit my job, I didn't take out huge loans and kept my costs very low. One of the biggest challenges and costs for Grindr when we started to grow was scaling our technology platform to allow millions of users to create profiles and deliver a great service. The advent of cloud services has made it more cost-effective for start-ups like us to scale. Having a revenue model from the beginning has enabled us to invest in the technologies and achieve our growth.

Eren Bali | www.udemy.com

I was inspired to start Udemy based on my own personal experience using the Internet to teach myself mathematics. I came from a small village in Turkey where I went to a one-room schoolhouse and eventually found myself learning math via the Internet. This led to a successful academic career in mathematics and opened up many doors. Without the Internet, I wouldn't have been able to progress so quickly.

My personal journey helped me deal with uncertain and risky situations. I certainly did take on a huge risk. I moved to the U.S. and left my family and friends behind in Turkey. I also left a well-paying job at Speed Date to dedicate my full attention to Udemy. I also lived with 2 other roommates during the early days of the start-up to keep my costs down.

Christy Ferer | www.vidicom.com

At the time I had no children and that was key in being able to pour myself into this, although I did have a husband and a full time job, but when you love an idea and you work hard you someone how find the time; nights or weekends. Part of the risk was underwritten by friends who threw in camera work or editing and even writing. They had faith that if there was a success they would be part of it. And many were.

I must admit the risk was not huge because I did keep my "*day job*" but it was scary when I jumped off the "*cliff*" and stopped working to try the venture full time. And because the fashion industry had the "*crowd*" mentality many jumped into the fashion video marketing concepts.

Scott Perkins & Shawn Boday | www.vube.com

Big rewards come with big risks. Investing time and money into something you are passionate about is an invigorating experience. One of the most satisfying feelings in life is seeing something you created through hard work succeed.

Bas Beerens | www.wetransfer.com

We have always been a bootstrapped start-up and that is something we are extremely proud of. We invested a lot into the business at the start – my whole pension plan went into it – but thanks to the advertising, paid subscription and a whole load of seriously hard work from everybody in the team, we are now profitable and are producing nice margins. We have gone from scraping by every month to pay the hosting, pushing everyone to pay on time, and only being able to pay the bill once all advertisers had paid, to knowing we can comfortably pay Amazon Web Services at the beginning of the month.

A small, independent team doesn't allow us to move fast. This means that we do things at our own pace. It might not be the 'Silicon Valley way' of doing business, but it works for us. I believe in creations that have been thoroughly tested and are optimal at the moment of release. If you release a product you should be 100% happy with it and not just release it because you've hit a specific deadline that has been breathing down your neck.

Across all of my companies, we have always started by identifying and thinking about real user needs. By being bootstrapped and moving at our own pace, we are able to thoroughly interrogate the data and test it in the real world. Between Alpha, Beta and full-launch, we are able to add features when necessary and refine the product based on feedback from real users. This process allows for iteration, which in turn reduces our risks. It makes big failures unlikely and turns all of those small failures into constructive criticism.

We're taking our time to optimize our service and market from our bellies. We do tests, look into different approaches but in the end we feel what's best for our users and for us, and that decides our direction.

Jason Cohen | www.wpengine.com

I started my first company with savings from my job. I started early enough that I didn't have many expenses. Whether you're starting with two kids and a husband or with no personal ties and a $2000/mo burn rate, the calculation is the same – you have $X in the bank, and you spend $Y/month on personal expenses, and thus you have X/Y months before you run out of money.

Unless X is high relative to Y – which is usually isn't – this doesn't give you enough time to build a business. Most people either work a day job to cover costs, or try consulting work. Both are good options, but both are traps if you're not careful.

The trap of a day job is that you can only have two full-time jobs, including social life and family. That is, you can have a normal day job (1) and be an attentive, present parent (2), but that's all your time. Or you could put off having a family so that you can sustain a day job (1) and your business on the side (2). In my experience, people who claim they can have a family, and a day job, and start-up, inevitably end up sacrificing one or two. So the trap of the day job is that you have to decide that you will not also meaningfully develop a personal life or family if you're going to give your start-up the time required to make it successful.

The trap of consulting is that it's hard to devote the time necessary to do your start-up instead. Finding clients, keeping them happy, doing the work, and doing the finances, is itself a start-up! So if that's your path to an "*actual*" start-up, you're really doing two start-ups, and again that's almost impossible for anyone to pull off.

Beth Shaw | www.yogafit.com

Luckily I had a very good business partner in the beginning. We were able to make the business plan together, and from there I was able to build my business. There is no such thing as a start-up with any risk. I had to take an enormous risk to get YogaFit off the ground. I was lucky to have an initial investor who believed in my idea. My family was remarkably supportive, but I am sure they didn't always trust in my idea or my vision. I was taking a huge risk because I didn't have a set income! When I was a yoga instructor, I knew that I would be getting a paycheck. But when I started YogaFit, I had to constantly worry about budgeting enough money for myself.

Sometimes I would invest too much in my business and realize I didn't have much money left over to eat!! The best way to overcome these types of challenges is to believe in you. I know that sounds corny, but you have to follow your own ideas and passions. There are going to be hundreds of people giving you advice and suggestions -- and it is good to listen to them once and a while. But overall, you have to be true to yourself and do what you think is correct. There were many times when I was told that I couldn't start my own yoga school because the market was already saturated. But I kept meeting people who were interested in my type of yoga and were interested in my products. I didn't let these naysayers get in the way of my dreams.

Jill Foucré | www.marcelsculinaryexperience.com

I predetermined what I was willing to invest in the start-up of the business and, more importantly, I segregated the funds that I promised I would not touch. Again, I had a strong financial plan and I was realistic about what I was going to spend. I do not see failure as an option but we are only 2 ½ years in so it requires constant vigilance and driving to performance standards. This was an enormous risk for my family because, as stated earlier, I am the only wage earner in my family (and always have been the only one) and I was leaving a very high income situation. My position was that I had been entrusted all these years to take care of us financially and I had done very well at that and that I had earned the right to try this. I worked very hard to get us in the financial position we are in and I was not going to be stupid and jeopardize that. My husband supported me in this position.

Chapter 24 : Selling Your Business

Not everyone is fortunate enough to grow a business big enough to be able to sell it. But not all businesses are sold with an exit in mind. Michael Kawula has been a serial entrepreneur at heart. At its peak, his cleaning business was making him as much as $24,000 a week.

But in 2012, his focus shifted toward his online business that was growing pretty swiftly and was ranked the 144th fastest growing business in the US. The shift in focus and priorities meant the revenues from the cleaning business tanked and it fell to under $20,000. Michael realized the change in priorities and decided to put his cleaning business for sale - "*I had manager turnover and knew I'd have to come back in to restructure or sell the business while it still had great value. I put the business up for sale to focus on my online company which I've also recently sold because of partnership differences. I think you always need to be looking forward at what could impact your business both positive and negatively and make decisions based on that.*"

Myra Roldan | herbanluxe.etsy.com

I sold my original business in 2008. I had appeared on the Oprah Winfrey show as a finalist in her search for the next big idea. After the show, things got crazy from all angles and I was not prepared for the deluge of calls, emails, sales and threat of law suits. My business exploded; something that I had completely underestimated. I found myself drowning, losing sleep, feeling like I was wondering lost, unsure of what to do or where to find help. Although the demand had grown overnight I lacked the capital to take the business to the next level, so I put my business up for sale in a desperate move to pull myself back up. My business sold within a month of listing.

Looking back, I don't think I could have prepared better for what was going to happen. It was like pouring soda over baking soda – the situation just got out of my control. I did, however, learn some valuable lessons.

1) Don't be afraid to take risks.
2) When you set a goal and reach it, be prepared for the outcome.
3) The dollar is KING!
4) Don't bite off more than you can chew.
5) Always be honest with yourself.
6) Slow and steady wins the race for real.

Arnon Rose | www.localmaven.com

I have always grown my businesses for an exit at some point and it's important to remember that. Deals are made when there is value for both the buyer and the seller. As a seller you always need to remember that and to leave something on the table to make a deal viable. I have always been open to overtures from potential buyers and believe it's important to listen to everyone. I think an entrepreneur should always be thinking about that day and build a business that is ready for that day. That means you must keep records always in order, build a solid management team, and maintain business plans and outlines on your strategy.

Of course, if you believe in your business, you need to stick with it and continue to grow it to its potential, but there is nothing wrong with periodically taking some chips off the table. My last business was sold and I retained a large stake in the business and continued to run the business under the new ownership structure. Together we had a fantastic return and it was rewarding for both me as a seller and for the private equity buyer. The reason I bring up this example is because often sales don't have to be binary, you can sell part of your business to create some liquidity for yourself while retaining a substantial enough stake to remain engaged and excited about the future.

As for my latest business LocalMaven.com, we think we are on to something big and the inclination is to take this as far as I can take it, but with that said, if the right buyer came along, who could offer great strategic value as assist with our growth, I'd again be willing to take the ride alongside a partner.

Jason Cohen | www.wpengine.com

Selling a business is very personal. The phrase "*it's not personal, it's business*" is never more incorrect than when a small business owner sells her business. You should think about selling your business periodically. Not because you necessarily want to or are able to, but because it helps you get perspective on your own state of mind. There are times during a start-up where you wouldn't sell for 100x the value because you're deriving so many fulfillments from it that money could never replace. There are other times where you're so burnt out you would trade it for a "*normal job.*" It's useful to check in with yourself, and thinking about what it would be like to sell and what would cause you to do so is an interesting foil for that process.

The biggest learning is to separate your personal identity from the business. Most small business owners can't do this. It means selling the business feels like a loss, and in fact a recent study showed that almost all sellers have feelings exactly mirroring post-partum depression. But if you can't make this separation, not only does it mean you can't sell without difficult emotions, it means the same difficulty if the business falls on hard times, or changes in other ways as they inevitably do.

Dan DeLuca | www.grownsmall.com / www.classchatter.com

There are many reasons you could be looking to sell your business. For me it was to breathe new life into the venture. At a certain point I had run out of the enthusiasm to grow the business, but I was not ready to dismantle it. I had explored selling the site before and had only found people who were interested in cannibalizing its traffic.

I was not interested in having my site destroyed. I knew it was time to sell when I found someone who was enthusiastic about growing the site as part of a suite of other high quality educational tools. Of course there is also the business side of it, I sold when e-learning, MOOC's, blended learning and flipped classrooms where '*hot.*' A sector getting attention does not mean your business is magically worth more but it does help you get attention from the right kind of people.

Nellie Akalp | www.corpnet.com

I had no intention of selling my first business and did not even have an exit strategy. When we were approached by Intuit to sell, we thought about it, and the timing was perfect for us as an entrepreneurial couple. It allowed us to focus more of our resources on our then growing family.

I think entrepreneurs in general should think about selling their business if there is a normal life-cycle associated with their business or in there industry. For us, although the timing was perfect, we had never been involved in an acquisition so we did not know what to expect other than what was relayed to us so it was a bit of a shocker. What I realized is how people change and you truly get to know who your friends are during the process.

Philip Masiello | www.800razors.com

Generally there is an event that occurs to prompt an exit. In one particular case, the business needed more capital and expertise than I could provide in order to grow it to its potential. An acquirer happened to emerge at the right time and assisted with the failing business. What you need to decide is whether or not you are in the game for ego or success. If it is success, you make decisions that are good for the growth of the business. If it is ego, you make decisions that are best for you. Other times I had to sell because the business was not working and it was the only option to salvage anything out of the business.

Jason Schultz | www.jason.me

You have to figure out what you want in life and in business. After you build your company you have to decide if selling it is right for you. When I've sold businesses in the past it was to free my time up and/or to give the company more potential towards a bigger success with the acquirer.

J'Amy Owens | www.billthebutcher.com

My partners and I sold Laptop Lane in 1999, when we got an offer for $45 million in a stock transaction from a Chinese broadband company. It ended up being the wrong buyer and the lesson was that we should have sold it to Kinkos, who had offered $35 million in cash. We sold the business because of the offers, but we picked the wrong buyer. The lesson? Know thy buyer.

Ashok Subramanian | www.liazon.com

We weren't thinking about selling but were presented with an aggressive opportunity that would allow us to grow Liazon faster than we ever could have without our new owner. Focus on building your company and not on selling. And, if you are so lucky to find yourself in a position to sell, make sure it's to someone who offers your company true growth opportunities. I think it's a shame to build something and not have the opportunity to have it stay around for a while.

Jake Sigal | www.livioconnect.com

Corporate development is like dating. When you know, you know. We knew where the automotive industry was going. We have great products, great people, and great intellectual property. Ford's vision of the world as it relates to connecting apps to cars was something that we all believe in. It just made sense!

I think an entrepreneur should always be thinking about selling if they have taken in other people's money. As a venture back entrepreneur, you have a responsibility to your shareholders, (and sometimes those include friends and family) to get their money back, hopefully with a profit. Options are always good for the business. How proactive or passive you want to be is a decision between the board of directors. A few companies to buy Livio approached us. Once the offers were high enough, we knew it was time.

Iftach Orr | www.pix.do

Selling your business depends on so many elements: your financial situation; time invested; growth; revenue; personal goals; your personal connection to the product; and so many more. In rough terms there are three types of sales: bailing out, cashing out and acqui-hire. If you're out of resources and hope, then it's better to sell than to flush your technology down the toilet. If someone is offering you a profitable deal, you should ask yourself if your goal is to get a bit richer or if you believe your start-up will be bigger and you want to change the world or be much richer (or both). If you get an offer for acqui-hire (i.e., buying you for your talents), you should consider if you'll get paid enough in order to become a corporate soldier and whether or not that's what you want reflected in your resume.

Dianne Crowley | www.wildwingcafe.com

We sold our business in January of 2012. We thought at the age of 60, it was a good time to move on. My recommendation to others that our considering selling their business is to wait until they are absolutely ready for the transition. If you are selling your business purely for the cash infusion, I would recommend finding a minority partner rather than a majority partner.

Everyone runs his or her business differently. Our restaurant was our life. We loved Wild Wing Cafe to it's core. We still do. We weren't quite ready for the lifestyle change. We grew Wild Wing Café to 35 restaurants. Every one of the franchisees is a close friend of ours. Our employees are like our children. This has been a fun and wild ride and we certainly wouldn't change it for the world.

Mark McClain | www.sailpoint.com

Selling your business is a very personal decision, although less so when you have external funding (and investors who are expecting a return). For many people, thinking through what really motivates them at the beginning (e.g. independence, financial return, a creative drive, new technology, etc.) will help determine where the business should go later. The first company I founded, Waveset was a VC-backed company, which meant we had to get to a *"liquidity event"* (IPO or M&A). Therefore, it was pretty clear that selling would be a viable option from the beginning.

Chapter 25 : The Lows Of Entrepreneurship

Entrepreneurship can be an extremely lonely journey. When Kyle James started his coupons and deals website, Rather-Be-Shopping.com, the internet was still at its infancy and the dotcom world was still recovering from the crash of 2000. The first six months were exciting – the internet world was new and Kyle was enjoying the entrepreneurial venture he ran on the side of his full time job.

But with little to no visitors, Kyle lost the motivation to work. He was ready to give up completely. But then, something interesting happened. Kyle noticed a small trickle of visitors coming to his website from another site called "*Google*". He had never heard of this new search engine before but quickly realized that he was ranking fairly well on this brand new site. That got him his interest back and Kyle started investing in learning about Search Engine Optimization to give his website a new lease of life.

I asked entrepreneurs about the lows that they experienced at business that made them want to quit. Reading such stories from other entrepreneurs teach us the power of persistence and the attitude that is required to see these challenges through. Here are some stories that these business owners shared.

Mike Glanz | www.hireahelper.com

Our business faced a major lawsuit from U-Haul. I thought we were going to lose everything - not just our jobs, but jobs for the small team we had hired. It was their livelihoods as well. My parents had also just barely scraped enough together to invest in our idea. To lose their money, their retirement, and let them down was too much to bear some days.

But the fear of losing it all is what ultimately drove our determination not to close the company. Our focus on revenue only intensified as we realized that after we offered several settlement options, that their goal wasn't to settle. Their goal was to crush us in legal fees. Every decision we made was centered on what would make us our next $1, so we could keep paying the mounting legal expenses.

I remember our lawyer having an honest conversation with us and outlining a worse-case scenario of staying open and fighting the lawsuit. He explained it would impact future income for years and years to come, and that we couldn't declare bankruptcy to escape it. It was terrifying.

There was no "*plan B*" and the threat of ruining lives was very real. I literally felt hopeless. I used to stand in the shower for hours too paralyzed to go to work. Ironically, the mounting legal fees kept us focused. The notion that our legal costs were growing day by day - and that we weren't cash-flow positive yet, and we didn't have money to pay our lawyer - drove us hard to succeed. We knew we were in the fight for our livelihoods - and our families' livelihood - and it kept us laser focused on generating revenue.

Month over month, we accounted for the fees like any other business expense, and it gave us an aggressive, yet concrete sales goal to hit. I just stayed focused on building revenue to cover what legal costs we could, and trusted our lawyer to do his thing. In the meantime, I, my wife, my co-founder Pete, Pete's wife, and our few employees prayed a lot. Our lawyer shares our faith in God, so we started praying with him every time we met.

Monique Tatum | www.beautifulplanning.com

This has not happened once, it has happened multiple times. There have been times when I have had to terminate large chunks of staff and I freaked out emotionally or felt really down because I grow so connected to my employee. There have been times when a client project that I thoroughly believed in capsized or shut down due to items that had nothing to do with their PR, but their bad business practices. There was a day in 2013 when we were planning a large event and everything that could go wrong seemed to be going wrong. I walked in the house and sat on the floor and cried. You don't hear business owners say these things but highs and lows don't just happen in the start-up phase.

The key is to have a strong support system around you. By that I mean staff, loved ones, family members and friends that care. Those days come and go. You resolve it because you have to. It makes a difference when you wipe your eyes and then realize "*I HAVE to do this because that staff member that I love believes in me and counts on me for her paycheck.*" Or "*I HAVE to do this because I need to show myself.*" To be an entrepreneur means trying again and again.

There was one time our largest client pulled their contract due to the direction their new investor wanted them to go in. This was after they had just re-signed a new contract with us for a second year. Per that contract, I hired new staff. I was heartbroken. Was I going to fire all of these newly hired people? Well, I didn't. I paused their account, sent it to legal and gave them a date to get it together by, and then began working full force on a new project. The new project kept me afloat and I managed to pull through. The early days in business are hard, but the middle days in business are also hard. The thing is I can think of a tremendous number of anecdotes with which to answer your question.

But, on the flip side, the amazing moments are definitely doubled. It is all worth it.

Chris Thierry | www.etelesolv.com

While I never really considered selling the business, in 2009 I went through a tough time both financially as well as from a company culture perspective. In talking to my mentor and partner, we decided it would be the right time to look for a CEO. I was 32 at the time, so my thinking was maybe I wasn't the right guy the lead the company and an experienced CEO would be the silver bullet to turn things around.

I went through a search and found someone I really liked. After a few months of his doing due diligence on us, I got him signed to an employment contract for more money than I was paying myself. However the day before he was supposed to start he called to say he accepted another offer. I was stunned, but looking back it was a defining moment for me as an entrepreneur. After a sleepless night, I decided to re-invent myself and learn about leadership, strategy and culture. I took courses, listen to audiobooks in the car and worked to educate my management team along the way. It's been 5 years since that time, but it was a key turning point for me as well as my company. Today the result of this is that we are debt free, profitable and are ranked as one of the top 50 employers in Canada.

Sam Tarantino | www.grooveshark.com

(In 2012, Grooveshark faced a very torrid time with lawsuits) As hard as the first few years of Grooveshark were, 2012, I would say was even harder because in the early days we didn't really have anything to lose. So while missing payroll was no fun and being rejected by a hundred VC's was tough, we never really knew any better. The more difficult (and humbling) lesson was to go from being the cool darling child of the tech world, to within just a few months, losing almost everything and being the shunned black sheep. We went from 35M users to 10M users within 6 months of being hit with the big lawsuits.

Throughout that first half of 2012, I saw the best and worst in people. I saw people bail in fear, but at the same time I witnessed the most inspiring people who stepped up in spite of the scary $3Bn lawsuits. My former assistant took on the challenge to lead our ad networks team after our old leader left; an intern of ours with two jobs around town and little experience learned to code and then built an entire platform from scratch while other developers fled to Google or other start-ups; my Operations leader learned Accounting from the ground up in order to transition our accounting system to someone new after our CFO bailed; and a new marketing hire from a big company came aboard and kept the whole sales department afloat after our head of sales left. I overcame my own doubts because of these amazing people who I continue to work with every day. Their stories of overcoming their own odds powered me through this period even when I stopped believing in myself.

Chandler Crouch | www.chandlercrouch.com

After I had been in business for 5 years a guy that bought 30 houses through me (and had an addition 30 more under contract) offered me a "*sweet heart deal.*" He had built tremendous trust with me. I had some cash and was looking for opportunities to grow bigger faster. He offered me the opportunity to lend him money secured by a piece of real estate at a great equity position (evidenced by an appraisal).

I should have done my due diligence. I made a lot of mistakes with this deal. I ended up losing a bunch of money and going into debt pretty bad. As when I first started, I remembered stories of highly successful people and the really low times that it seems all of them talk about. I was really depressed for 1-2 weeks. It was sad – no other way to put it. I screwed up and I felt like I had failed my family. Luckily I was able to work through the depression and put it all into context before the weight of everything hit my wife. I really turned the corner mentally when I asked myself how all these other ultra-successful people recovered from similar failures.

I concluded that they learned from them somehow. So instead of thinking of all the ways I screwed up, I took time to write down every lesson I could possibly learn from the situation. The clarity of the lessons in a moment like that are crystal clear. After I got done writing everything down, it was very easy to see that the lessons I learned would make me way more money than it cost me. This was definitely a course changing moment for my company. I'm happy to report 7 years later that we've paid off all the debt (several hundred thousand dollars) and are on a path I would never have been on if I hadn't gone through that. It also helps to have the best wife in the whole world.

Andrew Stanten | www.altitudemarketing.com

When we started this thing, Stan and I had one rule: There would be no elephants in the room. Because we were friends first, we wanted to be sure – first and foremost – that that relationship would stay solid. We knew that making a commitment to being open and honest with each other – no matter how difficult or uncomfortable it might be at the time – would be what would make us or break us in both a professional sense and a personal sense. I believe that that rule laid the foundation and tone for the culture of Altitude today.

While there certainly have been highs and lows, I never once considered abandoning Altitude. We have 10 full-time employees and I take my commitment to them very seriously. I see it as supporting 10 families. We love what we do. We love our clients. And we have become a family. Quitting is simply not an option.

During the low times, that's what I think about my commitment to Altitude's extended families. And I begin to think about how to make it work. Budgets ebb and flow. When it's flowing, it's all good, but there are some times when we are paying more attention to what we're spending and have to make difficult decisions based on those challenges. Last year, for example, we made the decision to stay at our current address rather than moving to a newer, bigger space because we didn't need it.

Micha Kaufman | www.fiverr.com

A few weeks after launching Fiverr we experienced a situation that looked very grim. A story that the WSJ ran on Fiverr hit the homepage of Yahoo! This was the first major media coverage we had received. After the stories ran, we got so much traffic that our servers melted down. Because we were then began sending an unusually high amount of emails, all major email providers rejected our welcome emails for new customers. This prevented users that had just read about Fiverr from registering to our service.

At that point in time it looked like all efforts were lost. It is not uncommon in these situations that the first reaction is panic and devastation. Entrepreneurship is a roller-coaster. I believe that it is crucial for entrepreneurs to be born optimists and resourceful. It is the only way to get perspective and understand that you can turn most situations around.

We took long and deep breaths and figured out an action plan to overcome the setback. We quickly issued a message to our customers asking for their patience. We added servers and we worked to solve the email situation. Eventually we managed to salvage most of the positive media impact, minimized the damage and learned how to be prepared for these types of spikes.

Myra Roldan | herbanluxe.etsy.com

I've had a lot of experiences, good and bad. I've learned the biggest lessons from the bad experiences. I think can think of one particular experience that had me completely stressed out. I had received a cease and desist letter from a women who had a 20 year old patent for an item that was similar than mine. I contacted a patent lawyer who gave me the run around for about 2 weeks before we finally connected. I had a provisional design patent for my item which is valid for a year and gives you the time to work on applying for a full patent. The attorney told me in so many words – the only way you can fight it if you get sued is to have deep pockets. Something I didn't have. I became so afraid of a lawsuit that I lost sleep over it. Lack of serious funds and with no potential backers, I decided to let my provisional patent expire and not go forward with my product.

At first the decision was devastating but within a few days I felt like a weight had been lifted off my chest and I could breathe again and concentrate on the things that I really needed to take care of. I was able to refocus and in the end I saved myself a ton of headaches. I also learned that a patent can only protect you once it has been issued, non-disclosures are only valid for a year and competitors can work on developing a similar product or improving on your design and beat you to market.

Matthew Griffin | www.bakersedge.com

Before the business was selling stuff, we thought about never starting many times. It was risky and bad timing (new marriage, kids, mortgage, etc.). Not starting was a real possibility. Once the business started we had boundaries in terms of cash and time. If those were crossed we would quit as a function of failure, not out of "*giving up*". We never took a risk so large that it would destroy our futures. Sure – we have had tons of low points. There was a time when we spent 18 months of profits on tooling for a new pan – only to learn that our size calculations were off. One simple goof-up like this set us back considerably in both time and money. The only way from going crazy about this was to keep it in perspective. This was money that the business had generated – to use a gambling term it was "*house money*". We learned a lesson, and kept moving forward.

Mike Matousek | www.flashnotes.com

During my lows, I have slept in my car for multiple nights with no money and no way of getting home. It's times like these where you question everything and learn a lot about yourself.

These are the nights that you either wake up with the same energy you did the day before, or you crumble. In my eyes, a true "*entrepreneur*" is someone who is so confident in their mission, that no person, event, or situation can break them. Before I go to bed, I always think that today I did not stay the same -- I either got better, or I got worse. To get you through lows, it's important to remember that it's the war that matters, not the battles.

One last thing that specifically helped me though those difficult nights was a call from my top student-seller on Flashnotes.com at Florida State University. He had no idea what I was going through, and he simply called to say he loved the opportunity Flashnotes.com had given him. Having passionate users and never forgetting that they're the only people that matter will get any entrepreneur through those low nights.

Courtney Ilarrazza | www.babybodyguards.com

There have been times where we sunk much of our profits into something for the business and left ourselves with very little or no cushion. It's scary but sound investments in your business are always a good play. It should always pay off better than it would sitting in a savings account or as stock in someone else's company. During those times we'd freak out that we had no cushion and we'd work harder to build it back up. As we did the investment would begin to pay for itself and we'd be ahead of the game. Sometimes you'll make an investment that doesn't pan out as well as you'd like. All failures are learning opportunities if you're smart about it. Even successes can be learning opportunities if you consider how you may have been able to do even better. At this point that's what drives us now. How can we be even better!

We had a setback in 2012. We lost our office and all our inventory, computers and hard drive during Hurricane Sandy when we got flooded with over 8 feet of water. Those first few days when we had no power, no office and no gas, I was so freaked out. I couldn't imagine rebuilding again. As soon as the power was back on, the phone was ringing again and we put one foot in front of the other and kept going. We kept looking forward and ended up finishing the year stronger than ever.

Betsy | www.betsyandiya.com

We've never wanted to quit. We've both cried, felt overwhelmed, anxious, exhausted, but never ready to throw in the towel. Fortunately, our lows are never coincidental, so one of us is there to talk the other through it. From those lows, we re-strategize, rebuild, refocus, or just retry. Eventually, that leads back to a high. For some, marriage and business don't work; it would be disastrous, but for us, there's a collaboration, support, and trust that I don't think we could find in any other business partner. I think that success in business is resilient optimism coupled with honest and continuous self-criticism and I think we're both pretty good at those things.

J'Amy Owens | www.billthebutcher.com

Having a cause and a purpose and a mission drives me. Of course I have difficult days and raising over $5 million dollars in a start-up, coming out of the recession was no picnic. My thought process every day is, "Figure out how to make it work". Quitting was never an option because of my fiduciary duty to our shareholders. I remain beholden to the gods of will power and elbow grease because nothing pulls me out of a ditch faster than action.

Aditi Kapur | www.deliverychef.in

You can't be a true entrepreneur without facing such situations. Sometimes, everything goes wrong at once, and you consider giving up and calling it a day. But it's up to you to keep strong and see through the tough times. When you become an entrepreneur, you need to resolve firm and hard, that you will keep at it no matter what. If you have limitations (time, funds, etc), take those into account at the very beginning. Don't give up unless you have hit those.

Adam Simpson | www.easyofficephone.com

Yes, I hit quite a low four years ago. The company's co-founder and CTO, who was also an old friend, passed away suddenly and at a young age. I had already been grappling with other issues in the business as a result of the recession, and the loss seemed insurmountable. My team gathered that night at one of our houses and all of us spoke openly. We realized that everyone's hearts and minds were still very much in the business, and that the best way to honor our co-founder was to carry on and create something he would have been proud of.

Michael Kawula | www.selfemployedking.com

Back in 2010 my online company grew so fast that PayPal froze our account to investigate our business to assure we were doing everything on the up & up. I was unaware they did this and learned it's normal. The problem was though I kept all the cash in the account until bills were due at the end of the month.

We had $200,000 in cash and vendors wanting to be paid. They froze our shipments and customers were starting to cancel orders. It was a complete mess but luckily I was able to get through it or our business would have closed.

Zalmi Duchman | www.freshdiet.com

There were times when I thought we would go bankrupt. We were growing very fast & our liabilities were catching up. I remember those days were very dark & I could barely sleep at night. We got thru those times by being creative with cash flow & bills. More than anything having the support of my family helped me get thru those tough times & knowing that in the end I had their support no matter what happened.

Chris Grant | www.grantfamilyfarm.com

I was once asked *"what keeps you from quitting?"* I replied, *"I am probably too dumb to know when to give up"*. I love what I do, and even though everyone else I went to school with has jobs all over the country,

I know where I belong. Entrepreneurship is tough, but if you love what you are doing it will all be worth it. Not every day will be sunshine and lollipops, and not everyone goes to work with a smile on their face, but for all the bad times, there has to be good times that outweigh them. When I think about quitting, I think why not just get a "*real*" job. Throw it all away so I can do a normal everyday 9-5 job. When I am at farmers' markets, or on my tractor, or collecting eggs, no matter how bad things seem, I know that I am right where I belong. Maybe someday this will all change for me, but I will deal with that when it comes.

Kathy Crifasi | www.hipzbag.com

There were several occasions where I questioned having my own business. Then, I would look at where my thoughts were coming from. Were my concerns about the viability of business model (was I trying to make a business out of something that should not be a business) or was it about something I needed to push through to persevere? Let's face it, if it were easy, everybody would have a business. Every time I would look at the situation objectively, I would discover that my trepidation was always about something I needed to push through: my belief system, my expertise, my story—or it was something I just plain did not want to do.

When you have a business, the buck stops with you, so until you are making lots of loot – you get to do the not so fun things. Once I defined where the breakdown was occurring, I challenged myself to push through, whatever that meant. That "*completion*" always freed up space in me to do what I needed to do for the business and my life. Everything is how you look at it, and I try to find a way to look at things as a way to evolve personally--- that seems to work for me!

Mike Townsend | www.homehero.org / www.flowtab.com

Our low point was a failed Flowtab pub crawl with hundreds of people. We partnered with Thrillist and DAMA Tequila to throw a 3-bar pub crawl in Santa Monica on Maine Street with 31Ten Lounge, Basement Tavern and Finn McCools. Overall, it was a rough day. There was limited cell service at 31Ten, Finn McCools was severely short staffed and our server crashed for a solid 20 minutes during the event. The event cost $1,800 total, we got 130 new users, sold $1,200 in drink volume and suffered a few 1-star reviews in the App Store. Stressful day with way too many drunk people, but it was the fastest way to learn.

Iftach Orr | www.pix.do

This probably happens to me once a week, and has happened with every one of my ventures over the years. In some cases I did quit and I don't regret it -- knowing when to quit is just as important as the virtue of dedication. When I lose hope I turn to my users and post what I'm working on. Hearing their excitement about a new feature gives me strength to continue and the knowledge that I'm not alone. Talking to friends and family about my start-ups and using them as a sounding board focuses me on what's really important and gives me motivation when I feel overburdened by tasks. Make sure that your surrounding environment, your spouse and loved ones, support you because if they don't you are bound to fail, no matter how good your idea and execution is. Also, be sure to move your body once a day go for a 20 minute walk or jog for example. You'll find that shortly afterward; will be by far your most creative time of the day.

Jeb Blount | www.salesgravy.com

If I had a dime for every time I wanted to quit I could retire. The highs and lows of entrepreneurship are often extreme and on days can feel debilitating. One of the worst experiences was in the summer of 2010 when our database crashed and our entire website was down for three days. My advertisers were screaming at me and I thought at the time that all of the work and pain I had endured to get to that point was wasted. I was so depressed and I really wanted to quit – just walk away. But I didn't quit. We finally got the website back up and I became even more determined that something like that would not happen again. That was when I started the process of getting new developers and build redundancy into our servers. At the time it was horrible but getting through that low made me and my company much stronger.

Greg Tseng | www.tagged.com

Yes, my lowest point was when the economy crashed in 2008-09 and we were also faced with legal and PR issues. I thought about quitting but never really got that close. I really leaned on my co-founder, board of directors and full team for support. What really kept me going was the belief in our vision and the positive impact we were having on our members every day. We resolved it through grit, persistence and hard work. Business goes in cycles and I like to say *"you must get through the current valley to be there for the next peak."*

Akbar Chisti | www.seamusgolf.com

When I left the big trade show the first year, I thought I had failed drastically. I didn't open any new accounts at the show, and thought we didn't make a dent. But then some phone calls started coming along. Throughout the first year and a half I was continuously concerned about whether our hobby could survive as a business, and in many ways that worry is what drove me to continue to innovate and sell. If we had good times from the beginnings, we'd be out of business. Innovation is the result of forced creativity, and when you have no options but to think outside the box an entrepreneur is born.

Is jumping off a bridge the same as quitting? Because I went over the Brooklyn Bridge every day and thought about jumping! The early days of a start-up are extremely hard and miserable but you cannot give up (even if you do think about jumping off a bridge sometimes). Everything is working against you and you have to be able to brush off all the issues and keep coming in everyday with a positive attitude. I don't consider failure an option so somehow I always find a way.

Zeb Couch | www.offmarketformula.com / www.speedhatch.com

When DealFlow was struggling, my savings account was dwindling and my credit card bills were growing. I remember having something like $48 in my checking account, $500 in my savings and $2,400 in credit card debt along with over $17,000 in student debt. I remember my old entrepreneurship professor from Boston College had a hardwood flooring business and he hired me to install wood floors. I was on my hands and knees installing hardwood floors during the day and working on Speedhatch and Off Market Formula at night. I put another $500 on my credit card to help grow Speedhatch and it took off, and Off Market Formula followed.

Things have a funny way of working out. Be humble, know what you need to do and do it. Recognize that to achieve success, you must sacrifice. Most people aren't willing to do that. As Thoreau said, they live in *"quiet desperation"* forever. Spending 6 months installing floors was the greatest learning experience of my life.

Lawson Nickol | www.allamericanclothing.com

Yes, debts did add up at times. However, we had a strong, proven plan that showed growth for almost every year we have been in business. So the key to getting through these tough times is really about having a good plan and strong relationships. By having a solid history of paying our bills and a proven business plan we were able to obtain favorable terms with our vendors and operational loans through the bank. This allowed us to get through some of the growing pains.

Justyn Howard | www.sproutsocial.com

There have been challenges that seemed insurmountable at the time, but giving up never factored in. Over time you might even come to enjoy the personal growth involved with overcoming larger and larger obstacles. Something that would have crippled you even a year earlier becomes a simple exercise.

Early on we decided to rebuild our product from scratch, which is normally a great way to kill a software company. However, it ended up changing the trajectory of our business and strengthening our team's resolve and tenacity. After that, it's pretty hard to make us sweat.

Danny Maloney | www.tailwindapp.com

Entrepreneurship is a roller coaster, full of great moments and gut wrenching ones. But I've never wanted to give up. When you care about your mission, team, customers and investors, giving up simply isn't an option. I've survived by surrounding myself with other entrepreneurs and helping them. My wife Megan is an entrepreneur, which is a huge plus. When one of us is down, the other's ready with a pep talk or a kick in the pants, as needed.

Raj Sheth | www.recruiterbox.com

We have had this recurring low throughout the first three years – I am being super honest. When you hear of a new competitor, or a customer leaves you because you did not add the feature that you meant to, it always hurts. But then there are also highs! That well-known brand that starts using you and paying, or that record breaking revenue month. We live for the highs! We resolve the lows by hoping for a high the next day and just going to bed.

Cricket Allen | www.theperfectsnaque.com

Entrepreneurship is exhilarating. No two days - and no two hours - are alike! You will wear more hats than you knew existed. As an entrepreneur, I've learned how to build a pallet, configure a margin, set up an LLC, obtain trademarks, interact with customers, learn the trade and lingo and much more. There was never a time we ran the risk of selling, but that simply was not an option I would have ever considered. I was too determined and committed (and too stubborn!) to make it work. You will not believe how resourceful you become when you run into perceived, unsolvable obstacles. We are not shy in calling people to gain advice or ask a favor. If you start with the crawl, walk, run approach in all areas of starting your own business, you will become more formidable and make smart decisions that will hopefully ward off some of those lows.

Josh Rosenwald | www.unroll.me

Which of the last six times that I've thought about quitting would you like me to discuss? Of course there are lows. When you're carrying a business on your shoulders, you're accountable for all your stakeholders - owners, employees, customers. It's scary as hell! The times that I've thought about walking away have been when we hit a wall in the company - growth wise, financially - or when I've hit a wall personally - losing confidence. So far, the company has always rebounded as have I. This is also where having a great co-founder, a true partner, becomes so important. When one of you is down, the other one is able to say *"we got this," "we'll get through this," "let's fix this."* Simply having a great supporting team can help you get through any low. But I guess that's true of life in general.

Christy Ferer | www.vidicom.com

Most of the highs and lows came from outside—personal life, not the business: Births of children, divorce, death in the family, etc. Those were the only times I questioned priorities of working and having to be so self-propelled. At first it feels lonely and there is no one to *"edit"* ideas, pitches, or even the choice of hires. But you keep saying to yourself, *"nothing ventured, nothing gained"* and go for it.

Scott Perkins & Shawn Boday | www.vube.com

If quitting is in your personality, you're not an entrepreneur. It is those that refuse defeat regardless of their circumstances or environment that will succeed in business. This is a personality trait that you either have or you don't. Motivation is the number one key to success.

Tracey Noonan | www.wickedgoodcupcakes.com

The only time I thought about quitting was the very first day we opened our doors for our first location. We had a line out front before we opened. Halfway through the day we still had a line, we were blowing through product, and there was no end in sight.

Looking back, I think I was so overwhelmed and tired from all of the work we put in ahead of time. We never anticipated the size of the crowd. I went out back had a good cry. My in-laws were there that day to lend a helping hand. My mother in law came out back and we had a lovely chat. I put on my big girls pants and dragged myself back in. We sold over 2,000 cupcakes out of the shop that day. I went back the work the next day and never looked back. I laugh to myself when I think about that first day. Ironically, I now welcome chaos. As Mario Andretti says: If everything seems under control, you're not going fast enough.

Beth Shaw | www.yogafit.com

In my business, there are always ups and downs. Sometimes you get a lot of students signing up and buying your products, and sometimes you don't. It correlates closely to the economy. I stuck with my business because of all of the people who loved my services. If it weren't for my devoted base of customers, then I would not have been able to make it through the hard times.

Joshua Dorkin | www.biggerpockets.com

In the 9+ years that I've been in business, I've considered quitting dozens of times. Running your own company can be incredibly stressful and there are a lot of bad people in the real world. When you run across these folks, it can seriously damper your enthusiasm. Additionally, my business is a 24/7/365 one — that can also be very stressful. When I see my friends are making the same amount of money with much less stress, it is easy to think twice about what I do.

What has always kept me going has been the support, encouragement, and love of my wife, and that of our community overall. Not a day goes by where I don't hear from one of our users who tells me how our website has changed their life for the better. In the tough times, going back and seeing the impact we've made on our industry quickly gets me out of my rut.

Monica Wreede | accessoryconnectz.com

Just last week my daughter wrote me a letter that truly broke my heart into pieces! In a nutshell, I need to spend more time with my family! Sometimes I almost wish I had a 9-5 job so I can turn it off at some point! I am working around the clock to try bettering my family every day of the week! It is a lot for any entrepreneur to process when it comes out of family assets! I really haven't come to a good conclusion for that yet;-(I hope to have some answers in the coming months!

Jordan Eisenberg | www.urgentrx.com

For me, selling the business has been and would be a high, but there is no question entrepreneurship is not for the faint of heart. Don't be fooled by how much the life of a start-up CEO is romanticized in our culture – it is always much prettier on the outside than it is on the inside. The truth is that getting a new venture off the ground is all-encompassing (say goodbye to your social life), grueling, extremely stressful, will take more effort and time and energy than you could've ever imagined, and can be a very lonely existence early on (if your friends and family haven't been there themselves, there are not many you can turn to for advice and guidance).

But, if you ask me, it is extremely fun and fulfilling, and in the end that's all that matters. Along the roller-coaster ride that is entrepreneurship, I have encountered countless "*lows*" – ranging from nearly running out of money to dealing with difficult investors to hiring the wrong employee to having issues with the product that threaten everything you've worked so hard to build. If there is one trait that is absolutely critical as an entrepreneur, it is extreme resilience. Said differently, you need to have an extremely high threshold for pain. Not giving up and pushing forward no matter what is key to making it as an entrepreneur.

Eric Schiffer | www.digitalmarketing.com

There was a time in my mid 20s when I was kicked hard in the teeth. I literally had to pull myself up and do a reset! The great thing about doing that is you can only go up. Once you get that first win, it's incredibly inspiring! You go from knocked down to standing up straight, with a victory on your shoulder. It can be a great rush.

It's important to believe in yourself and stick to the core principles that work. If you work hard and you sort by the facts, you're going to win — it's just a matter of fact. In my experience, it's the law of business. In time, the system will reward you.

Philip Masiello | www.800razors.com

Prior to 800razors.com,, I launched a start-up in the natural skin care industry. We launched it at the height of the capital crash in 2008 so we went into the start-up phase under capital pressure. When the business did not work as a shopping channel product line, we focused it on retail as a way to keep the business growing and alive. But the continual need for capital was draining and I wanted to just give up and walk away.

Alicia Weaver | www.prestigeestateservices.com

I really never thought about throwing in the towel. My worst days of owning my own company are still better than any days working for someone else. If worst case scenario happens and the company folds despite my best efforts I'd just try and try again. I've caught the bug now, there's no going back!

Eren Bali | www.udemy.com

You have to really enjoy what you do as an entrepreneur. Being an entrepreneur is a tough journey most of the time. In our case, if we were not obsessed, we would have given up at least five times.

Most start-ups fail, so the odds of success are really low in the early days. We never ran the risk of quitting the business because we focused all our efforts on succeeding. When we were first rejected by VCs it was a blow but we doubled-down and kept our focus on getting the traction we needed to convince investors.

Chapter 26 – Lessons From start-up Journey

Despite the challenges and debts that entrepreneurship throws at you, one thing that all entrepreneurs agree on is that it is a pretty fulfilling journey. So what did the entrepreneurs I talked to learn from their start-up journey? Here are some wonderful lessons for aspiring entrepreneurs to take home.

Sam Tarantino | www.grooveshark.com

The single greatest lesson in life I've learned is that anything you have can be taken from you. Who you are and what you stand for cannot. That is eternal and the root of happiness. Money, fame, status, power, people, things, all can be lost. Purpose and happiness can't. One thing I always look back on when we faced impossible odds was that I assumed every day that tomorrow I could lose everything.

When you accept that anything can be taken from you at any second, constricting fear dissolves and you operate from a place of infinite potential and ability. You suddenly have superhuman strength. When you look at man's accomplishments through history, they were mostly from people who had nothing to lose. The founding fathers were traitors guaranteed to be hung, the Wright brothers were bicycle shop owners who loved to create, and Steve Jobs was a college dropout who loved to make things "*insanely great.*" Being able to put yourself perpetually in this detached, warrior state of mind is not only the greatest challenge but the greatest personal power you can wield in the startup called "*life.*"

Chris Grant | www.grantfamilyfarm.com

Never assume you know everything about anything. Every day in business is a giant learning process. Do not sell yourself short by thinking you know it all, and be open to new ideas.

The hardest part of business is minding your own. Don't worry if another business has a nicer office than you, more people, better equipment, or more customers. If you worry about everyone else, you will suffer the most. Be aware of your competition, but don't lose sleep over them. Like in the third grade, you need to mind your own business.

Matt Shoup | www.mandepainting.com

Realizing that any business is just an extension of the person running it. If I don't live by the qualities I state my company stands for, my company will never stand for them. Doing everything the right way as a leader, a man and a father is essential to making sure that my company lives up to the high standard I have set and allows me to inspire my team to do the same.

Jill Foucré | www.marcelsculinaryexperience.com

What everyone said at the beginning is true – everything will take more money and more time than you expect so plan for that. Also, if you are not self-motivated and prepared to treat your business like a business (and not a hobby), then don't start. It will just lead to financial losses and a lot of heartache.

Eric Schiffer | www.digitalmarketing.com

The most important thing in business is to retain your customers by providing a top-tier quality service, having great relationship management skills, ensuring they feel like a VIP at all times, and providing an experience that is great at all times. Experience is king. Great experience builds empires.

Mike Glanz | www.hireahelper.com

I can't do it alone - the success of the company depends largely on how much I lean on God, my wife, and my employees. All my senior management make jokes about how I'm a "*delegator*," - when in reality I've learned that the more I trust them to do big important tasks, the better they turn out.

My wife is a rock star. She convinced me to start the company and has never wavered in her support of HireAHelper.com; even when she was working full time with a one month old, and I wasn't getting a paycheck and we were on the brink of bankruptcy from the U-Haul lawsuit.

Mike Townsend | www.homehero.org / www.flowtab.com

An important lesson to remember is to constantly grow your skills and not be intimidated by things you don't know. If you don't know how to code, design, or raise venture capital, just jump in and try. Have the mentality that you will solve any problem that comes your way and you will attract talented people looking for a leader.

Raghu Kulkarni | www.idrive.com

It is very challenging. It takes a lot out of your personal and professional life. Be ready to sacrifice a whole lot. It is not for everyone. Most do not succeed. But for the ones who do, it is well worth it and nothing in the world comes close to the joy of achieving success in a startup.

Michael Folkes | www.mafolkes.com

It's very important to establish and maintain a mutually beneficial relationship with the right partners - customers, suppliers, & employees.

Kyle James | www.rather-be-shopping.com

Never let somebody tell you that you can't do something. If I had listened I would have quit a long time ago or never started to begin with. Find a niche, create a website and content that is the best resource available, helps people solve problems, and the customers will follow. Oh yeah, and don't forget to find the influencers in your niche and befriend them in any way possible as they'll be your best ally when it comes to gaining links and growing your brand.

Rick Martinez | www.senorsangria.com

Keep it simple. Be humble, Work hard, sacrifice and lead by example

Zeb Couch | www.offmarketformula.com / www.speedhatch.com

So many people talk about "*changing the world*," being their own boss, setting their own schedule. They see the IPOs, the balance sheets, the cash, the apparent freedom. Forget all that. The world belongs to the meat eaters. Those who see what they want, drool at the mouth at the thought of tasting it, and aren't afraid to get battered and beaten in order to take a bite. Behind every IPO, every company like Facebook, Twitter, Instagram and Roc-A-Fella there's a meat eater who's scraped and clawed to win. Guaranteed. If that sounds too painful, too unappealing, this life just isn't for you.

Greg Tseng | www.tagged.com

It really is about the journey not the end goal. Pick something you're passionate about and enjoy the action-packed journey full of highs and lows and the associated full range of emotions. Go into it with an open mind and an open heart – you'll learn a lot about yourself and you'll experience lots of personal growth. Then any "*business success*" that comes will just be icing on the cake.

Christy Ferer | www.vidicom.com

Don't be afraid to fail. That is the best experience of all because once you survive that, you can do anything. Use it to propel you forward

Beth Shaw | www.yogafit.com

Always listen to your customers. Even if you only have a few, those are the ones who are most devoted.

J'Amy Owens | www.billthebutcher.com

What lesson have I learned? To be true, kind, fierce and courageous. Identify those people that are the "*trippers and askers*". They are the black holes of destruction who take and do not contribute. Get them out of your life and business as fast as possible.

Aaron Skonnard | www.pluralsight.com

A library of online video tutorials for coders, developers and IT pros.

Adam Simpson | www.easyofficephone.com

A leading provider of cloud-based business phone services.

Adi Bittan | www.ownerlistens.com

Mobile app to privately send feedback and complaints to business owners.

Aditi Kapur | www.deliverychef.in

Online food ordering portal in India

Akbar Chisti | www.seamusgolf.com

Makers of handcrafted golf accessories including their signature Scottish clan tartan head covers.

Alex Brola | www.checkmaid.com

On-demand cleaning service

Alicia Weaver | www.prestigeestateservices.com

Providers of personal property liquidation and appraisal services

Andrew Gazdecki | www.biznessapps.com

DIY mobile app builder for small businesses

Andrew Stanten | www.altitudemarketing.com

A full service, integrated marketing firm for technology-oriented B2B companies

Andy Hart

Entrepreneur with a clothing line business

Arnon Rose | www.localmaven.com

Tech platform that monetizes word of mouth referrals

Ashok Subramanian | www.liazon.com

Operator of industry-leading private benefits exchanges for businesses

Audrius Jankauskas | www.impresspages.org

Open-source PHP framework for content management

Bas Beerens | www.wetransfer.com

Online file sharing service

Beth Shaw | www.yogafit.com

Yoga fitness school with a network of over 250,000 instructors.

Betsy | www.betsyandiya.com

A handmade jewelry brand in Portland, OR

Blaine Vess | www.studymode.com

Portal offering online learning tools and resources for students

Blake Smith | www.cladwell.com

Free, online personal stylist for men

Bryan Knowlton | www.appraiseallrealestate.com

A private club for real estate appraisers to teach marketing techniques

Chandler Crouch | www.chandlercrouch.com

Real Estate company from Fort Worth, Texas

Chris Grant | www.grantfamilyfarm.com

Farm owner producing vegetables, cut flowers and eggs for farmer markets

Chris Thierry | www.etelesolv.com

B2B software that tracks telecom expenses for enterprises

Christy Ferer | www.vidicom.com

Branded custom video solutions distributor for enterprises

Courtney Ilarrazza | www.babybodyguards.com

Full service child safety company, providing home safety consultations and baby proofing.

Cricket Allen | www.theperfectsnaque.com

New Jersey-based manufacturer of whole sprouted lentil, quinoa and other super food snack blends

Dan DeLuca | www.grownsmall.com / www.classchatter.com

ClassChatter offers web tools for blended learning. GrownSmall connects small growers to customers

Danny Maloney | www.tailwindapp.com
   Pinterest analytics suite offering social media marketing tools for business

Debra Cohen | www.homeownersreferral.com
   A pre-screened network of local home improvement contractors

Dianne Crowley | www.wildwingcafe.com
   Restaurant chain in the south and southeastern United States

Edward DeSalle | www.netirrigate.com
   Manufacturer of Wireless Agricultural Irrigation Monitoring (WAIM) technology

Eren Bali | www.udemy.com
   Marketplace for online courses

Eric Schiffer | www.digitalmarketing.com
   Digital marketing agency

George Burciaga | www.elevatedigital.com
   Developer and provider of interactive, touch screen digital displays

Giancarlo Massaro | www.viralsweep.com
   Online tool for running sweepstakes and giveaways

Greg Tseng | www.tagged.com
   Fourth largest social network in the world with 330 million users

Heidi Lamar | www.spalamar.com
   Privately owned resort-style spa in Scottsdale, Arizona

Hill Ferguson | www.zong.com (Chief Product Officer, Paypal)
   Mobile payment service

Iftach Orr | www.pix.do
   Website discovery and incentivizing service

J'Amy Owens | www.billthebutcher.com
   Seattle based "new school" butcher shop chain

Jake Sigal | www.livioconnect.com
   Music platform designed to work in cars, various devices, and online.

Jason Cohen | www.wpengine.com
   Wordpress hosting solutions

Jason Richelson | www.shopkeep.com
   iPad "Point of Sale" solution

Jason Schultz | www.jason.me
   Serial entrepreneur and angel investor

Jay Barnett | www.prioritypickup.com.au
   Private chauffeur booking service in Perth, Australia

Jeb Blount | www.salesgravy.com
   Sales jobs community

Jeff Kuo | www.ragic.com
   Flexible cloud database for businesses

Jill Foucré | www.marcelsculinaryexperience.com
   Gourmet retail store and recreational cooking school

Joel Simkhai | www.grindr.com
   Locality based mobile social network for gays

John Brady | www.protempartners.com
   Management consulting for businesses in transition

Jojo Hedaya | www.unroll.me
   Email newsletters subscription management service

Jordan Eisenberg | www.urgentrx.com
   Fast-acting over-the-counter flavored powder medications

Josh Rosenwald | www.unroll.me
   Email newsletters subscription management service

Joshua Dorkin | www.biggerpockets.com
   Online social network and content platform for real estate investors

Julie Busha | www.slawsa.com
   CPG grocery product that has placement in over 6,000 retail locations in the US & Canada

Julien Smith | www.breather.com
   Service that lets you find beautiful, practical spaces that you can reserve on the go

Justyn Howard | www.sproutsocial.com
   Social media engagement and analytics tool for businesses

Kathy Crifasi | www.hipzbag.com
   Manufacturer of a functional accessory worn with a waist-looped strap

Kevin Lavelle | www.mizzenandmain.com
   Innovative men's lifestyle brand - ecommerce and brick & mortar

Kyle James | www.rather-be-shopping.com
   Coupons and deals website launched in 2000

Lawson Nickol | www.allamericanclothing.com
   Apparel company where everything is 'Made in USA'

Mark McClain | www.sailpoint.com
   Identity and access management solutions

Mary Apple | www.prettypushers.com
   Manufacturer and retailer of labor gowns, maternity apparel and post-baby products

Matt Barrie | www.freelancer.com
   Marketplace for freelancers

Matt Keiser | www.liveintent.com
   Email newsletters ad exchange

Matt Shoup | www.mandepainting.com
   Painting company in North Colorado

Matthew Griffin | www.bakersedge.com
   Manufacturer of Edge brownie pan and simple Lasagna pan

Micha Kaufman | www.fiverr.com
   Marketplace for micro-gigs costing $5 a gig

Michael Folkes | www.mafolkes.com
   Packaging and value added logistics services company

Michael Kawula | www.selfemployedking.com
   Serial entrepreneur with cleaning business and an online dropship business

Michael Lindell | www.mypillow.com
   Pillow manufacturers

Michael Wayne | www.deca.tv
   Production house for mainstream digital entertainment

Michelle MacDonald | www.sweetnotebakery.com
   Gluten-free bagel factory

Mike Glanz | www.hireahelper.com
   Online service to compare and book moving labor for loading/unloading services

Mike Matousek | www.flashnotes.com
   Student marketplace for study guides, class notes and video tutorials

Mike Niederquell | www.quell.com
   Integrated brand communication firm

Mike Townsend | www.homehero.org / www.flowtab.com
   Homehero is an online service to find and hire senior home caregivers

Monica Wreede | accessoryconnectz.com
   Inventive solution to interchanging accessories

Monique Tatum | www.beautifulplanning.com
Fast growing PR firm in New York

Morris Miller | www.xenex.com & www.rackspace.com
Xenex manufactures germ-zapping robots for hospitals. RackSpace is a cloud based web hosting service

Myke Nahorniak | www.localist.com
Unique and interactive event calendaring platform

Myra Roldan | herbanluxe.etsy.com
Etsy based cosmetic products company

Nellie Akalp | www.corpnet.com
Online legal document filing service

Nick Paradise | www.threadbuds.com
Manufacturer of colorful earbuds that do not tangle

Patrick DeAmorim | www.decate.no
Norwegian social networking website

Peter Mann | www.oransi.com
Manufacturer of air purifiers

Philip Masiello | www.800razors.com
Razor blade manufacturer and subscription service

Raghu Kulkarni | www.idrive.com
Online data backup and file sync service

Raj Sheth | www.recruiterbox.com
Recruiting software and applicant tracking system

Rick Martinez | www.senorsangria.com
Manufacturer of ready to serve bottled Sangria

Rob Biederman | www.hourlynerd.com
Marketplace for small businesses to hire MBA students for consulting assignments

Rob Infantino | www.openbay.com
Online marketplace for car repair

Rob Walling | www.getdrip.com
Email marketing tool for lead generation

Robert Livingstone | www.royaltext.com
National mobile text messaging marketing company

Robin Ian Turner | Keyzi
Property search website for real estate investors

Ryan Wallace | www.iphoneantidote.com
US-based iPhone buyback company

Sam Tarantino | www.grooveshark.com
Online music streaming website

Scott Perkins & Shawn Boday | www.vube.com
Viral video engine for content creators

Stacey Lindenberg | www.growyourtalent.com
Learning and organizational development support company for businesses

Tracey Noonan | www.wickedgoodcupcakes.com
Cupcake manufacturing company

Zalmi Duchman | www.freshdiet.com
Doorstep delivery service for fresh meals

Zeb Couch | www.offmarketformula.com / www.speedhatch.com
Brick & mortal residential real estate company

Printed in Great Britain
by Amazon

28930078R00141